Programming and GUI Fundamentals

IEEE Press
445 Hoes Lane
Piscataway, NJ 08854

Programming and GUI Fundamentals

Tcl-Tk for Electronic Design Automation (EDA)

Suman Lata Tripathi
Lovely Professional University
Phagwara, India

Abhishek Kumar
Lovely Professional University
Phagwara, India

Jyotirmoy Pathak
Lovely Professional University
Phagwara, India

Published by John Wiley & Sons, Inc., Hoboken, New Jersey.
Published simultaneously in Canada.

For general information on our other products and services or for technical support, please contact our Customer Care Department within the United States at (800) 762-2974, outside the United States at (317) 572-3993 or fax (317) 572-4002.

Wiley also publishes its books in a variety of electronic formats. Some content that appears in print may not be available in electronic formats. For more information about Wiley products, visit our web site at www.wiley.com.

Library of Congress Cataloging-in-Publication Data applied for:

Hardback: 9781119837411

Cover Design: Wiley
Cover Image: © whiteMocca/Shutterstock

Set in 9.5/12.5pt STIXTwoText by Straive, Chennai, India

Contents

About the Authors

Dr. Suman Lata Tripathi received her Ph.D. in the area of microelectronics and VLSI from MNNIT, Allahabad. She received her M.Tech in Electronics Engineering from UP Technical University, Lucknow, and her B.Tech in Electrical Engineering from Purvanchal University, Jaunpur. She is a Professor at Lovely Professional University and has more than seventeen years of experience in academics. She has published more than 74 research papers in refereed journals and conferences. She has organized several workshops, summer internships, and expert lectures for students. She has worked as a session chair, conference steering committee member, editorial board member, and reviewer in international/national IEEE journals and conferences. She has received the "Research Excellence Award" in 2019 and "Research Appreciation Award" in 2020, 2021 at Lovely Professional University, India. She received the best paper award at IEEE ICICS-2018. She has published the edited books *Recent Advancement in Electronic Devices, Circuit, and Materials*; *Advanced VLSI Design and Testability Issues;* and *Electronic Devices and Circuit Design Challenges for IoT Application*. She is also an editor of the book series on *Green Energy: Fundamentals, Concepts, and Applications* and *Design and Development of Energy Efficient Systems*, which are yet to be published. She is currently working on an accepted book proposal specifically on *Electronic Device and Circuits Design Challenges to Implement Biomedical Applications*. She is working as a series editor for a title, *Smart Engineering Systems*.

Her area of expertise includes microelectronics device modeling and characterization, low power VLSI circuit design, VLSI design of testing, advanced FET design for IoT, embedded system design, biomedical applications, etc.

Mr. Jyotirmoy Pathak has completed his post graduation in VLSI Design and graduation in Electronics and Communication Engineering from Anna University, India. He holds more than 10 research papers in a refereed journal. He holds 9 patents and 1 copyright. He has been the reviewer of many journals such as the *IETE Journal of Research* etc. He has also played the role of session chair for many international conferences.

His area of expertise includes VLSI signal processing, hardware security, FPGA prototype development, and low power ASIC design.

Dr. Abhishek Kumar obtained his Ph.D. in the area of VLSI Design for Low Power and Secured Architecture from Lovely Professional University, India. He received his M.Tech in Electronics Engineering from the University of Mumbai, India, and graduated from The Institution of Engineers (India). He has been an Associate Professor at Lovely Professional University for 11 years. He has published more than 35 research papers in refereed journals and conferences. He has organized workshops, summer internships, and expert lectures for students. He has worked as a session chair, conference steering committee member, editorial board member, and reviewer in international/national journals and conferences. He has published the book *Intelligent Green Technologies for Sustainable Smart Cities* with Wiley-Scrivener and another book *Machine Learning Technique with VLSI* is in production with Wiley-Scrivener.

His area of expertise includes VLSI design, low power architecture, memory design, data converters, ASIC-SoC, cryptology, and side channel attacks.

1

Introduction

Language is a structured system of communication used by humans. When a human wishes to communicate with a computer system, a programming language is required. A programming language is able to convert a set of instructions, known as the source code, to perform a specific task. There are a number of common programming languages, such as C, C++, and JAVA. Each programming language requires a specific compiler, which is able to translate the source code into machine code. There are also other mechanisms to produce machine code that are interpreter-based, and these use step-by-step executors of the source code. A language can be implemented with either a compiler or interpreter. A combination of both platforms is possible too where the compiler generates the machine code and then passes it to the interpreter for execution [1].

Tcl stands for Tool Command Language. It is an interpreter-based scripting language, designed to be easy to embed into the application. A scripting language is a programming language that automates the execution of tasks. Scripts are written for the run time execution and are interpreted rather than compiled. Some popular scripting languages are Python, Ruby, Bash, Node Js, and Perl. Scripting languages are required in web applications, system administration, gaming, and plugin development for an existing system. Scripting languages are preferred owing to the (i) ease of learning, (ii) fast editing, (iii) interactivity, and (iv) functionality.

The shell script is a set of instructions in the specific programming language to be run by the UNIX shell, a command-line interpreter. Tcl (pronounced as tickle) is high-level, interpreted, dynamic programming. Tcl is very similar to the UNIX shell languages, namely Bounce, C, Korn, and Perl, and therefore offers a wide range of programmability [2]. Tcl supports a wide range of programming paradigms, like object-oriented programming, and the imperative and functional procedural styles offer the ability for applications to communicate with each other. It is possible to associate Tcl with the toolkit (Tk) used for building a graphical user interface (GUI). Tk is a cross-platform, which offers a wide range of widget libraries that can also be associated with other programming languages.

Tcl and the X-window toolkit were developed by Prof. John Ousterhout of U.C. Berkeley to solve the difficulty associated with a programming language. It was initially developed for UNIX, then ported to Windows, MAC, DOS, and QS/2. Its ability to integrate a Tcl interpreter with existing applications and to interact with the program set is what differentiates it from other programs. Table 1.1 presents a comparison between programming and scripting languages.

Programming and GUI Fundamentals: Tcl-Tk for Electronic Design Automation (EDA), First Edition.
Suman Lata Tripathi, Abhishek Kumar, and Jyotirmoy Pathak.

Table 1.1 Programming and scripting language comparison.

Programming language	Scripting language
Set of instructions executes a task	Based on script written for run time environment
Compiler based	Interpreter based
Develop from scratch	Can integrate with existing
Run independent of parent program	Run inside another program
Compiled into a more compact form, does not need to be interpreted	Can be interpreted within another program
Offer full usage of language	Faster execution
One-shot conversion	Line-by-line conversion
Long development time	Shorter development time since less coding
C, C++, C#, Java, VB, COBOL, PASCAL	JavaScript, Tcl, Perl, PHP, Ruby, Lua, Shell

1.1 Features of Tcl

- Low development time
- Easy integration with Tk
- Cross-platform independence can access with Windows, Mac, Unix
- Inclusion into another programming languages
- Open-source
- Command-based operation
- Dynamically redefined and overridden
- Data types are based on strings
- Event-driven interface

A Tcl application requires a Tcl interpreter and a text editor. Nomenclature and version of the editor would be different depending on the operating system. Vi is preferred for UNIX or LINUX systems and notepad for Windows as a .tcl file. A Tcl script development with a text editor must be saved with the extension .tcl, which is known as the source file. The interpreter enables us to execute the Tcl command line by line. The latest version of the Tcl installer for the Windows operating system can be downloaded from http://activestate.com. The latest stable version is tcl8.6.

There is a different mechanism to access the Tcl interpreter

```
Search → tclsh
```

Figure 1.1 shows a command-line interpreter based on the Windows environment.

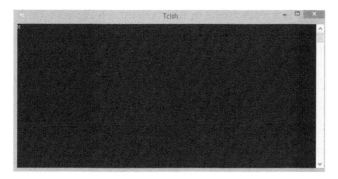

Figure 1.1 Command-line interpreter.

`Search → wish`

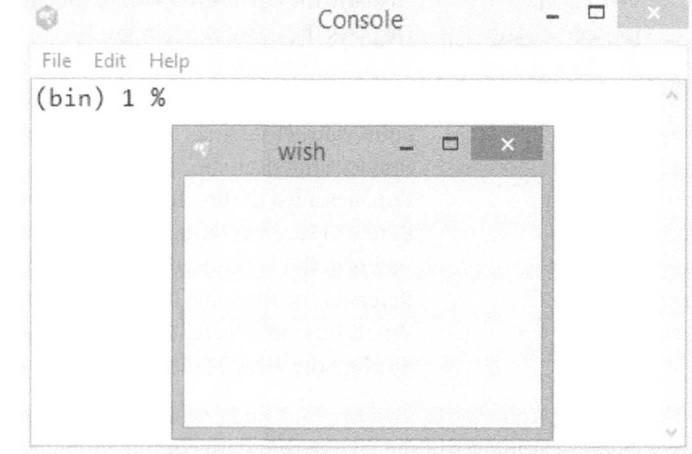

Figure 1.2 Wish interpreter.

Wish, i.e., Windowing Shell, is a Tcl interpreter, as presented in Figure 1.2, embedded with Tk; the Tcl command is read from a standard text editor or notepad. The Tcl command can be edited in the console window and wish in a smaller window to display the Tk widget. Alternatively, users can interact via importing the source file into the interpreter. A set of Tcl commands edited with notepad saved with the .tcl extension can be imported into the console.

`File → Source → locate the file → open search → tkcon`

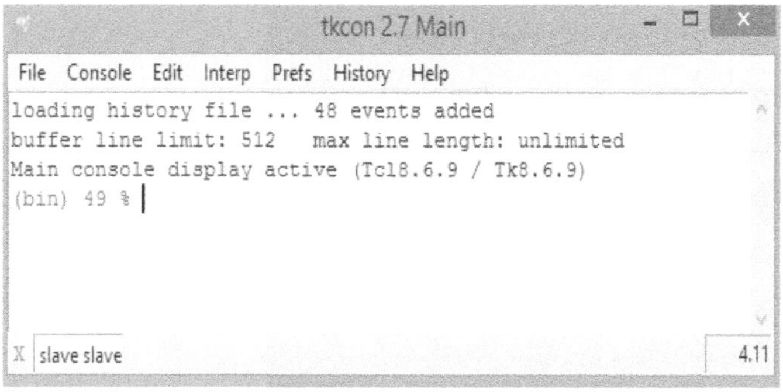

tkcon 2.7 Main

File Console Edit Interp Prefs History Help

```
loading history file ... 48 events added
buffer line limit: 512   max line length: unlimited
Main console display active (Tcl8.6.9 / Tk8.6.9)
(bin) 49 %
```

X slave slave 4.11

Figure 1.3 Tkcon interpreter.

The tkcon interface shown in Figure 1.3 is a replacement of the standard console with Tk. It provides a GUI while the Tk commands are used in the program. Users can enter the program using a standard text editor or can import a source file.

File → Load file → Locate the file → Open

1.2 Special Variable

Tcl includes some special variables that present their usage (see Figure 1.4). The following is a list of the special variables [3].

`tcl_library`	Sets the location of Tcl library.
`tcl_version`	Displays the current version of the interpreter.
`tcl_patchLevel`	Displays the current patch level.
`tcl_interactive`	Switches between interactive (1) and non-interactive (0) mode.
`tcl_precision`	Displays the number of digits to generate when converting floating-point values to strings.
`tcl_rcFileName`	Provides the user-specific startup file.
`tcl_pkgPath`	Provides a list of directories where packages are installed.
`Argc`	Refers to several command-line arguments.
`Argv`	Refers to the list containing the command-line arguments.
`argv0`	Refers to the filename being interpreted.
`env (PATH)`	When Tcl starts, it creates the env array and reads the environment. It displays the array of elements for the environment variable.

Tk is the most common extension of Tcl, and enables the creation and manipulation of the interface widgets. Advantages of the GUI design with command-line arguments are (i) faster development, (ii) a higher level of interface than other standard library toolkits, (iii) interface can be factorized with user application.

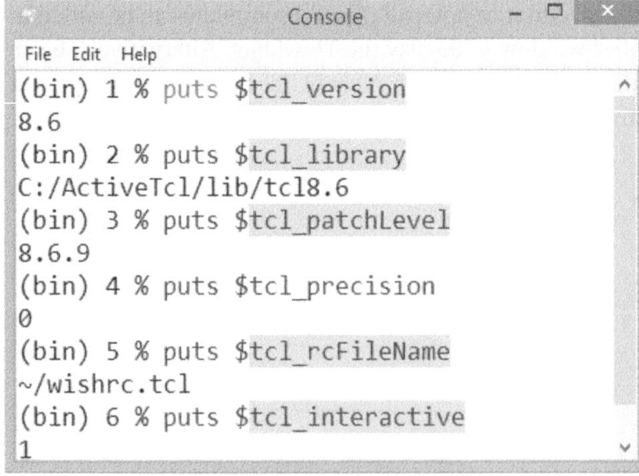

Figure 1.4 Tcl special variable.

The following online platforms prove that an online interpreter does not need to be installed:

https://onecompiler.com/tcl
https://rextester.com/l/tcl_online_compiler
https://ideone.com/l/tcl

1.3 Tcl First Program

The following Tcl script displays a statement at the std. output [4]:

```
puts "Hello Tcl World"
```

Each line of the script can be terminated by a newline or semicolon (;). A script can be stopped from execution via commenting by adding a hash (#) at the beginning. Figure 1.5 displays a simple program to display.

Figure 1.5 Tcl simple program.

1.4 Tcl Identifiers

Tcl is a case-sensitive language. Identifiers are the names used to identify the variable (defined by the user). An identifier can start with an alphabetical letter (A–Z/a–z), underscore (_), or numeric digit (0–9). It avoids characters such as @ and %.

Examples: var., Var, St1, s_1, prog50.

Whitespace in Tcl is known as a blank statement and the interpreter ignores it. Whitespace describes the blank, newline, tab character, or comment. It separates one part of the statement from another.

1.5 Applications of Tcl

There are several reasons a developer may prefer a Tcl scripting language. The following are the most favorable applications for the Tcl language.

a) Cross-platform application
b) Graphical user interface development

c) Software testing via API of the application
d) Scalable website
e) Embedded application
f) Web-server hosting

References

1 https://www.tcl.tk/software/tcltk/choose.html
2 https://www.tutorialspoint.com/tcl-tk/index.htm
3 https://www.activestate.com
4 Beebe, N.H. (2013). *A Bibliography of O'Reilly & Associates and O'Reilly Media. Inc. Publishers.* Department of Mathematics, University of Utah.

2

Basic Commands

2.1 Introduction

Tcl is a script-based language that was developed by John Osterhout in 1989 (University of California, Berkeley). It has a lower number of keywords and syntax compared with others making it easy to learn. Windows-based Tcl shells can be used as *tclsh* or *wish*, as shown in Figures 2.1 and 2.2, respectively. The first is similar to a C-shell while the second is a Tcl interpreter that extends its Tk command to create and manipulate widgets. The console window executes the Tcl program and the graphical user interface (GUI) developed with Tk widgets appears in the wish window. Console and wish are intractable. Both shells print a % prompt and execute the Tcl command and print the result sequentially. A Tcl program saves with an extension of .tcl.

Figure 2.1 Tclsh screen.

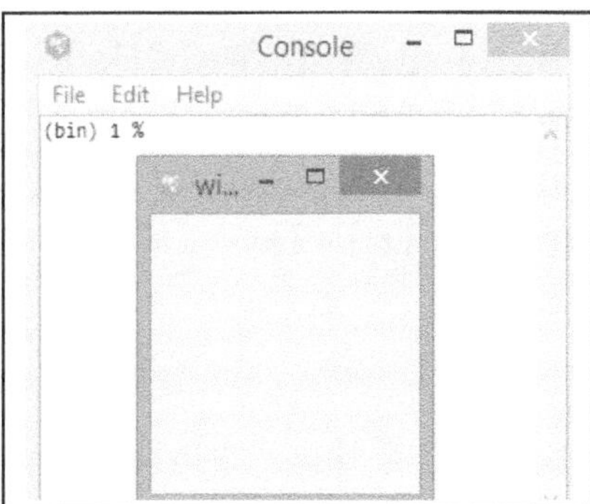

Figure 2.2 Wish screen.

The basic syntax of a Tcl program is

```
Command arg1, arg2 ,............ Argn
```

Here, the command can be either built-in or a user-defined procedure followed by arguments separated by whitespace. Whitespace separates the commands and their arguments, and a newline or semicolon ends a Tcl statement. Arguments are string values. In the case of more than one argument, each argument must be enclosed by curly braces { }.

- `Tcl command` One or more arguments separated by whitespace.
- `Tcl script` Sequence of commands separated by newlines, a semicolon is a terminator.
- `Comments` Individual Tcl statements can be commented with symbol #.
- `puts` Writes the result string along with a new line.

Programming and GUI Fundamentals: Tcl-Tk for Electronic Design Automation (EDA), First Edition.
Suman Lata Tripathi, Abhishek Kumar, and Jyotirmoy Pathak.

To display the value or string on the monitor screen, the following scripts are used:

```
puts stdout  {Welcome to Tcl World}
puts  {Welcome to Tcl World}
```

In this example, `puts` is a command to write the result as a standard output (stdout). The default stdout device is a monitor screen. A group of arguments must be enclosed within {}, else the result is an error.

The system-defined command starts with *(bin) number %* and results appear immediately following the statement [1]. Figure 2.3 shows that the `puts` command displays the argument, and the `puts` command identifies the I/O stream identifier and a string. The `puts` command writes the string to the I/O stream along with the newline character.

The output can be re-structured in a different format with a backslash sequence, namely `\a (Bell), \n (newline), \t(tab)`. Figure 2.4 displays the output "Hello Tcl-Tk" controlled by the `(\)` sequence. Appendix II summarizes the backslash sequence.

2.2 Set Command

The `set` command initializes variables with a constant value. A variable can be initialized with a `set` command and holds a value. The variable is case sensitive, a reference to computer memory where the value is stored. It takes two argument set names of variables where the second is their

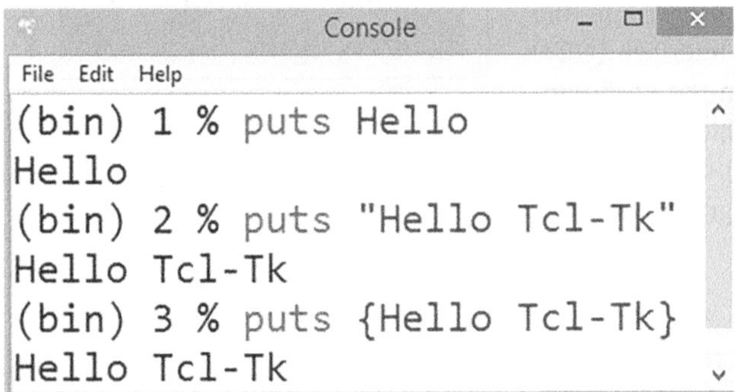

Figure 2.3 The `puts` command in Tcl.

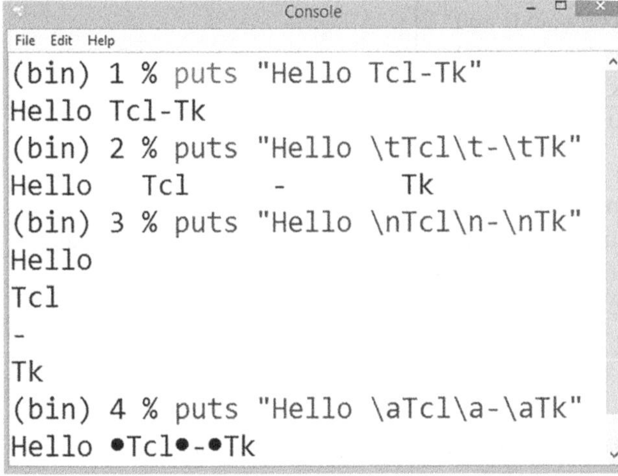

Figure 2.4 The `puts` command with (\) sequence.

Figure 2.5 Variable declarations with the `set` command.

```
(bin) 1 % set a 22
22
(bin) 2 % set b "Welcome to Tcl Script"
Welcome to Tcl Script
(bin) 3 % set c a+b
a+b
(bin) 4 % set d a - b
wrong # args: should be "set varName ?newValue?"
```

value. The variable can be of any length. The interpreter can create value implicitly [2]. Figure 2.5 shows the variable declaration with the `set` command, *(bin) 1* and *(bin) 2* declare a constant value of 22 to `a` and the string "Welcome to Tcl Script" to `b`. *(Bin) 3* assigns (`a + b`) to variable `c` but returns an error in the case of *(bin) 4*. Since the variable (`a - b`) is separated by whitespace, it is interpreted as a different variable. A Tcl variable can accept a single variable, and grouping requires the avoidance of errors.

2.3 Variable Substitution

The value of a variable can be updated via the $ symbol; an argument declared with the $ symbol can be rewritten by the substitution of a value for the variable. A previously declared variable can be substituted in the current statement, as shown in Figure 2.6, where the string "Welcome to Script World" is assigned to a variable "a." The command `puts` displays the string substituted by `$a`, and displays the string "Welcome to Script World."

2.4 Grouping

Grouping is required when more than one word or integer needs to be assigned to a single variable. There are two ways to group the argument: double quotes " " or curly braces { }. Since Tcl is a string-based language, a string may contain one or more arguments. A single argument does not need to be a group, but more than one argument needs to be a group. The difference between " " and { } grouping is the permission for substitution; grouping with double quotes results in complete substitution of the whole group while that with braces does not allow substitution. Therefore, grouping of variables should be performed with double quote else grouping with braces is sufficient. A variable grouped with braces prints the arguments similar to the grouping. Here `&` is considered as a normal character, not for substitution purposes. Thus, *curly braces are used when substitutions on the argument need to be delayed. Grouping and substitution are employed by the Tcl interpreter before it runs a command.*

Figure 2.6 Variable substitution.

```
(bin) 1 % set a "Welcome to Script World"
Welcome to Script World
(bin) 2 % puts $a
Welcome to Script World
```

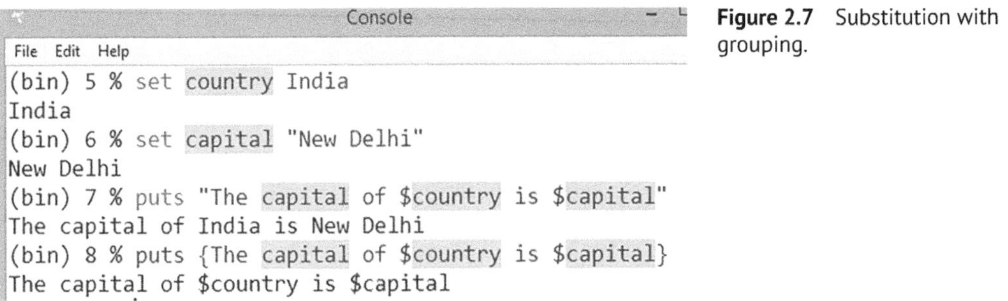
```
(bin) 5 % set country India
India
(bin) 6 % set capital "New Delhi"
New Delhi
(bin) 7 % puts "The capital of $country is $capital"
The capital of India is New Delhi
(bin) 8 % puts {The capital of $country is $capital}
The capital of $country is $capital
```

Figure 2.7 Substitution with grouping.

Figure 2.7 explains the grouping feature of Tcl, where `bin(7)` groups the two strings via " " and creates a single string with substitution $country substituted with India and $capital substituted with New Delhi; while in `bin(8)`, grouping is performed via { }, where `$country` and `$capital` are considered as a single variable and new string without substitution.

2.5 Command Substitution

A Tcl command is shown within square brackets `[ ]`. An argument written in `[ ]` is considered as a command and evaluated accordingly. A Tcl command has two arguments: the first is a variable declared via a set and the second is in `[command]` after evaluation, where the result gets updated onto a variable.

Figure 2.8 presents the implicit declaration of a string's `script` and command `string length`, enclosed in `[ ]`. Variable x gets updated with the evaluation, i.e., `6`. (bin) 2 shows variable substitution of x.

Command substitution can relate to a single or more than one (nested) command, where the order of execution is followed from left to right (default). Each right bracket encountered in the command is evaluated one after another. The space inside the bracket is ignored. The interpreter evaluates the nested command by considering everything left of the right bracket as a single character and the results are updated with the remaining nested command, as presented in Figure 2.9.

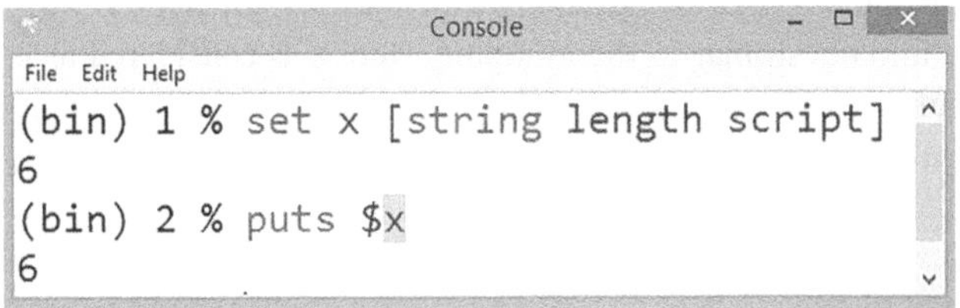
```
(bin) 1 % set x [string length script]
6
(bin) 2 % puts $x
6
```

Figure 2.8 Command substitution.

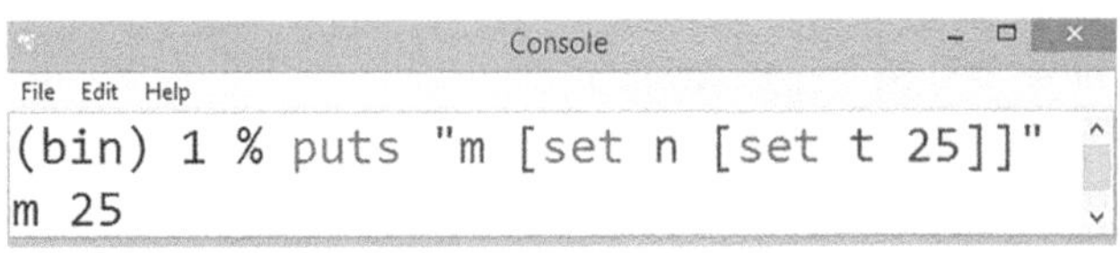
```
(bin) 1 % puts "m [set n [set t 25]]"
m 25
```

Figure 2.9 Nesting of commands.

```
(bin) 1 % puts "sum of 25 and 35 is [expr 25 + 35]"
sum of 25 and 35 is 60
(bin) 2 % set x 25
25
(bin) 3 % set y 35
35
(bin) 4 % puts "sum of $x and $y is [expr $x + $y]"
sum of 25 and 35 is 60
```

```
(bin) 6 % set x 25
25
(bin) 7 % set y 35
35
(bin) 8 % set z [expr $x + $y]
60
(bin) 9 % puts $z
60
```

```
(bin) 1 % set a 7
7
(bin) 2 % set b 8
8
(bin) 3 % puts [expr $a + $b]
15
```

Figure 2.10 Math expressions with the `expr` command.

2.6 Math Expressions

A mathematical expression starts with `expr` inside `[ ]` (square brackets). This command is equivalent to the C-expression syntax. A Tcl interpreter treats the `expr` command like other Tcl commands and leaves the expression upon implementation. The command `expr` deals with a primary integer, floating number, and binary value, and the logical operation returns a true (1) or false (0). Integer results are promoted over floating as the requirement and the floating number is presented in scientific notation [3]. An example of variable and command substitution with `expr` helps to implement a mathematical expression, as shown in Figure 2.10; where the symbol (+) stands for summation.

2.7 Backslash Substitution (\&)

Backslash substitution is slightly different from regular substitution `(&)`, and it is presented by `\&`. It disables substitution and returns the character as written in the string prefixed with \$. It prefers to quote special characters. Backslash substitution `\&` does not allow substitution, since the interpreter interprets a single string. Here, `(\)` disables the substitution of a single character immediately following the backslash. Any character immediately following the backslash will stand without substitution. In the case to disable multiple substitutions, multiple backslash symbols are to be used.

Figure 2.11 explains an example of disabling substitution, `(bin) 3` combines the variables `z1` and `z2` by substitution but `(bin) 4` (uses \$) does not substitute in the values of `z1` and `z2`. It treats `$z1` and `$z2` as new variables and simply prints the variable `$z1 $z2`.

Figure 2.11 Disable substitution.

```
(bin) 1 % set z1 "The capital of India is"
The capital of India is
(bin) 2 % set z2 "New Delhi"
New Delhi
(bin) 3 % puts "$z1 $z2"
The capital of India is New Delhi
(bin) 4 % puts "\$z1 \$z2"
$z1 $z2
```

2.8 Tcl Operator

A Tcl operator is a symbol that instructs the compiler to perform a specific operation. An operator applies to the data (variable) known as the operand. Operators that work with only one operand are called unary operators. Those which work with two operands are called binary operators. There is also ternary operators that work with three operands. The Tcl script is a rich built-in operator and provides the following [4]:

- Arithmetic operators
- Relational operators
- Logical operators
- Bitwise operators
- Ternary operators

2.8.1 Arithmetic Operators

Table 2.1 lists the arithmetic operators supported by the Tcl language. Figure 2.12 describes the arithmetic operator, where each symbol there has the usual meaning similar to the C-language.

Table 2.1 Arithmetic operator.

Symbol	Description
+	Performs addition
−	Performs subtraction
*	Performs multiplication
/	Performs division
%	Returns the remainder after division

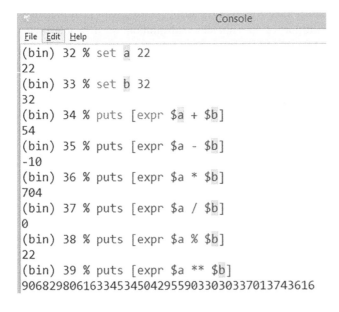

```
Console
File Edit Help
(bin) 32 % set a 22
22
(bin) 33 % set b 32
32
(bin) 34 % puts [expr $a + $b]
54
(bin) 35 % puts [expr $a - $b]
-10
(bin) 36 % puts [expr $a * $b]
704
(bin) 37 % puts [expr $a / $b]
0
(bin) 38 % puts [expr $a % $b]
22
(bin) 39 % puts [expr $a ** $b]
90682980616334534504295590330303370137436l6
```

Figure 2.12 Arithmetic operator.

2.8.2 Relational Operators

The relational operators shown in Table 2.2 require two different operands. It evaluates the relation between operators and returns the result 1 for true and 0 for false. The relational operator presented in Figure 2.13 compares the variables a = 20 and b = 10 and displays the result according to the operator in the expression.

Table 2.2 Relational operator.

Symbol	Description	Output
==	Checks the value of the two operands are equal	Returns 1 if same, else 0
!=	Checks the value of two operands are not equal	Returns 1 if not equal, else 0
>	Checks left operand is greater than the right operand	Returns 1 if true, else 0
<	Checks left operand is less than `arg2`	Returns 1 if true, else 0
>=	Checks left operand is greater than or equal to the right operand	Returns 1 if true, else 0
<=	Checks left operand is smaller than or equal to the right operand	Returns 1 if true, else 0

Figure 2.13 Relational operator.

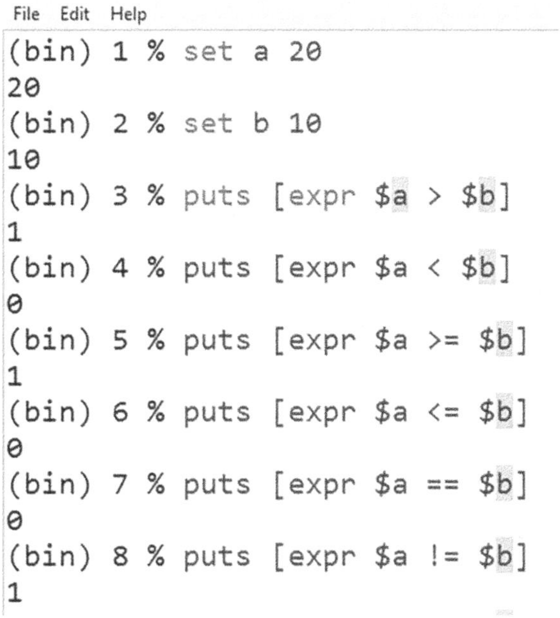

```
File  Edit  Help
(bin) 1 % set a 20
20
(bin) 2 % set b 10
10
(bin) 3 % puts [expr $a > $b]
1
(bin) 4 % puts [expr $a < $b]
0
(bin) 5 % puts [expr $a >= $b]
1
(bin) 6 % puts [expr $a <= $b]
0
(bin) 7 % puts [expr $a == $b]
0
(bin) 8 % puts [expr $a != $b]
1
```

2.8.3 Logical Operators

A logical operator is used to create the condition in the program. The three logical operators supported by the Tcl language are presented in Table 2.3. Two different operands may be combined and create a condition to return either 0 (false) or 1 (true).

Figure 2.14 evaluates the relation with variables a and b initialized as 0 and 1, respectively. Here, `[expr $a && $b]` returns 0 since both operands are not 1. Additionally, `[expr $a || $b]` returns 1 since one of the operands is 1 and `[expr !$a]` returns 1 since the negation of a is 1.

Table 2.3 Logical operator.

Symbol	Description	Output
&&	Logical AND	Returns 1 if both operands are non zero, else 0
||	Logical OR	Returns 1 if any operand is non zero, else 0
!	Logical NOT	Reverses the style of the operand

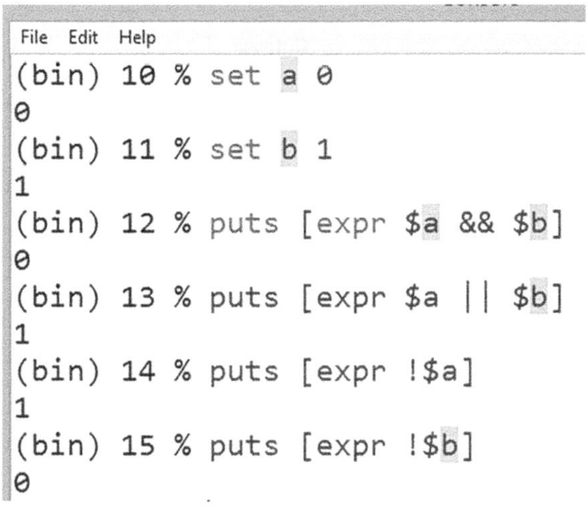

```
File  Edit  Help
(bin) 10 % set a 0
0
(bin) 11 % set b 1
1
(bin) 12 % puts [expr $a && $b]
0
(bin) 13 % puts [expr $a || $b]
1
(bin) 14 % puts [expr !$a]
1
(bin) 15 % puts [expr !$b]
0
```

Figure 2.14 Logical operator.

2.8.4 Bitwise Operators

The bitwise operator works on bits of two different operands and performs a bit-by-bit operation. The Tcl language supports three bitwise operators `"&" -bitwise AND`, `"|" -bitwise OR`, and `"^" -bitwise XOR`, which updates each bit of the operand according to the truth table given in Table 2.4.

Figure 2.15 describes the bitwise operator; variables "a" and "b" are initialized as 10 and 20, respectively. Bitwise operator `[expr $a & $b]` evaluates the binary conversion of each operand, evaluates in binary, and returns the result in decimal equivalent.

Table 2.4 Bitwise operator.

Input		Bitwise AND	Bitwise OR	Bitwise XOR
a	b	a & b	a | b	a ^ b
0	0	0	0	0
0	1	0	1	1
1	0	0	1	1
1	1	1	1	0

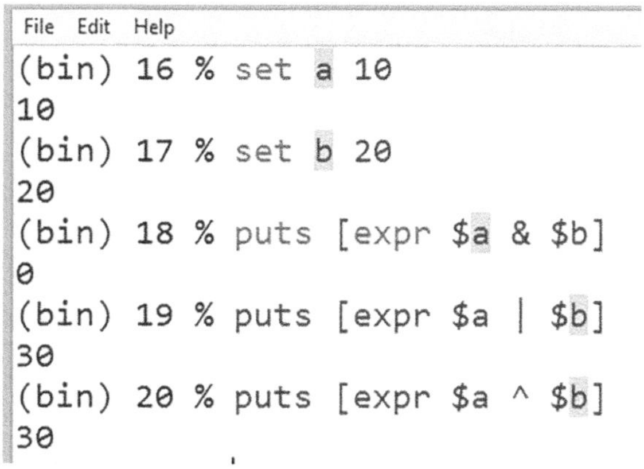

Figure 2.15 Bitwise operator.

```
File Edit Help
(bin) 16 % set a 10
10
(bin) 17 % set b 20
20
(bin) 18 % puts [expr $a & $b]
0
(bin) 19 % puts [expr $a | $b]
30
(bin) 20 % puts [expr $a ^ $b]
30
```

2.8.5 Ternary Operators

The ternary operators are based on three operands and map the function as a 2:1 multiplexer. A ternary operator consists of three segments: a condition; true expression; and false expression. The syntax of the ternary operator is shown as follows:

Condition? True: False

It evaluates the true statement if the condition is true else a false statement since the condition is formed with a mathematical operator necessary to use the `expr` command in [ ]. As shown in Figure 2.16, variable `z` updates as `x` if the condition is true else `z` will update with the value of `y`. A relational operator is used to create the condition.

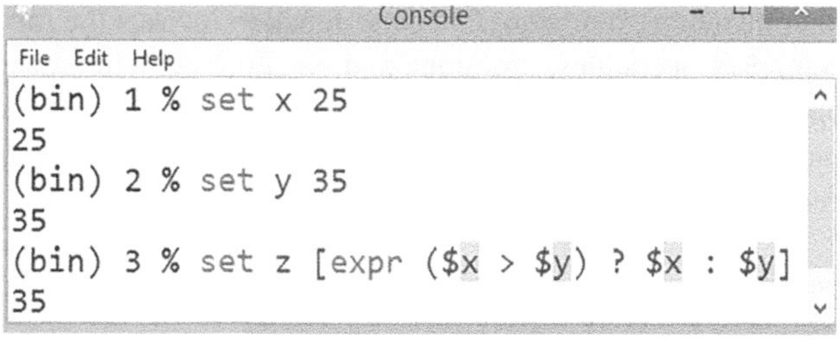

Figure 2.16 Ternary operator.

```
Console
File Edit Help
(bin) 1 % set x 25
25
(bin) 2 % set y 35
35
(bin) 3 % set z [expr ($x > $y) ? $x : $y]
35
```

2.8.6 Shift Operators

Shift operators move each bit of the operand. They apply to a single operand and shift the bits either left or right by a defined number of bit positions and displays the result as a default decimal equivalent. The shift operator is necessary to execute within an `expr` command in [ ]. A list of shift operators is provided in Table 2.5.

Table 2.5 Shift operator.

Symbol	Description
<<	Shift bits of arg left by n-times, where n is an integer. Inserts 0 in blank bits positions on the right
>>	Shifts bits of `arg` right by n-times, where n is an integer. Inserts 0 in blank bits positions on the left

Figure 2.17 describes the shifting of the value of `a` = 7 left and right twice. Operand `a` is presented as an 8-bit binary equivalent 00000111. Shifting left twice inserts two zeros in the least significant position and

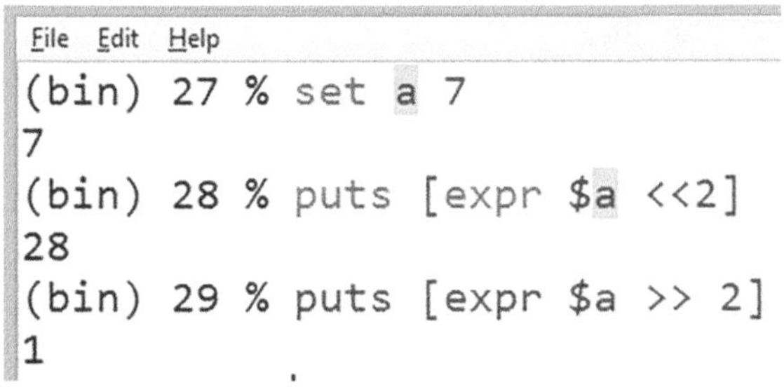

```
File  Edit  Help
(bin) 27 % set a 7
7
(bin) 28 % puts [expr $a <<2]
28
(bin) 29 % puts [expr $a >> 2]
1
```

Figure 2.17 Shift left and shift right.

results in 0011100 = 28. Similarly, shifting right twice and inserting two zeros in the most significant position results in 0000001 = 1.

Note – If the operand value is an even number, shifting the content left is equivalent to multiplying by 2 and shifting the content right is equivalent to dividing by 2.

2.8.6.1 Operator Precedence

An operator in the expression applies to the operand. Precedence and order of associativity of the Tcl operator determine the order of execution in a grouped expression. The operator with the highest precedence will be evaluated first and the operator with the lowest precedence will be evaluated at the end. Table 2.6 lists the precedence order of the operators supported by the Tcl language.

2.8.7 Tcl In-built Math Function

Tcl offers several in-built functions for math operations, which are included in Appendix I. These functions are applied to one or more than one argument. A command with `expr` within `[ ]` is used to evaluate an expression. The math function invokes the math library function. The Tcl expression comprises operations, operators, and parentheses. Whitespace is used to separate the operator and operand and can be ignored. The evaluation of the Tcl expression is similar to the C language; their meaning and precedence are similar. The Tcl expression evaluates a numerical result as either an integer or float.

Table 2.6 Operator precedence order.

<table>
<tr><th>Category</th><th>Operator Symbol</th></tr>
<tr><td>Sign, bit-wise, logical NOT</td><td>– + ~!</td></tr>
<tr><td>Exponentiation</td><td>**</td></tr>
<tr><td>Arithmetic</td><td>+ - * / %</td></tr>
<tr><td>Shift</td><td><< >></td></tr>
<tr><td>Relational</td><td>== != < > <= >=</td></tr>
<tr><td>Bitwise</td><td>& | ^</td></tr>
<tr><td>Logical</td><td>&& ||</td></tr>
<tr><td>Ternary</td><td>? :</td></tr>
</table>

2.9 Procedure

The procedure in Tcl is similar to the function/task/subroutine in other programming languages. A set of scripts that are repeated multiple times in the program can be written separately as a procedure and can be called in the program. This offers reusability of the code; a group of code performs a specific task, written separately, and can be called in the main program by its *procedure_name* [5].

A procedure in Tcl is defined with `proc`.

```
proc procedure_name {arguments} {
    Body
}
```

Each procedure has a unique name through which it can be identified; remember, the name is case sensitive. The procedure name and variable name should not have a conflict. Each procedure has its variable to present the expression and the body contains a series of commands. A Tcl procedure is ended with a return command and returns a single value of the result.

An addition procedure, as presented in Figure 2.18, calls a user-defined procedure to add, which returns an addition of two values. The mapping of local values 10, 20 to the procedure variables a, b, respectively, follows the order of declaration. A procedure acts as a user-defined command. It must follow the hierarchy of the command substitution and thus it gets called in square brackets.

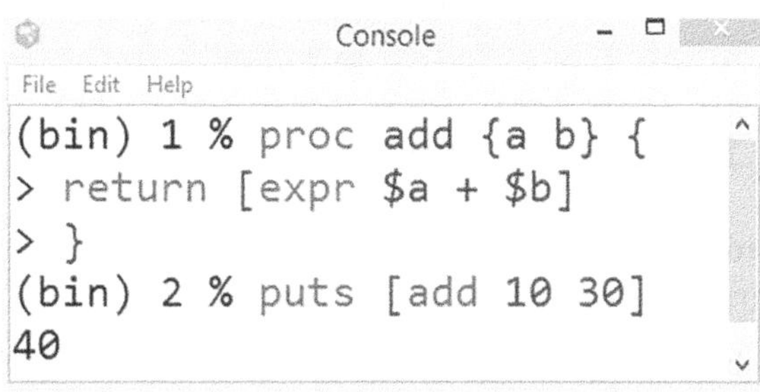

Figure 2.18 Addition with the procedure.

Figure 2.19 performs a summation with the help of a procedure where the variable is implicitly declared. An argument is inside a procedure grouped within curly braces. Opening of the curly brace on the end of the first line ignores the newline character and gobbles up text until a matching right brace is found.

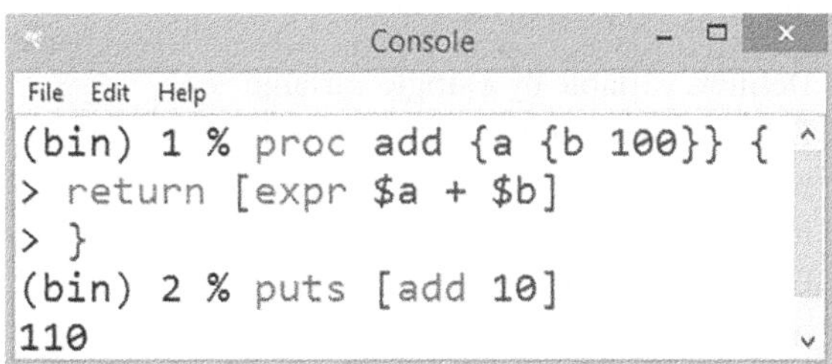

Figure 2.19 Using `proc` with default variable.

2.9.1.1 Advantages of a Procedure

Use of a procedure in the script includes the following advantages:

a) reduces the duplication of code;
b) decomposes the complex variable into smaller species;
c) improves clarity and readability of code;
d) reuses code;
e) hides information.

2.10 Eval Commands

For evaluation-involved substitution, Tcl will allow an executing program to create new commands and execute them during evaluation. The Tcl command is defined as a list of strings, commands, or procedures. The `eval` command takes one or more arguments, and comprises a Tcl script containing one or more command. The `eval` command concatenates all its arguments like the `concat` command, passes the concatenated string to the Tcl interpreter recursively, and returns the result of that evaluation. The `eval` command returns the final value of the commands being evaluated.

```
File Edit Help
(bin) 1 % set x {"Hello World"}
"Hello World"
(bin) 2 % set cmd {puts $x}
puts $x
(bin) 3 % eval $cmd
"Hello World"
```

Figure 2.20 The `eval` command.

The above example assigns a string to variable `x` and puts the command assigned to variable `cmd`. The `eval` command evaluates the nested substitution of the `cmd` and `x` values (Figure 2.20).

2.11 Solved Questions

Problem 2.1

Write Tcl script to convert Celsius to Fahrenheit.

Solution

The mathematical procedure to convert the numerical value of temperature from °C to F is given as follows.

- Define a variable by a single variable
- Express the conversion formula which returns the temperature value in Fahrenheit
- Call the procedure inside square brackets

A procedure is preferred that express a mathematical relation as a function; there is no limit to calling a procedure any number of times (see Figure 2.21).

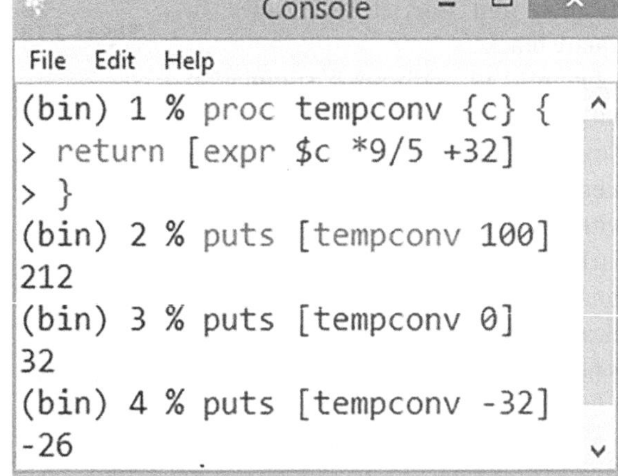
Console
File Edit Help
(bin) 1 % proc tempconv {c} {
> return [expr $c *9/5 +32]
> }
(bin) 2 % puts [tempconv 100]
212
(bin) 3 % puts [tempconv 0]
32
(bin) 4 % puts [tempconv -32]
-26

Figure 2.21 Temperature conversion with `proc`.

Problem 2.2

Write Tcl script to generate a random number.

Solution

There is an in-built function `rand()` to generate random numbers in the range of 0 to 1 (including both ends) with 16 points after the decimal. Every time this function is called inside square brackets, a unique random number is produced, as shown in Figure 2.22. The range of numbers can be extended to 0–10 by multiplying the function by 10, i.e., rand()*10, and extended to 0–100 by multiplying by 100, i.e., rand()*100, and so on. To remove the fractional part, round(rand()) is preferred to display only the integer part.

```
Console
File Edit Help
(bin) 1 % set r1 [expr rand()]
0.5714269669593437
(bin) 2 % set r1 [expr rand()]
0.9730336856902734
(bin) 3 % set r1 [expr rand()*10]
7.771553964247719
(bin) 4 % set r1 [expr round(rand()*10)]
7
(bin) 5 % set r1 [expr round(rand()*100)]
12
```

Figure 2.22 Random number generation with rand() function.

Problem 2.3
Write the Tcl script to find the maximum in the given number.

Solution

- Define a procedure with two variables
- Define a decision with an if condition; which returns a maximum of two
- Call procedure maps the variable over the procedure variable

In the example shown in Figure 2.23, a procedure is defined with variables x and y; a relational operator compares two variables and returns x if (x>y) else y. In the main program, two variables a and b are assigned with local variables 23 and 32, respectively. The procedure is called any number of times and maps the variable to proc in the same order as defined. It returns the result from proc mapped back to the variable val from where proc has been called.

```
Console
File Edit Help
(bin) 1 % proc maximum {x y} {
> if {$x > $y} {
> return $x
> } else {
> return $y
> }
> }
(bin) 2 % set a 23
23
(bin) 3 % set b 32
32
(bin) 4 % set val [maximum $a $b]
32
(bin) 5 % set max [maximum 0 1]
1
```

Figure 2.23 Using proc to find the maximum of two numbers.

Problem 2.4 (Recursive Procedure)
Write a Tcl script to compute a factorial using a recursive procedure.

Solution
Recursion in the Tcl script is a way of defining a function in which a function is applied in its function itself. A function calls the same function. There is a limit of 1000 recursion calls in Tcl (Figure 2.24).

```
Console
File Edit Help
(bin) 1 % proc factorial {number} {
> if {$number <= 1} {
> return 1
> }
> return [expr $number * [factorial [expr $number-1]]]
> }
(bin) 2 % puts [factorial 5]
120
(bin) 3 % puts [factorial 10]
3628800
```

Figure 2.24 Factorial computation using proc.

Problem 2.5
Write Tcl script to find an Armstrong Number.

Solution
An Armstrong number is observed if the sum of cubes of individual digits is equal to the number itself.

371 is an Armstrong number as 3^3 + 7^3 + 1^3 = 371.

Some other Armstrong numbers are 0, 1, 153, 371, 407.

```
set str 153
set len [string length $str]
set num1 [string index $str 0]
set num2 [string index $str 1]
set num3 [string index $str 2]
if {[expr ($num1*$num1*$num1) + ($num2*$num2*$num2) +
($num3*$num3*$num3)] == "$str"} {
puts "str is an Armstrong number"
} else {
puts "given string is not an Armstrong number"
}
```

2.12 Review Questions

1) Write Tcl script to compute arithmetic functions using the procedure.
2) Write a Tcl script to generate random number ranges 0–100 if input1 is greater than input2 else 0–1000.
3) Write Tcl script to identify a given number of odd numbers.

2.13 MCQs Based on Tcl Basics

1 Command interpolation is caused by which of the following?
A \ Disable Substitution
B $ Enable Substitution
C % Format
D [ ] Command

Solution (d)

2 What is the output of the following TCL program?

```
set x 4;
set y x+10;
```

A 4
B 5
C x+10
D None of the above

Solution (c)

3 What is the extension of a Tcl program?
- **A** .tcl
- **B** .wish
- **C** .tk
- **D** .script

Solution (d)

4 What is used to decode a Tcl script?
- **A** Compiler
- **B** Interpreter
- **C** Assembler
- **D** None of the above

Solution (b)

5 Which will generate random numbers in the range of 0–1?
- **A** `rand()`
- **B** `rand()`*10
- **C** `rand()`*100
- **D** `rand()`*1000

Solution (a)

6 Variable interpolation or substitution is caused by which of the following?
- **A** whitespace
- **B** \
- **C** #
- **D** $

Solution (d)

7 What is the advantage of using a Tcl procedure?
- **A** Removes duplication of script
- **B** Simplifies the program
- **C** Hides information
- **D** All of the above

Solution (d)

Important Points

`$`	enables substitution
`\$`	disables substitution
`[ ]`	square brackets for command substitution
`" "`	grouping with double-quotes allow substitution
`{ }`	grouping with curly braces prevents substitution
`proc`	procedure must exist before being called

References

1 Welch, B.B., Jones, K., and Hobbs, J. (2003). *Practical Programming in Tcl/Tk*. Prentice Hall Professional.
2 https://zetcode.com/lang/tcl/basiccommands
3 https://www.tutorialspoint.com/tcl-tk/tcl_basic_syntax.htm
4 Ousterhout, J.K. (1994). *Tcl/Tk Engineering Manual*. Sun Microsystems.
5 Flynt, C. (2012). *Tcl/Tk: A Developer's Guide*. Elsevier.

2.A Appendix I (Built-in math functions)

`abs (x)`	Calculates the absolute value of `arg` either integer or floating
`acos (arg)`	Calculates arccosine of x
`asin (arg)`	Calculates the arcsine
`atan (arg)`	Calculates arctangent of `arg`
`ceil (arg)`	Calculates the smallest integer of `arg`
`cos (arg)`	Calculates the cosine of `arg`
`cosh (arg)`	Calculates hyperbolic cosine of `arg`
`double (arg)`	Returns floating value; if arg is integer, converts into floating, then returns
`exp (arg)`	Calculates the exponential value of `arg`
`floor (arg)`	Calculates largest integer equal or less than `arg`
`fmod (x/y)`	Performs division x/y and returns floating-point reminder, reports error in case $y = 0$
`hypt (x,y)`	Calculates the length of the hypotenuse of a right-angle triangle
`int (arg)`	Returns integer with the same width of the machine
`log (arg)`	Calculates the natural logarithmic value of `arg`
`log10 (arg)`	Calculates base 10 logarithmic value of `arg`
`pow (x,y)`	Calculates x raised to y
`rand ()`	Returns a random number between 0 and 1, the internal clock of the machine is used to set the seed
`round (x)`	Rounds the value of x to the nearest integer
`sin (arg)`	Calculates sine of `arg`
`sinh (arg)`	Calculates the hyperbolic sinc of `arg`
`sqrt (arg)`	Calculates the square root of `arg`
`srand arg ()`	Calculates a random number between 0 and 1. Value of arg resets the seed of the random number generator. Each interpreter has its seed
`tan (arg)`	Calculates the tangent of `arg`
`tanh (arg)`	Calculates the hyperbolic tangent of `arg`
`wide (arg)`	Returns a 64-bit wide integer

2.B Appendix II (Tcl Backslash sequence)

`\a`	Bell
`\b`	Backspace
`\f`	Form feed
`\n`	Newline
`\r`	Carriage return
`\t`	Tab
`\v`	Vertical tab
`\\`	Backslash ("\")

3

Program Flow Control

Program flow control controls the order of execution of the individual states. By default, when a Tcl program is run, it is executed from the top of the source file to the bottom sequentially, but there are certain control flow commands that can alter the order. These commands can be conditional and executed when certain specific conditions are met. Flow control has a command body to be executed and returns the value of the last command chosen to execute. The loop-based command enables execution of a set of instructions to be executed a specific number of times repeatedly and there are some fine-tuning controls, like break, continue, return, and error. Every programming language supports the conditional statement [1].

3.1 If–Else Command

The `if` command is used to verify a Boolean condition. If the condition is true, it executes `body1` else `body2`. To avoid substitution, it is necessary to group the command body (group of instructions) by curly braces. Control of the flow command triggers the evaluation when the condition is met, as shown by the flow chart in Figure 3.1.

```
if {Condition } then  {
        body1
}
```

```
if {Condition } {
        body1
} else {
                body2
}
```

These are two formats of syntax. The `if` command verifies the condition and evaluates `body1` if the condition is true, and then is optional. The `else` command in the other syntax creates a branch. If the condition is true, it executes `body1` else `body2` when conditions are false. Here the `else` commands are optional. Since the Tcl interpreter uses the `expr` command internally, one does not need to use it explicitly. Conditions are created with the use of Tcl operators. Example 3.1 shows the expression controls with a single condition; however, if the condition is not met, it returns a blank statement.

Programming and GUI Fundamentals: Tcl-Tk for Electronic Design Automation (EDA), First Edition.
Suman Lata Tripathi, Abhishek Kumar, and Jyotirmoy Pathak.

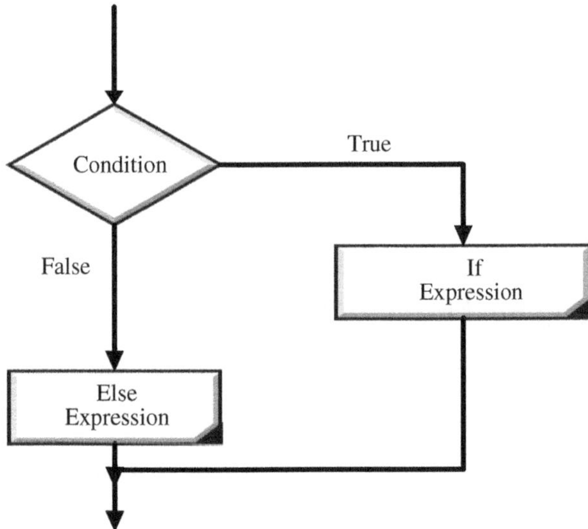

Figure 3.1 `If-else` condition flowchart.

Example 3.1 The value of `x` is set internally for the comparison, but is not substituted due to the curly braces. If the condition executed is true, it executes the `if` expression otherwise the `else` expression.

```
set x 100
if {$x > 50} {
puts "x is greater than 50"
}
```

```
x is greater than 50
```

```
set x 100
if {$x > 50} then {
puts "x is greater than 50"
}
```

```
x is equal to 100
```

```
if {$x == 2} {
puts "$x is 2"
} else  {
puts "$x is not 2"
}
```

```
1 is not 2
```

```
set x 1;
if {$x != 1} {
  puts "$x is != 1"}
  else {
  puts "$x is 1"
  }
```

```
1 is 1
```

```
set x 1;
if {$x==1} {
puts "GOT 1"
}
```

```
GOT 1
```

3.1.1 If-Elseif-Else Commands

The `else` command is used whenever two branches need to be implemented, and multiple branches are implemented with the `elseif` command. The `elseif` command evaluates the second condition when the first condition is not met and may extend to the third or more condition. The last expression does not follow any condition considered as the default statement and gets evaluated if the earlier listed conditions are not met. Any number of conditions can be chained to create branches, as shown in Figure 3.2.

```
if {condition1} {
        body1
} elseif {condition2} {
        body2
} elseif {condition3} {
        body3
        .
        .
} else {
        bodyn
```

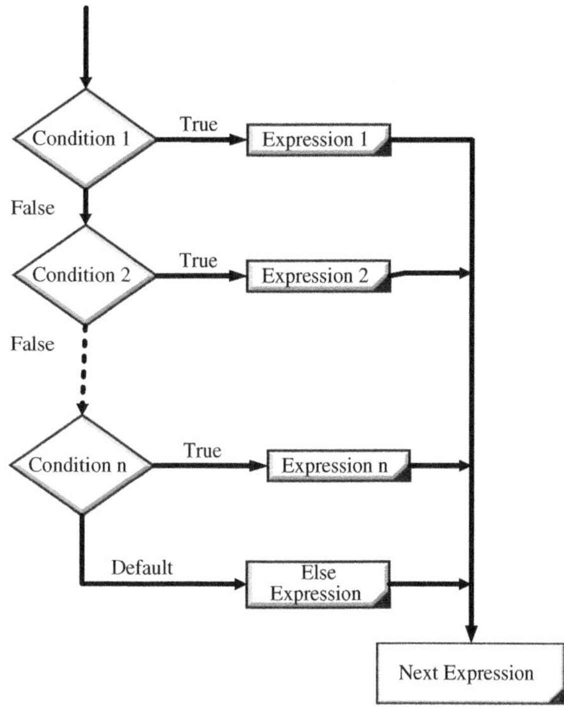

Figure 3.2 `If-elseif-else` condition flowchart.

Example 3.2 Verify the input character is a vowel with an `if-elseif-else` condition. Set a variable character and compare five times with vowels a, e, i, o, u with `if-elseif`, and a default expression is last with the `else` branch. If the character matches with a vowel, display "char is a vowel" else "char is not a vowel".

```
set char u
if {$char == "a"} {
        puts "char is a vowel"
} elseif {$char == "e"} {
        puts "char is a vowel"
} elseif {$char == "i"} {
        puts "char is a vowel"
} elseif {$char == "o"} {
        puts "char is a vowel"
} elseif {$char == "u"} {
        puts "char is a vowel"
} else {
        puts "char is not
a vowel"
}
```

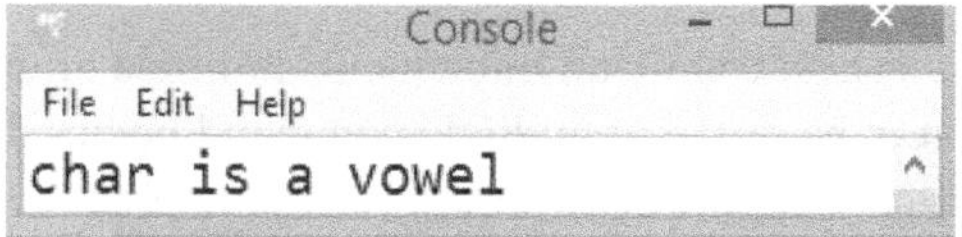

Example 3.3 A student scores 40, 60, and 60 in English, Math, and Science subjects, respectively. Criteria followed for awarding the division are based on the average score of the three subjects: more than 60, first division; more than 50 and less than 60, second division; more than 33 and less than 50, third division; and below 33, fail. Write Tcl script to calculate the division of the student.

Solution

Define three variables to initialize the scores in English, Math, and Science.

Total = English + Math + Science

Average = Total / 3

An `if` statement condition evaluates based on the value of the condition average of the score obtained by a student in English, Math, and Science and decides which division to be awarded.

```
set english 40
set maths 60
set science 60
set total [ expr
$maths+$english+$science]
set averagr [expr $total/3]
if { $average >60 } {
        puts "First division "
} elseif { $average >50} {
        puts "Second division "
} elseif { $average > 33} {
        puts "Third division "
} else {
        puts "Failed "
}
```

```
Console
File Edit Help
Second division
```

3.2 Switch-Case Command

A `switch` command implements multiple branch links to a case expression. It contains a condition to be tested at multiple command bodies depending on the value of the expression, as presented in Figure 3.3. The body contains either a simple expression or pattern matching. As soon as the pattern match evaluates the following expression, it returns the following body expression. The last condition is the default and gets evaluated when no earlier condition has been evaluated. In case the default string is not available and no condition is met, the switch command returns an empty string. The body must be grouped by curly braces to avoid substitution. The value/pattern to the switch case is numeric, alphabetic, or a string.

```
switch switchingString {
matchString1 { body1}
matchString2 { body2 }
        ...
matchStringn { bodyn }
 }
```

Figure 3.3 `Switch` case flowchart.

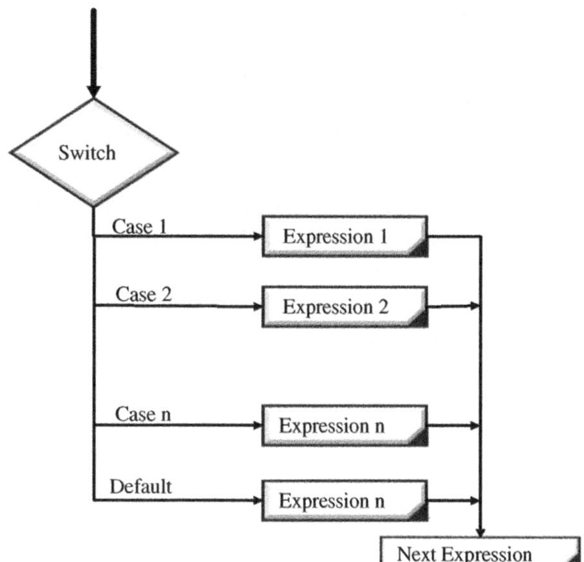

Example 3.4 Evaluate the grade of a candidate given in Example 3.3 based on switch-case conditions.

Solution

The condition `per` is set to evaluate the average. The switch condition is framed according to the level of the score and decodes the grade.

```
set english 60
set maths 60
set science 60
set total [ expr
$maths+$english+$science]
set per [expr $total/3]
switch $per {
60 {puts "First division "}
50 {puts "Second division " }
33 {puts "Third division " }
default {puts "Failed " }
}
```

Console
File Edit Help
First division

3.3 Loop Command

The `loop` command in Tcl enables execution of the set of expressions repeatedly based on the given condition. There are three types of loops supported in Tcl: while; for; and forever [2].

3.3.1 While Loop

The `while` command has two parts: a test condition and command body. It continuously executes the body till the condition is truly presented, as shown by the flowchart in Figure 3.4. Since the variable of the body gets updated on each loop, it is necessary to store the internal variable depending on the requirement. The test condition may be a single or group of statements which evaluate to true (1) or false (0). When the condition gets a false, it is removed from the loop and the control goes to the next immediate expression.

```
while {booleanExpr} {
        body
        }
```

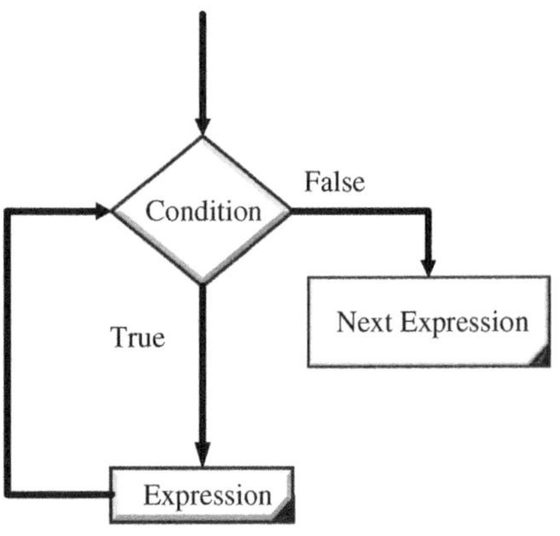

Figure 3.4 `While` loop flowchart.

Example 3.5 Write Tcl script to display the number ranges 0 to 10 using the `while` loop.

Solution
Set a variable `i` = 0; the `while` loop continues to evaluate the following expression until the condition is true, i.e., `i` ≤ 10. On every iteration, the value of i increments and is displayed. The `puts` command in the `while` loop after the `incr` command displays the incremented value on each iteration.

```
set i 0 ;
while {$i <= 10} {
            incr i
            puts $i
                  }
```

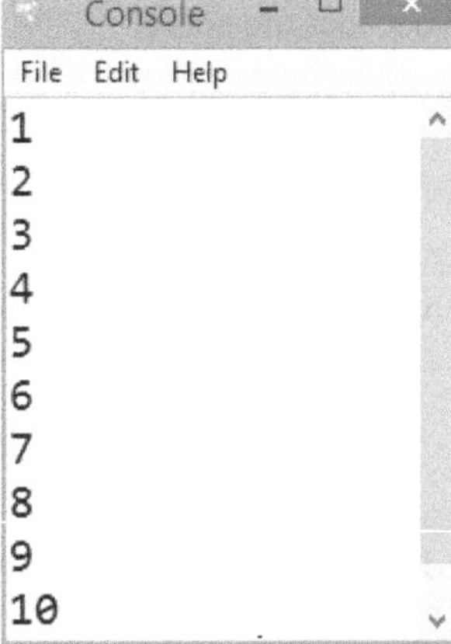

Example 3.6 Write a Tcl script to display only even numbers in the range 0 to 10 using the `while` loop.

Solution
A `while` loop continues to evaluate the following two expressions until the condition is true. The `puts` command in the `while` loop before the `set` expression verifies when the condition is true and it is displayed. On the last iteration, x is set to 10 but the (x < 10) condition becomes false and is not displayed.

```
set x 0;
while {$x < 10} {
    puts "x is $x an even";
    set x [expr $x + 2]
```

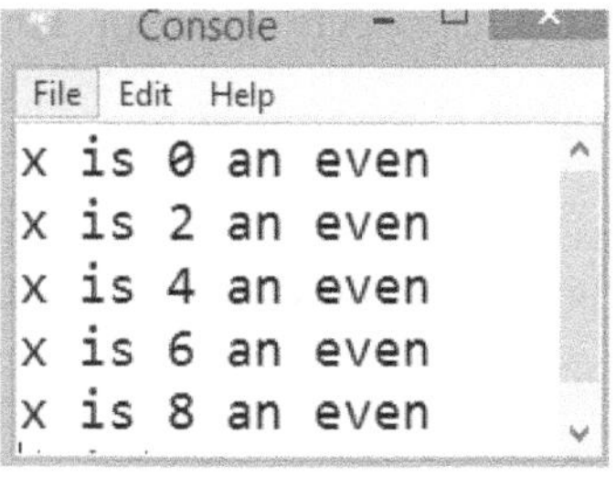


```
set a 10
while { $a < 20 } {
puts "value of a: $a"
incr a
}
```

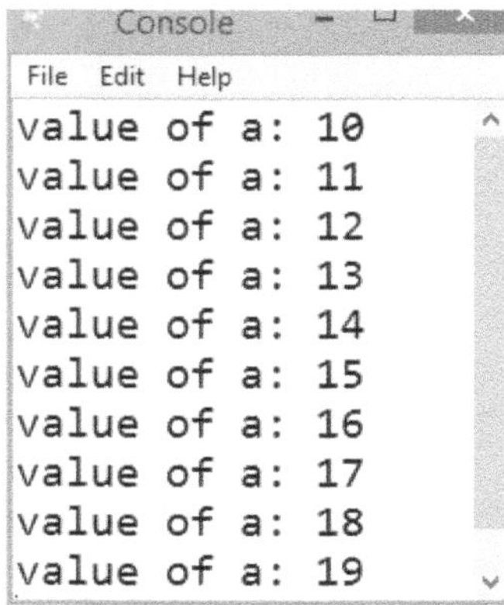

Here, the `puts` command in the `while` loop appears before the `incr` command. It verifies when the condition is found true and displays the `puts` command.

Note – Care is needed when using the `puts` command inside a `while` loop.

3.3.2 For Loop

The `for` loop supported in Tcl is similar to the for loop in the C statement. It contains four arguments: initialization; condition; increment; and expressions, as shown in Figure 3.5. The first argument initializes the loop once, and the loop control variable is declared in this step. The second argument is the condition that determines the number of times the loop will iterate if the condition is found true. If the condition becomes false, the loop is not executed, and the iteration control jumps to the next instructions after for loop. The third argument is after the iteration control jumps up to the increment statement. Here the variable can be updated. The fourth argument is/are expressions in the loop to execute and these repeat themselves.

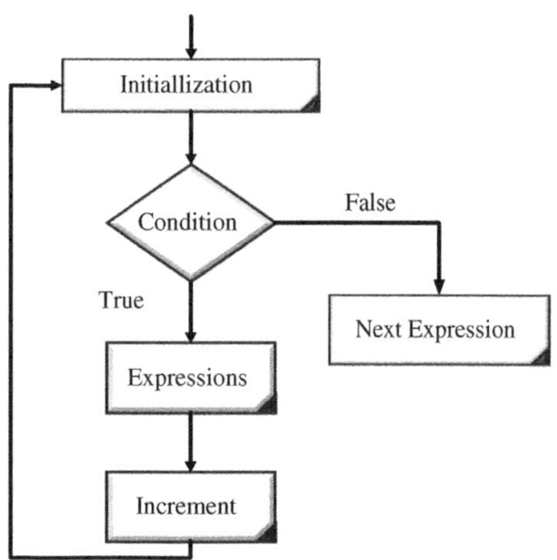

Figure 3.5 Flowchart of `for` loop.

```
for {initialization} {condition}
{increment} {
        expression(s)
    }
```

Example 3.7 Write Tcl script to display the range of numbers in the range of 0 to 9 using the `for` loop.

Solution
The variable `i` inside the `for` loop begins at 0. The value of `i` is displayed and increments until it is less than 10. The loop executes a certain number of times and displays for values from 0 to 9.

```
for {set i 0} {$i  < 10}
{incr i} {
        puts $i
}
```

Example 3.8 Write Tcl script to display only odd numbers between 0 to 10.

Solution
A `for` loop is required, similar to Example 3.7, to create a range of numbers from 0 to 9. It needs to select only an odd number if the condition inside the `for` loop divides the number by 2 and compares the remainder with 1. If the remainder is 1 display, else do not display.

```
for {set i 0} {$i < 10}
{incr i} {
       if {$i % 2 == 1} {
              puts "$i an
odd number"
              }
       }
```

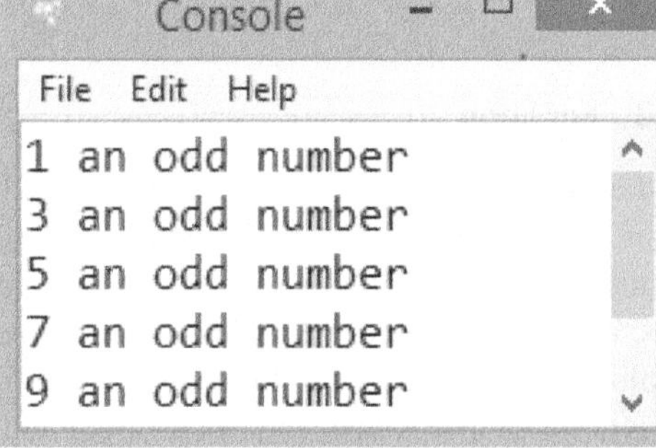

Example 3.9 Write Tcl script to display a truth table for logic gates (`AND/OR/NOT/NAND/NOR/XOR/XNOR`).

Solution
The procedure is used to present a Boolean equation of different logic gates and for a loop used to create a truth table. A separate `for` loop requires for each variable. Nesting of the `for` loop requires creating more than one input truth table. Each logic gate is declared as a separate procedure return with the defined equation of logic gates. The logical operator is used to present logical relations in the procedure. The `proc` invokes the procedure in the program wherever it is needed to evaluate the logical relation. Variable created through the `for` loop or nested `for` loop passes to the procedure to return the single value binary result.

$NOT = !A$
$AND = A \& B$
$OR = A \mid B$

```
proc not {a} {return [expr ! $a]}
proc and {a b} {return [expr
$a & $b]}
proc or {a b} {return [expr
$a | $b]}
puts "NOT Gate Truth Table"
puts "input\toutput"
for {set i 0} {$i < 2} {incr i} {
puts "$i\t[not $i]"
}
puts "AND Gate Truth Table"
puts "input1 input2    output"
for {set i 0} {$i < 2} {incr i} {
for {set j 0} {$j < 2} {incr j} {
puts "$i     $j       [and $i $j]"
}
}
puts "OR Gate Truth Table"
puts "input1 input2    output"
for {set i 0} {$i < 2} {incr i} {
for {set j 0} {$j < 2} {incr j} {
puts "$i     $j       [or $i $j]"
}
}
```

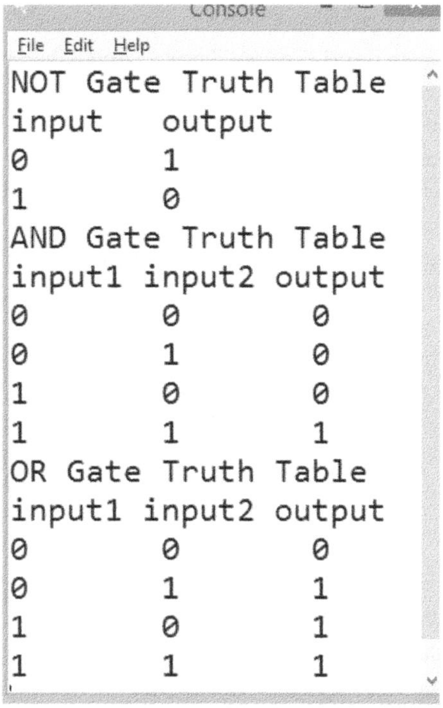

```
Console
File Edit Help
NOT Gate Truth Table
input   output
0       1
1       0
AND Gate Truth Table
input1 input2 output
0      0      0
0      1      0
1      0      0
1      1      1
OR Gate Truth Table
input1 input2 output
0      0      0
0      1      1
1      0      1
1      1      1
```

The NAND-NOR logic gate implements with nesting of the procedure described in the following. NAND logic requires a NOT and AND procedure while NOR requires an OR and NOR procedure. The order of the procedure needs to be carefully defined.

$NAND = !(A \& B)$

$NOR = !(A \mid B)$

```
proc not {a} {return [expr ! $a]}
proc and {a b} {return [expr
$a & $b]}
proc or {a b} {return [expr
$a | $b]}
proc nand {a b} {not [and $a $b]}
proc nor {a b} {not [or $a $b]}
puts "NAND Gate Truth Table"
puts "input1 input2   output"
for {set i 0} {$i < 2} {incr i} {
for {set j 0} {$j < 2} {incr j} {
puts "$i    $j      [nand $i $j]"
}
}
puts "NOR Gate Truth Table"
puts "input1 input2   output"
for {set i 0} {$i < 2} {incr i} {
for {set j 0} {$j < 2} {incr j} {
puts "$i    $j      [nor $i $j]"
}
}
```

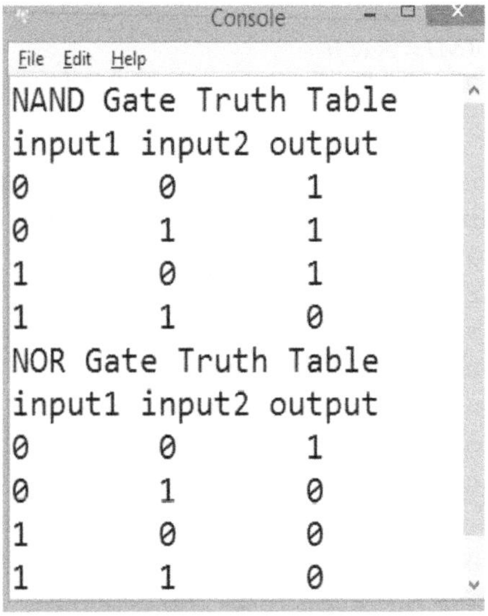

```
Console
File Edit Help
NAND Gate Truth Table
input1 input2 output
0      0      1
0      1      1
1      0      1
1      1      0
NOR Gate Truth Table
input1 input2 output
0      0      1
0      1      0
1      0      0
1      1      0
```

To define the XOR and XNOR gate, three nesting procedures are required with the careful declaration of the order of precedence.

$XOR = (!(A) \& B))|((A) \& !(B))$

$XNOR = (A \& B)|(!(A) \& !(B))$

```
proc not {a} {return [expr ! $a]}
proc and {a b} {return [expr $a & $b]}
proc or {a b} {return [expr $a | $b]}
proc xnor {a b} {or [and $a $b] [and
[not $a] [not $b]]}
proc xor {a b} {or [and [not $a] $b]
[and $a [not $b]]}
puts "XOR Gate Truth Table"
puts "input1 input2   output"
for {set i 0} {$i < 2} {incr i} {
for {set j 0} {$j < 2} {incr j} {
puts "$i     $j       [xor $i $j]"
}
}
puts "XNOR Gate Truth Table"
puts "input1 input2   output"
for {set i 0} {$i < 2} {incr i} {
for {set j 0} {$j < 2} {incr j} {
puts "$i     $j       [xnor $i $j]"
}
}
```

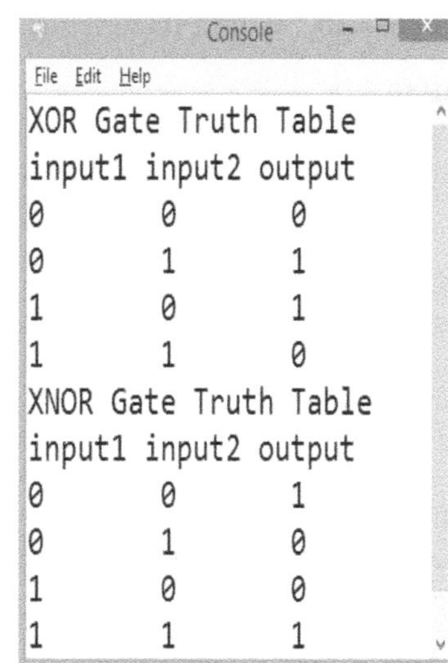

3.3.3 Foreach Command

The foreach command implements a loop with variables. The variable takes a value from the defined list or string, presented as a flowchart in Figure 3.6. Each element of the list (first to last) applies to the loop and executes the expression under the loop [3]. Each element is executed only once. The number of elements and loop iterations will not be the same if the number of elements is not sufficient for each loop variable, so empty values are used for the missing elements.

```
set x {    }
foreach i $x {
        expressions
}
```

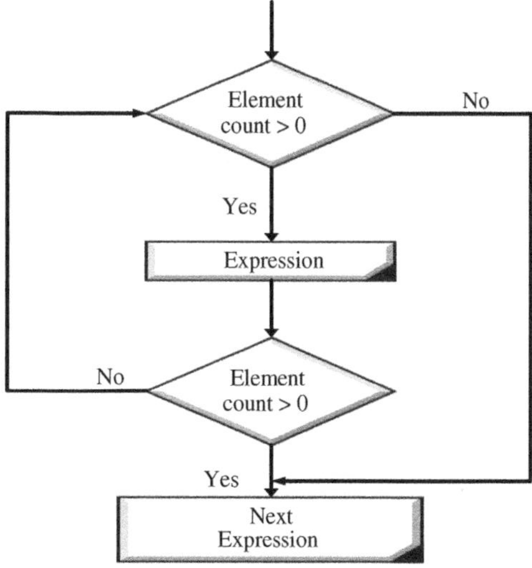

Figure 3.6 Foreach command flowchart.

Example 3.10 Write a Tcl script to display each element of the list individually.

Solution

By setting a list, a `foreach` loop requires a local variable and is applied to each element of the list, and the `puts` command is executed to display.

```
set numbers {1 2 3 4 5 6 7 8 9 10}
foreach x $numbers {
puts "x = $x"
}
```

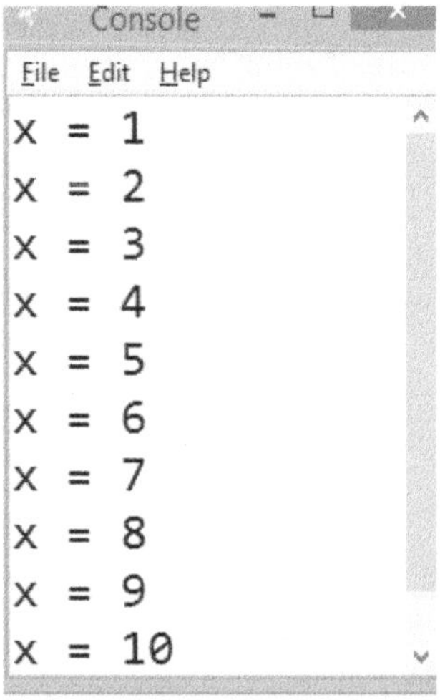

```
Console
File Edit Help
x = 1
x = 2
x = 3
x = 4
x = 5
x = 6
x = 7
x = 8
x = 9
x = 10
```

Example 3.11 Write Tcl script to display each element of a string along with the index number.

Solution

The index of the string begins with zero. A string `x` contains three elements. The `foreach` loop consists of a local variable `j` and applies on each element of `x`, and executes the `puts` statement and increments by a variable `i`.

```
set x "a b c"
set i 0;
foreach j $x {
  puts "$j is item
number $i in list x"
  incr i
}
```

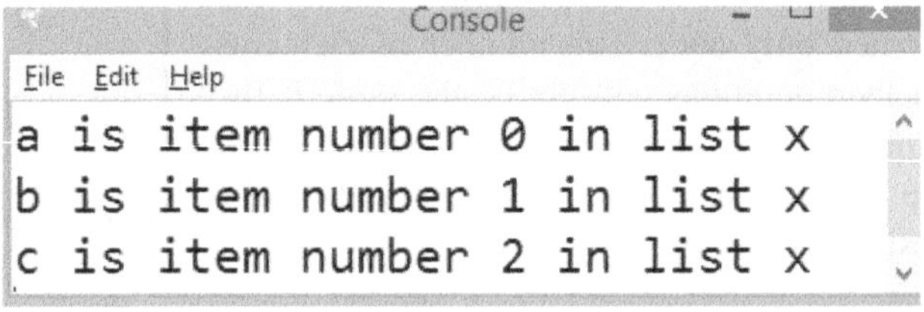

```
Console
File Edit Help
a is item number 0 in list x
b is item number 1 in list x
c is item number 2 in list x
```

Example 3.12 Write Tcl script to find the sum of all elements in a list.

Solution

Declare a list (`m`) and a variable (`n`) with an initial value of zero. The `foreach` command creates a loop to each element one by one in `m` and an updated value of `n`.

```
set m {1 2 3 4 5}
set n 0
foreach i $m {
set n [ expr $n + $i]
}
puts "Sum of all elements in
list=$n"
```

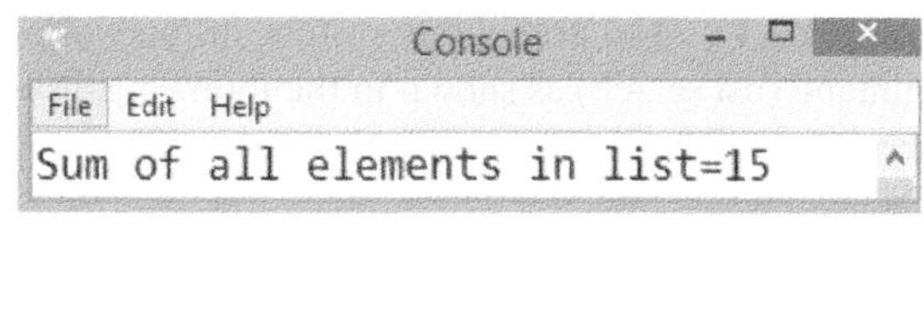

3.4 Continue and Break

The execution loop can be controlled by the `break` and `continue` statements. These statements continue to check for the conditional test. The `break` command says to immediately exit from the loop and the `continue` command says to continue the loop for the next iteration.

```
set i 0
set sum 0
while { 1 } {
    incr i
    if {$i == 5} { continue }
    if {$i > 10} { break }
    set sum [expr $sum+$i]
}
puts "Sum = $sum"
```

Console
File Edit Help
Sum = 50

In the above example, the value of `i` is incremented and added to the sum in the loop. When `i` = 5, the `continue` command allows to execute the next iteration until (`i` > 10), then the `break` command says to terminate the loop and execute the next `puts` statement.

3.5 Catch and Error

A command may raise errors due to wrong arguments or due to the wrong implementation. The error may cause the execution of the program to be aborted. In Tcl, errors are handled with the `catch` and `error` commands [4].

`Catch` command is used to detect the error in Tcl script:

```
catch { command } resultvar
```

Syntax of the `catch` command includes a command and a resultvar, which indicates the error message 0 if there was no error and 1 if it catches an error.

Example 3.13 The availability of files in the working directory can be populated with the `ls` command (list search) as shown in the following. If we try to open a file that is not available, the interpreter will catch the error, and a return of 1 indicates an error is detected.

```
ls
C:/ActiveTcl/bin:
bitmap-editor.tcl    cards.txt              critcl
critcl.tcl           diagram-viewer.tcl     dtplite.tcl
file                 input.txt              nns.tcl
nnsd.tcl             nnslog.tcl             one.csv
pt.tcl               sdx.kit                tcl86t.dll
tcldocstrip.tcl      tclkit.upx.exe*        tclkit.upx2.exe*
tclsh.exe*           tclsh86t.exe*          tclsht.exe*
tk86t.dll            tkcon.tcl              two.csv
wish.exe*            wish86t.exe*           wisht.exe*
catch {set file [open "myNonexistingfile.txt" r]} result ➔| 1
```

`Error` command raises an error condition that will terminate a script unless it is trapped with the `catch` command.

```
error "Error Message" "Error Info" "Error Code"
```

The `error` command enables the description of the detected error in detail. We can display the predefined error message, error information, and error code on detecting the error.

```
catch {set file [open "myNonexistingfile.txt" r]} result
puts "ErrorMsg: $result"
puts "ErrorCode: $errorCode"
puts "ErrorInfo:$errorInfo"
```

There is a possibility that a Tcl procedure can fall into error conditions. In such a case, the user may specify the error message when the catch returns 1. It will help in debugging but also enhance the length of the program.

```
proc errorproc {x} {
    if {$x >= 0} {
            error
"Error generated by
error" "Info String
for error" $x
    }
}
catch {errorproc
0} result
puts "ErrorMsg:
$result"
puts
"ErrorCode:$errorCode"
puts
"ErrorInfo:$errorInfo"
```

```
Console
File Edit Help
ErrorMsg: Error generated by error
ErrorCode:0
ErrorInfo:Info String for error
    (procedure "errorproc" line 1)
    invoked from within
"errorproc 0"
```

Example 3.14 Specify the error condition for dividing by zero in a procedure and display the error message.

Solution

```
proc Div {a b} {
   if {$b == 0} {
      error "Error generated"
"Error in string" 401
   } else {
      return [expr $a/$b]
   }
}
if {[catch {puts "Result = [Div
10 0]"} errmsg]} {
   puts "ErrorMsg: $errmsg"
   puts "ErrorCode:$errorCode"
   puts "ErrorInfo:$errorInfo"
}
if {[catch {puts "Result = [Div
10 2]"} errmsg]} {
   puts "ErrorMsg: $errmsg"
   puts "ErrorCode:$errorCode"
   puts "ErrorInfo:$errorInfo"
}
```

```
ErrorMsg: Error generated
ErrorCode:401
ErrorInfo:Error in string
    (procedure "Div" line 1)
    invoked from within
"Div 10 0"
Result = 5
```

3.6 Solved Problems

[1] Write a Tcl script to find the average of a given number in a list.

Solution
First, define a procedure to calculate the average. It can accept a list as input and return the single result average.

- In the procedure:
  - Define a variable sum initially zero
  - A `foreach` command with local variable x is applied to each element and added to the sum
  - Compute the average expression by dividing by the length of the list
  - Return the average
- Invoke the procedure with the list as input

```
proc avg {numbers} {
   set sum 0
   foreach x $numbers {
      set sum  [expr $sum + $x]
   }
   set average [expr $sum/
[llength $numbers]]
   return $average
}
puts "Average of {70 80 50
60}=[avg {70 80 50 60}]"
puts "Average of {70 80 50}=[avg
{70 80 50}]"
```

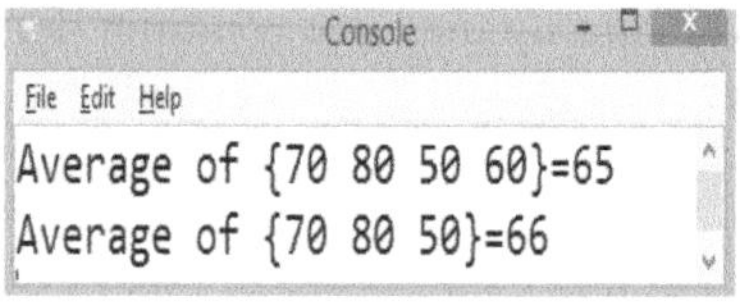

```
Console
File Edit Help
Average of {70 80 50 60}=65
Average of {70 80 50}=66
```

[2] Write a Tcl script to find the number of characters in your name.

Solution
Suppose the name is MANISH.

- Declare the name a string and a variable `len` to display the count value
- The `split` command splits each character of the string and separates them by whitespace
- A `foreach` loop on the split string is applied to each element and increments the variable `len`

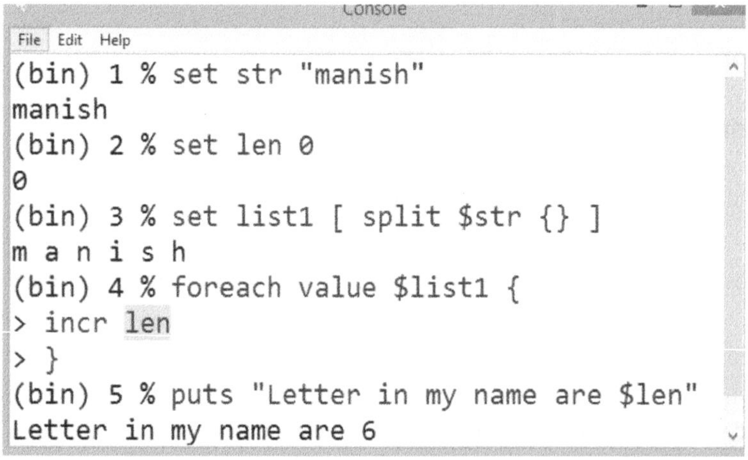

```
Console
File Edit Help
(bin) 1 % set str "manish"
manish
(bin) 2 % set len 0
0
(bin) 3 % set list1 [ split $str {} ]
m a n i s h
(bin) 4 % foreach value $list1 {
> incr len
> }
(bin) 5 % puts "Letter in my name are $len"
Letter in my name are 6
```

[3] Write Tcl script to calculate factorial using the `while` loop.

Solution

```
proc fact {n} {
set f 1
while {$n>=2} {
set f [expr $f*$n]
set n [expr $n - 1]
}
return $f
}
puts "Factorial of 5=[fact 5]"
```

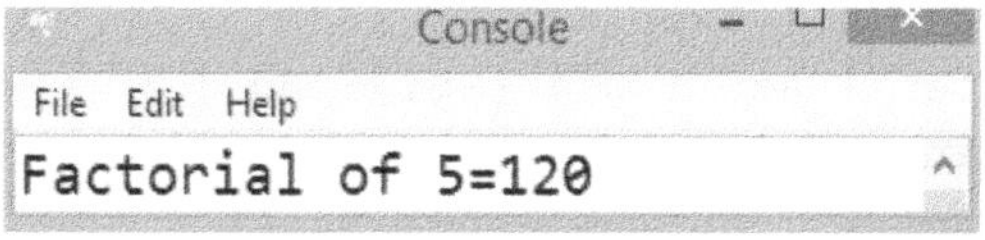

```
Console
File Edit Help
Factorial of 5=120
```

---

[4] Write Tcl script to display the following pattern.

Solution

```
0
0 1
0 1 2
0 1 2 3
0 1 2 3 4
0 1 2 3 4 5
```

```
Console
File Edit Help
(bin) 1 % set i 0
0
(bin) 2 % set out 0
0
(bin) 3 % puts $out
0
(bin) 4 % while {$i <= 5} {
> puts $out
> incr i
> append out $i
> }
0
01
012
0123
01234
012345
```

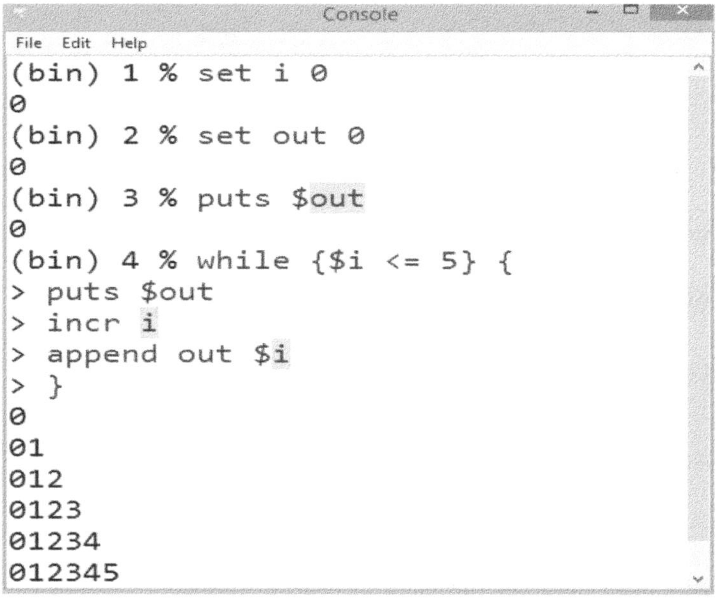

[5] Write a script to verify the given string is a palindrome.

Solution

- Define a string
- Calculate the length of the string
- Use a `for` loop on half of the string length
- Read the character in the first index assigned to var1
- Read the character in last index assigned to var2
- Compare `var1` and `var2`, if equal, print palindrome

```
set a "abcba"
set len [ string length $a ]
set n [ expr $len/2 ]
for { set i 0 } { $i < $n } {
incr i } {
set b [ string index $a $i ]
set c [ expr $len - 1 - $i ]
set d [ string index $a $c ]
if {$b != $d} {
puts "not a palindrome"
Exit
}
}
puts "Palindrome"
```

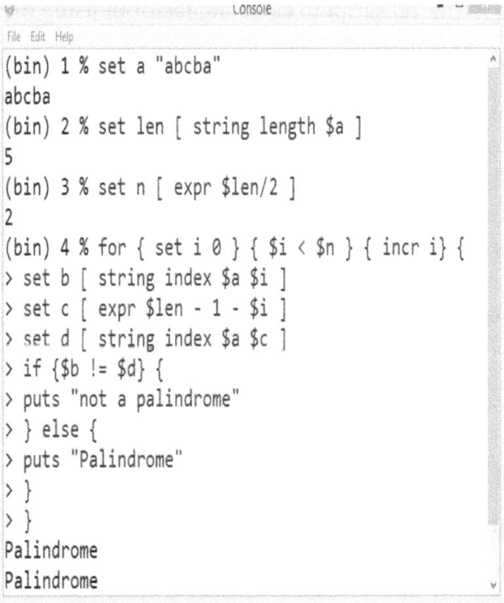

```
Console
File Edit Help
(bin) 1 % set a "abcba"
abcba
(bin) 2 % set len [ string length $a ]
5
(bin) 3 % set n [ expr $len/2 ]
2
(bin) 4 % for { set i 0 } { $i < $n } { incr i} {
> set b [ string index $a $i ]
> set c [ expr $len - 1 - $i ]
> set d [ string index $a $c ]
> if {$b != $d} {
> puts "not a palindrome"
> } else {
> puts "Palindrome"
> }
> }
Palindrome
Palindrome
```

3.7 Practice Questions

[1] Write Tcl script to find the factorial using the while loop.

[2] Write a Tcl script to find the number of vowels in your name.

[3] Comment on the following program:

```
for {set i 0; set sum 0} {$i <= 10} {set sum [expr $sum+$i];
incr i} {
}
puts "Sum = $sum"
```

[4] How many times will the following loop be executed?

```
        for {set i 0} {$i < 9} {incr i} {
    puts $i
}
```

[5] Comment on the result:

```
set c [list Mark Roy Brian]
foreach o $c {
    puts $o
}
```

3.8 MCQs

[1] Calculate the output value of s in the program:

```
set a 6
   set b 5
  set s 0
 for {set I 1} {$i<= $b} {incr i} {
  set s [expr $a + $s]
    }
puts $s
```

(a) s = 6
(b) s = 5
(c) s = 30
(d) s = 11

Solution (c)

[2] A foreach loop in Tcl executes the statement for ________ variable in the list.
(a) Selected
(b) Each
(c) Alternate
(d) Null

Solution (b)

[3] What will the following Tcl script return?

```
set list1 {a e i o u}
puts [lsearch $list1 o]
```

(a) 3,o
(b) o
(c) 4
(d) 3

Solution (d)

[4] What will the following Tcl script execute?

```
set k 1
foreach value {2 3 4} {
set k [expr $k * $value]
}
puts $k
```

(a) Multiply each element of a list by k
(b) Multiply each element of the list by k and update the value of k
(c) Multiply each element of the list by k, update values of k, and display 24
(d) None of the above

Solution (c)

[5] What will the following script display?

```
set c [list read write speak]
      foreach o $c {
            puts $o
         }
```

(a) read, write, speak
(b) write, read, speak
(c) speak, write, read
(d) None of the above

Solution (a)

References

1 Welch, B.B., Jones, K., and Hobbs, J. (2003). *Practical Programming in Tcl/Tk*. Prentice-Hall Professional.

2 Nadkarni, A.P. (2017). *The Tcl Programming Language: A Comprehensive Guide*. Createspace Independent Publishing Platform.

3 Harrison, M. and McLennan, M. (1998). *Effective Tcl/Tk Programming: Writing Better Programs with Tcl and Tk*. Addison Wesley Longman Publishing Co., Inc.

4 Flynt, C. (1999). *Tcl/Tk for real programmers*, 698. AP Professional.

4

Tcl Data Structure

The basic data structure of Tcl is a string and two higher levels of data structure are the list and array. The string is the default data type used to represent an integer, floating number, or text. In Tcl, a string contains 16-bit unicode and alphanumeric characters. A list is an ordered collection of numbers, words, or strings. Lists are implemented as strings [1]. The array is the indexed collection of variables. The index can be a string and the array variable another string. A string-list-array has its syntax and commands. These commands must execute in square brackets. The string-based command starts with `string [string ......]`, the list-based command starts with `l [l.......]`, and the array-based command starts with `array [array .......]`.

4.1 String and Matching Command

The string is the basic data type in Tcl. The string is a combination of alphanumeric character numbers or Boolean variables. A string declares with the *set* command, and does not require grouping in the case of a single word. More than one word in a string can be grouped using double quotes " " or curly braces { }. The declaration of a string is shown in Figure 4.1.

There is a large number of string-based commands, as presented in Table 4.1.

The syntax of a Tcl string command is

```
string operation stringname othertag
```

```
(bin) 1 % set st1 Hello
Hello
(bin) 2 % set st2 "Hello Tcl World"
Hello Tcl World
(bin) 3 % set st3 {Hello String of Tcl}
Hello String of Tcl
(bin) 4 % puts "$st1, $st2, $st3"
Hello, Hello Tcl World, Hello String of Tcl
```

Figure 4.1 String declaration.

Programming and GUI Fundamentals: Tcl-Tk for Electronic Design Automation (EDA), First Edition.
Suman Lata Tripathi, Abhishek Kumar, and Jyotirmoy Pathak.

Table 4.1 String-based command.

String-based command	Description
`string length string name`	Returns length of string
`string index stringname index value`	Returns character at the index position. Index position starts with 0 and keyword end can use for the last character
`string range string name first last`	Returns part of a string composed of first and last index numbers

`string compare string1 string2`	Compares two strings lexicographically, returns
	`-1 string1 sort before string2`
	`0 string1 equals string2`
	`1 string1 sort after string2`

`string first string1 string2`	Returns the index of the character in `string1` that starts the first match to `string2`, −1 if there is no match to `string2` in `string1`
`string last string1 string2`	Returns the index of the character in `string1` that starts the last match to `string2` −1 if there is no match to `string2` in `string1`
`string wordend string index`	Returns the index of the character just after the last one in the word which contains the index character of the string
`string wordstart string index`	Returns the index of the character just before the last one in the word which contains the index character of the string
`string match pattern stringname`	1 if the pattern matches the string name 0 if the pattern does not match
`string tolower stringname`	Converts all characters of the string to lower case
`string toupper stringname`	Converts all characters of the string to upper case
`string totitle stringname`	Converts the string into title case (first letter to uppercase and remaining in lower case)
`string trim stringname trimchar`	Removes the trim character from the string name from both terminals (left–right) Removes space if trim character is not specified
`string trimleft stringname trimchar`	Removes the trim character from the start (left) terminal of the string name
`string trimright stringname trimchar`	Removes the trim character from the end (right) terminal of the string name

The string-based command starts with a string; the second argument (operation) determines a specific operation; and the third argument (string name) and additional arguments are required depending on the command. A `string` command must be invoked within square brackets.

The string-based command is explained with an example:

`Defines a string st1= "This is my test string"`

A single operation command executes according to the description in Table 4.1. The nesting feature of the string command enables mixing of more than one command and executes the command focused on the initial string. `[String length [string range $st1 5 10]` → first, the string range execution results in the output `"is my test"` which acts as the input string for the outer command `[string length]` to compute the number of characters 11, as shown in Figure 4.2.

Figure 4.2 String basic command.

```
(bin) 1 % set st1 "This is my test string"
This is my test string
(bin) 2 % puts "There is [string length $st1] character"
There is 22 character
(bin) 3 % puts "There is [string index $st1 0] is the first character"
There is T is the first character
(bin) 4 % puts "There is [string index $st1 end] is the last character"
There is g is the last character
(bin) 5 % puts "There is [string range $st1 5 15] are character between 5th to 15th"
There is is my test  are character between 5th to 15th
(bin) 6 % puts "There is [string length [string range $st1 5 15]] are character between 5th to 15th"
There is 11 are character between 5th to 15th
```

```
(bin) 1 % set st1 "string based command"
string based command
(bin) 2 % set st2 "a"
a
(bin) 3 % puts "First occurance of $st2 in $st1 is [string first $st2 $st1]"
First occurance of a in string based command is 8
(bin) 4 % puts "Last occurace of $st2 in $st1 is [string last $st2 $st1]"
Last occurace of a in string based command is 17
(bin) 5 % puts "character at index 0 is $st1 is [string index $st1 0]"
character at index 0 is string based command is s
(bin) 6 % puts "Word end index in $st1 is [string wordend $st1 25]"
Word end index in string based command is 20
(bin) 7 % puts "Word start index in $st1 is [string wordstart $st1 25]"
Word start index in string based command is 13
```

Figure 4.3 includes the string trim example. The character to be removed can be declared separately or implicitly (Figure 4.4).

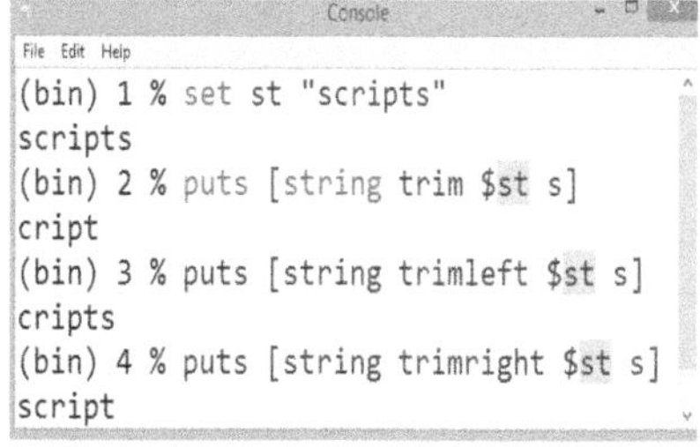

Figure 4.3 String trim.

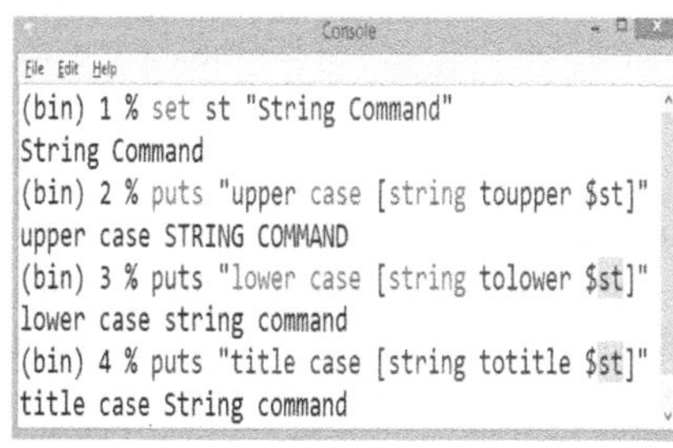

Figure 4.4 String case.

Figure 4.5 shows the comparison of two strings in lexicographical order. The string compare command compares two strings lexicographically (compares the strings character by character). If the first character of both strings is the same, continue with the second character and so on until the end. If both strings are equal `return 0`; if the non-matching character occurs first in `string 1 return -1`; and if the non-matching character occurs first in `string2 return 1`.

```
(bin) 1 % set st1 "scripting language"
scripting language
(bin) 2 % set st2 "TCL"
TCL
(bin) 3 % set st3 "programming language"
programming language
(bin) 4 % puts [string compare $st1 $st2]
1
(bin) 5 % puts [string compare $st2 $st3]
-1
```

Figure 4.5 String compare.

4.1.1 Append Command

As the name stands, the `append` command depends on the variable of the first argument, and then remaining arguments [2]. The variable will declare implicitly or not declare initially. It adds two new variables at the end of the string. It works on the memory allocation scheme to provide the extra space required for the expansion. In Figure 4.6, `st2` has been appended after `st1`, while the third string is not declared instantly appended.

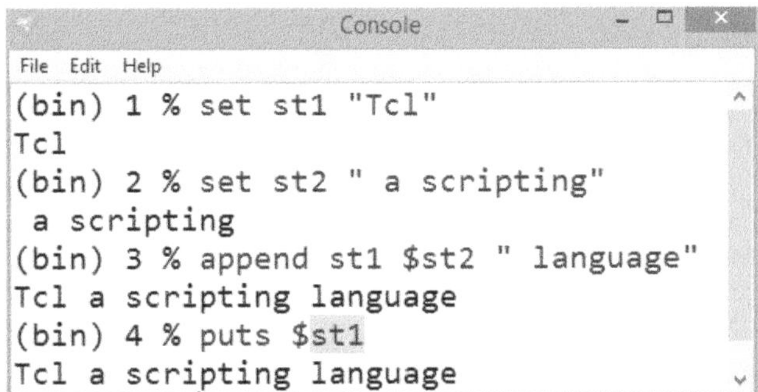

Figure 4.6 String append.

4.1.2 Format Command

The `format` command represents a string in the given format and converts the string according to the specifier presented in Table 4.2. Syntax of the command is

```
format spec value
```

Table 4.2 Format specifier.

Specifier	Description
`%d`	Signed Integer (decimal)
`%u`	Unsigned Integer
`%o`	Unsigned octal
`%x`	Unsigned hexadecimal
`%c`	ASCII
`%s`	String
`%f`	Floating number
`%e / %E`	Floating number with scientific notation

The `spec` is the combination of (i) literal place in the result and (ii) keywords indicating how to format. The keyword starts with %. It is similar to the *`printf`* command in the C language.

Figure 4.7 presents the floating-point presentation in regular and scientific format. The number of variables after the decimal is controlled by introducing the number of characters in the specifier, as shown in Figure 4.8. Precision indicates the period and a number. The specifiers `%f` and `%e` denote the number of digits after the decimal point. The specifier `%g` indicates the total number of significant digits and `%d` and `%x` indicate the number of digits to be printed with a padding of zeros if necessary.

```
Console
File Edit Help
(bin) 1 % puts [format %f 55.5]
55.500000
(bin) 2 % puts [format %e 55.5]
5.550000e+01
(bin) 3 % puts [format %s "Scripting Language"]
Scripting Language
(bin) 4 % puts [format "%u %s" 1 code]
1 code
```

Figure 4.7 Format command example.

```
Console
File Edit Help
(bin) 1 % set num 5.2477853
5.2477853
(bin) 2 % puts [format %0.7f $num]
5.2477853
(bin) 3 % puts [format %0.5f $num]
5.24779
(bin) 4 % puts [format %0.2f $num]
5.25
(bin) 5 % puts [format %0.0f $num]
5
(bin) 6 % puts [format %0.7e $num]
5.2477853e+00
(bin) 7 % puts [format %0.4e $num]
5.2478e+00
(bin) 8 % puts [format %0.1e $num]
5.2e+00
```

Figure 4.8 Format command with precision.

4.1.3 Number Base Conversion with the Format Command

Digital design frequently requires the conversion of a number into four popular formats: binary with base 2; octal with base 8; decimal with base 10; and hexadecimal with base 16. A method to perform conversion is described in Figures 4.9–4.12. The default number in the Tcl console is in decimal, and a number in binary starts with 0b, in octal 0o, and hexadecimal 0x.

```
(bin) 1 % set num 25
25
(bin) 2 % puts [format %b $num]
11001
(bin) 3 % puts [format %o $num]
31
(bin) 4 % puts [format %x $num]
19
```

Figure 4.9 Decimal to other formats.

```
(bin) 5 % set num 0b1101
0b1101
(bin) 6 % puts [format %d $num]
13
(bin) 7 % puts [format %o $num]
15
(bin) 8 % puts [format %x $num]
d
```

Figure 4.11 Binary to other formats.

```
(bin) 1 % set num 0o54
0o54
(bin) 2 % puts [format %d $num]
44
(bin) 3 % puts [format %x $num]
2c
(bin) 4 % puts [format %b $num]
101100
```

Figure 4.10 Octal to other formats.

```
(bin) 1 % set num 0xabc
0xabc
(bin) 2 % puts [format %d $num]
2748
(bin) 3 % puts [format %o $num]
5274
(bin) 4 % puts [format %b $num]
101010111100
```

Figure 4.12 Hexadecimal to other formats.

4.1.4 Scan Command

The scan command parses a string based on the format specifier, similar to `scanf` in C language, and operates by scanning the string and format together. This command parses substrings from an input string and returns a count of the number of conversions performed, or returns −1 if the end of the input string is reached before any conversions have been performed. The scan format uses square brackets; % indicates the start of a conversion specifier (Figure 4.13). The syntax of the scan command is

scan string {%[format]} variable

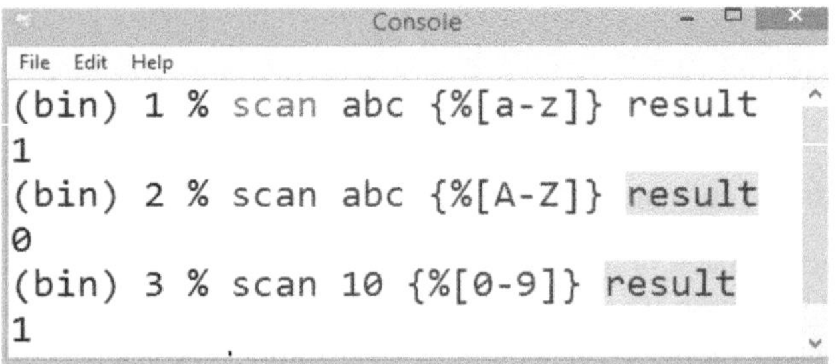
Console
File Edit Help
(bin) 1 % scan abc {%[a-z]} result
1
(bin) 2 % scan abc {%[A-Z]} result
0
(bin) 3 % scan 10 {%[0-9]} result
1

Figure 4.13 Scan command example.

4.1.5 Clock Command

The clock command is used to display the current time in seconds. Clock with a format command can be used to display the time in different formats. `[Clock seconds]` fetches the current system of time and display it in seconds. The current time is stored in the assigned variable. Every time its value would be updated is given in Figure 4.14. The clock command was added in Tcl7.5. The clock click is a high-resolution time value as a system-dependent integer.

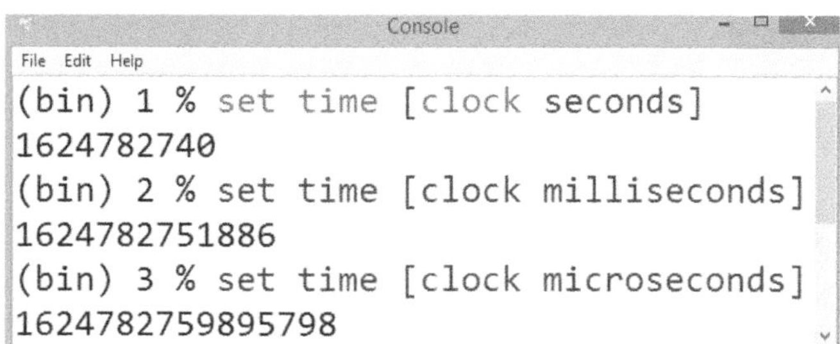

Figure 4.14 Clock seconds example.

- `clock click` Returns a high-resolution time value as a system dependent integer value
- `set time [clock seconds]` Updates the current value of time in seconds
- `set time [clock milliseconds]` Updates the current value of time in milliseconds
- `set time [clock microseconds]` Updates the current value of time in microseconds

Most `clock` commands deal with times represented as a count of seconds from epoch time, and this is the representation that `clock seconds` returns. The `clock click` command returns a platform-dependent high-resolution timer. Unlike `clock seconds` and `clock milliseconds`, the value of `clock click` is not guaranteed to be tied to any fixed epoch; it is simply intended to be the most precise interval timer available and is intended only for relative timing studies such as benchmarks.

4.1.6 Clock Format Command

The `clock` command provides access to the time and date. The clock command performs several operations that obtain and manipulate values that represent time. Digital devices display the time in different formats like HH:MM: SS, HH:MM:SS: AM/PM, HH: MM. The `clock format` command further converts the time variable into a specific format and returns it in a readable form. The syntax of the `clock format` command is

```
clock format clockvalue -format string -GMT boolean
```

`-GMT Boolean` acts as a switch, allowing selection of the timezone; `boolean 1` selects Greenwich meantime and otherwise Local Time. The `-format` string controls the format to be returned. The content of the string has content similar to the format command. Several % descriptors that can be used to describe the output are included in the following (Figure 4.15).

```
%H ....Hour (00 - 23)
%l .....Hour (00 - 12)
%M ....Minutes (00 - 59)
%S......Seconds (00 - 59)
%p ......PM or AM
```

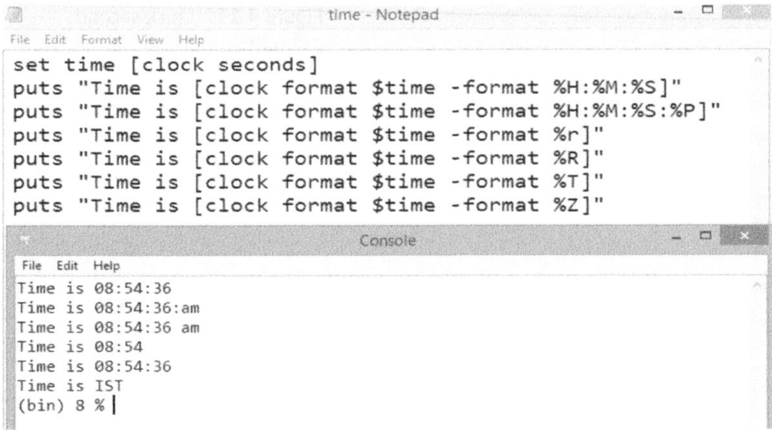

```
set time [clock seconds]
puts "Time is [clock format $time -format %H:%M:%S]"
puts "Time is [clock format $time -format %H:%M:%S:%P]"
puts "Time is [clock format $time -format %r]"
puts "Time is [clock format $time -format %R]"
puts "Time is [clock format $time -format %T]"
puts "Time is [clock format $time -format %Z]"
```

```
Time is 08:54:36
Time is 08:54:36:am
Time is 08:54:36 am
Time is 08:54
Time is 08:54:36
Time is IST
(bin) 8 %
```

Figure 4.15 Time representation with clock format.

There are predefined templates for the time representation (Figure 4.16).

```
%D . . . . Date as %m/%d/%y
%r. . . . . Time as %I:%M:%S %p
%R . . . . Time as %I:%M
%T . . . . Time as %I:%M:%S
%Z . . . . Time Zone Name
%a . . . . Abbreviated weekday name (Mon, Tue, etc.)
%A . . . . Full weekday name (Monday, Tuesday, etc.)
%b . . . . Abbreviated month name (Jan, Feb, etc.)
%B . . . . Full month name (January, February, etc.)
%d. . . . . Day of month
%m . . . . Month number (01-12)
%y. . . . . Year in century
%Y . . . . Year with 4 digits
```

```
set time [clock seconds]
puts "Date is :[clock format $time -format %d/%m/%y]"
puts "Date is :[clock format $time -format %d/%m/%Y]"
puts "Date is :[clock format $time -format %d/%b/%y]"
puts "Date is :[clock format $time -format %D]"
puts "Date is :[clock format $time -format %d:%m:%y]"
puts [clock format $time -format {Today is: %A, the %d of %B, %Y}]
```

```
Date is :10/08/20
Date is :10/08/2020
Date is :10/Aug/20
Date is :08/10/2020
Date is :10:08:20
Today is: Monday, the 10 of August, 2020
```

Figure 4.16 Clock format with predefined template.

A command that prints the current date and time of the system according to the default setting is shown in Figure 4.17.

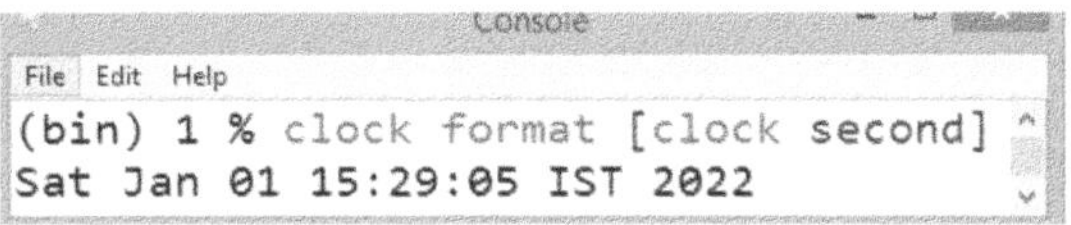

Figure 4.17 Clock format to display system time.

4.1.7 Clock Scan Command

The `clock scan` command accepts the time formatted as a string and converts it to the count value of seconds. It takes a `format` command followed by a string describing the expected format of the input.

`clock scan` *`dateString`* `-base seconds -format string -gmt` *`boolean`*

It converts `dateString` to an integer clock value, and year, month, and day are part of the string scan. It uses a format command that begins with % to represent the clock value of seconds presented in a specific pattern (Figure 4.18).

```
Console
File Edit Help
(bin) 1 % clock scan 2022
1641048720
(bin) 2 % clock scan 2022 -format %Y
1640975400
(bin) 3 % clock scan 01/2022 -format %m/%Y
1640975400
(bin) 4 % clock scan "2022-01-01" -format "%Y-%m-%d"
1640975400
```

Figure 4.18 Clock scan.

4.1.8 Clock Add Command

This command performs clock arithmetic on a value. It adds an offset to a time that is expressed as an integer number of seconds from the epoch time of 1 January 1970, 00:00 UTC. The other argument of the command is `-timezone`, where `-GMT.` and `-locale` have their usual meanings. The addition of seconds, minutes, and hours is straightforward to give an increment to the time values. The addition results in enhancement of the number of seconds from the epoch [3].

`clock add time value incremental value`

The example in Figure 4.19 explains the addition of seconds, minutes, and hours into the current time of the clock. The new value of clock time shows there is an increment of 5 hours, 35 minutes, and 25 seconds. The addition or subtraction of hours is defined in terms of absolute time, which means that it will add a fixed amount of time in the timezone. There is a surprising result that appears when crossing a point at which a leap second is inserted. The clock add command ignores the leap second; therefore, assumes that time comes in the sequence 23 : 59 : 59 then 00 : 00 : 00. Adding and subtracting days and weeks is accomplished by converting the given time to a calendar day and the time of day in the appropriate time zone and locale. The requisite number of days (weeks are converted to days by multiplying by seven) is added to the calendar day, and the date and time are then converted back to a count of seconds from the epoch time.

```
(bin) 1 % clock format [clock second]
Sat Jan 01 17:03:01 IST 2022
(bin) 2 % set time [clock second]
1641036786
(bin) 3 % set timenew [clock add $time 25 seconds]
1641036811
(bin) 4 % set timenew [clock add $time 25 seconds 35 minutes]
1641038911
(bin) 5 % set timenew [clock add $time 25 seconds 35 minutes 5 hours]
1641056911
(bin) 6 % puts [clock format $timenew -format "%d-%m-%y:%H:%M:%S %p"]
01-01-22:22:38:31 PM
```

Figure 4.19 Clock add.

4.1.9 Solved Problems

1. Write a TCL program to find the number of vowels in a string using string commands.

Solution

```
set str "scripting language"
set c 0
set l [string length $str]
puts " Length Of The
String = $l"
for {set j 0} {$j<$l}
{incr j} {
set b [string index $str $j]
if { $b=="a" | $b=="e" |
$b=="i" | $b=="o" | $b=="u"}
{incr c}}
puts " The Number Of Vowels
Is =$c"
```

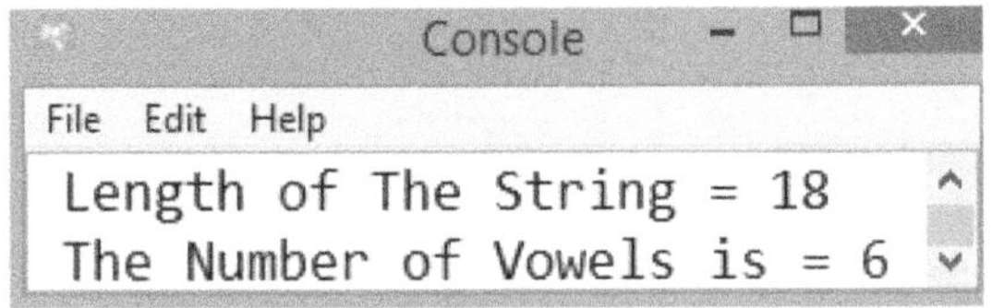
Console
File Edit Help
Length of The String = 18
The Number of Vowels is = 6

2. Write Tcl script to display your computer date in the following formats:

(a) dd : mm : yyyy

(b) mm : dd : yyyy

(c) yyyy : mm : dd

Solution

```
set time [clock
seconds]
puts "DD:MM:YYYY
Format [clock
format $time
-format %d:%m:%Y]"
puts "MM:DD:YYYY
Format [clock
format $time
-format %b:%d:%Y]"
puts "YYYY:MM:DD
Format [clock for-
mat $time  -format
%Y:%b:%d]"
```

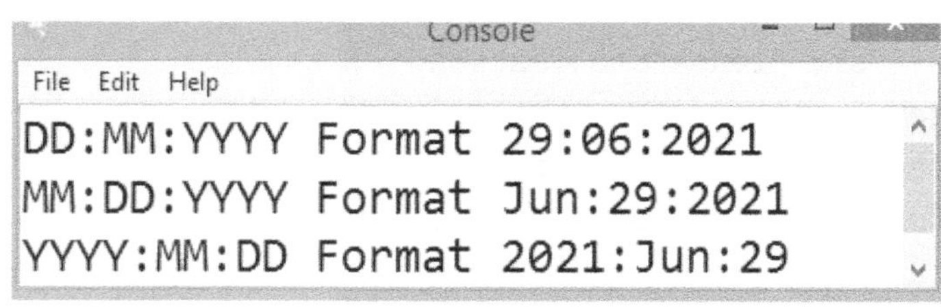

3. Write Tcl script to verify if a given string is a palindrome or not.

Solution

```
proc check {a} {
set len [string length $a]
set x [string reverse [string
range $a 0 $len-1]]
if {$a==$x} {
puts "Palindrome"
} else {
puts "Not Palindrome"
}
}
puts [check tata]
puts [check 12321]
puts [check rotor]
puts [check noon]
```

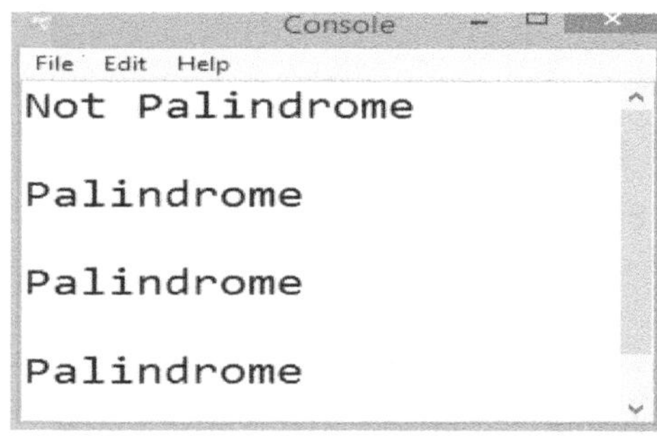

4. Write Tcl script to find the length of a string.

Solution

The following two methods find the length of the string.

Method 1: Split the string, separated by whitespace, and count each character.

```
set str "lenghtofthisstring"
set len 0
set list1 [ split $str "" ]
foreach value $list1 {incr len}
puts "Length = $len"
```

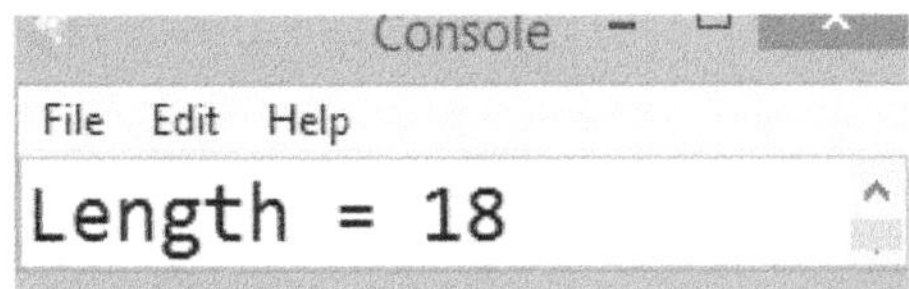

Method II: Convert a string into a list using the split command then with a list-based command

```
set str "lenghtofthisstring"
set lst [split $str {}]
puts $lst
set len [llength $lst]
puts "Length = $len"
```

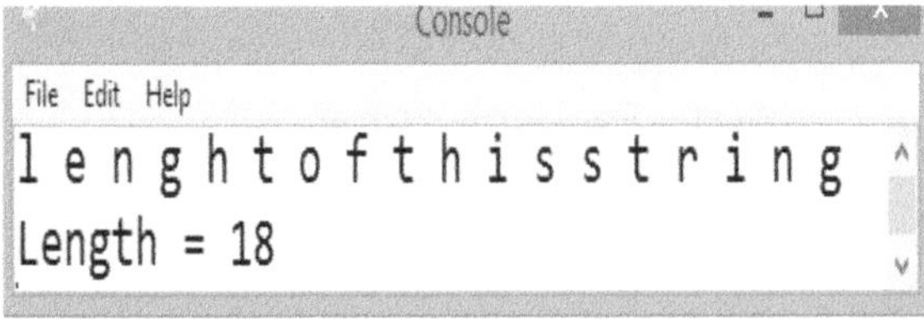

5. Write Tcl script to swap the content of two strings.

Solution

```
set st1 "12345"
set st2 "54321"
puts "Before Swap"
puts "st1=$st1"
puts "st2=$st2"

set st3 ""
set st3 $st1
set st1 $st2
set st2 $st3
puts "After Swap"
puts "st1=$st1"
puts "st2=$st2"
```

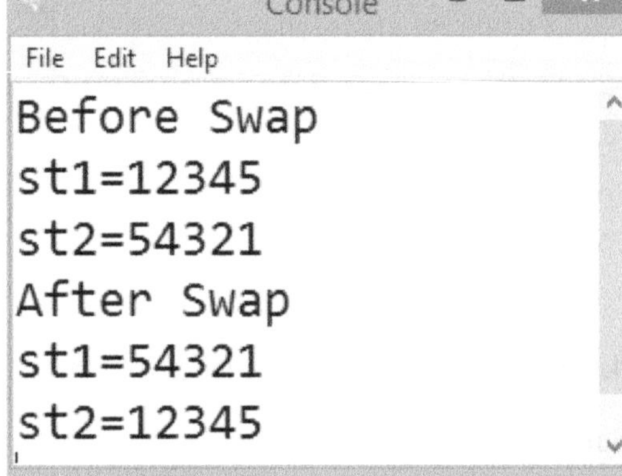

6. Write Tcl script to swap the set of characters in the given string.

Solution

```
set a "language"
set b [string range $a 4 5]
set c [string range $a 7 8]
set d [string replace $a 4 5 $c]
set e [string replace $d 7 8 $b]
puts "Before Swap $a"
puts "After Swap $e"
```

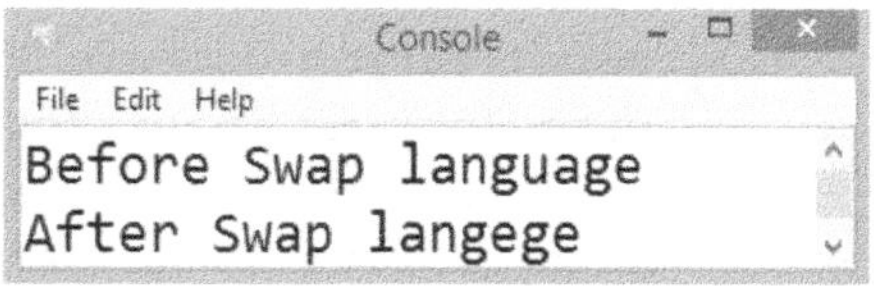

```
Console
File Edit Help
Before Swap language
After Swap langege
```

7. Write Tcl script to convert the current time of the system into a different time zone.

Solution

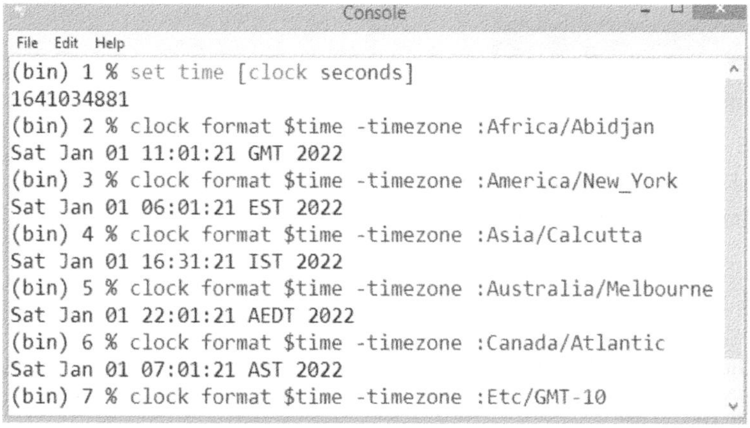

```
Console
File Edit Help
(bin) 1 % set time [clock seconds]
1641034881
(bin) 2 % clock format $time -timezone :Africa/Abidjan
Sat Jan 01 11:01:21 GMT 2022
(bin) 3 % clock format $time -timezone :America/New_York
Sat Jan 01 06:01:21 EST 2022
(bin) 4 % clock format $time -timezone :Asia/Calcutta
Sat Jan 01 16:31:21 IST 2022
(bin) 5 % clock format $time -timezone :Australia/Melbourne
Sat Jan 01 22:01:21 AEDT 2022
(bin) 6 % clock format $time -timezone :Canada/Atlantic
Sat Jan 01 07:01:21 AST 2022
(bin) 7 % clock format $time -timezone :Etc/GMT-10
```

4.1.10 Review Problems

1. Write the result of the following TCL string-based command.

```
set str1 "posco"
set str2 "calculator"
puts [string compare $str1 $str2]
puts [string index $str1 2]
puts [string length $str1]
puts [string range $str1 2 4]
puts [string range $str1 2 end]
puts [string toupper $str1]
puts [string tolower [ string toupper $str1 ]]
puts [string trim $str1 o]
```

2. Write the result of the following Tcl string-based command.

```
set str1 "cosco"
set str2 "ball"
puts [string compare $str1 $str2]
puts [string index $str1 2]
puts [string length $str1]
puts [string range $str1 2 4]
puts [string range $str1 2 end]
puts [string toupper $str1]
puts [string tolower [ string toupper $str1 ]]
puts [string trim $str1 o]
```

3. Write Tcl script to display the time in the following given formats.

01:44:37 AM

14:36
22 October, 2012

4. Design a computational engine that can accept numbers in any format (binary, octal, decimal, hexadecimal) and convert the equivalent into other formats.

4.1.11 MCQs on Strings

[1] What is the output of the following TCL program?

```
set a malayalam
set len [string length $a]
set n [expr $len/2]
```

A 8
B 9
C 4
D 5

Solution (c)

[2] What is the output of the following TCL program?

```
 set x 2
 set y 3
expr $x-1
expr $y-1
string compare $x $y
```

A −1
B 0
C +1
D None

Solution (a)

[3] The command `stringtrimremove` removes a character from ______

A Left end
B Right end
C Centre
D Both terminals

Solution (d)

[4] What does the output of the following program display?

```
set st "@@This is #my @world##}
set st1 [string trimright $st #]
set st2 [string trimleft $st1 @]
puts $st2
```

A @@This is @my @world##
B @This is #my @world#
C This is my world
D This is #my @world

Solution (d)

[5] What is the Tcl `format` command used for?

A Display the variable in a particular format
B Display the variable with precision
C Change the variable in a particular format
D All of the above

Solution (d)

[6] What is needed to convert a Tcl string to a list?

A Split
B Join
C Concat
D Append

Solution (a)

[7] What is the output of the following TCL program?

```
 set x 2
 set y 3
expr $x-1
expr $y-1
puts [string compare $x $y]
```

A −1
B −0
C +1
D +0

Solution (a)

4.2 Lists and their Commands

A Tcl list is an ordered string. It differs from a list in that the list elements are separated by whitespace. The `set` command is used to declare a list and grouping of elements requires double quotes and curly braces. Because of relationship between a string and a list, they can mutually be converted to each other. The following three ways are used to define a list.

(i) By declaring a list element – each element of the list can be defined separated by whitespace. Here, grouping requires curly braces.

```
set list1 {element1 element2 element3 ..........elementn}
```

(ii) By a `list` command – a `list` command followed by `list` element, grouped by square brackets.

```
set list2 [list element1 element2 element3 ..........
elementn]
```

(iii) By a `split` command – a `split` command can convert the unordered string into an ordered list, by splitting the string element via a special character. Whitespace is inserted in the place of a special character.

```
set list3
[split "stringsplcharcansplcharconvertsplchartolist" "splchar"]
```

Each element of the list can be accessed by its index number. The index number starts from the left and the first element has an index of 0. The list-based command begins with “l.”

Figures 4.20 and 4.21 describe the three methods to declare a string. `List1` is where each element is a programming language separated by whitespace, `list2` uses the list command, and `list3` splits a string by indicating a special character underscore `(_)`.

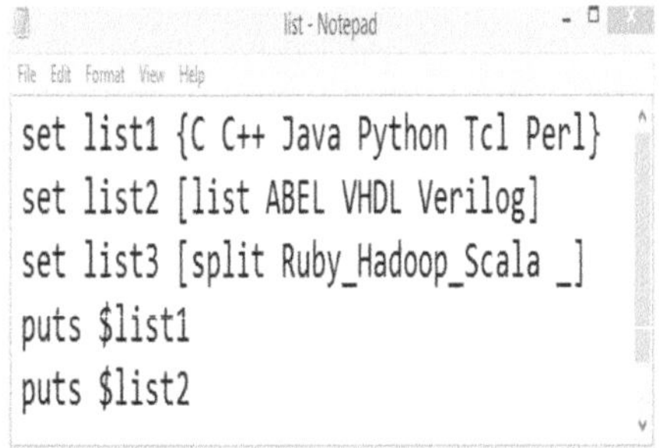

Figure 4.20 List declaration.

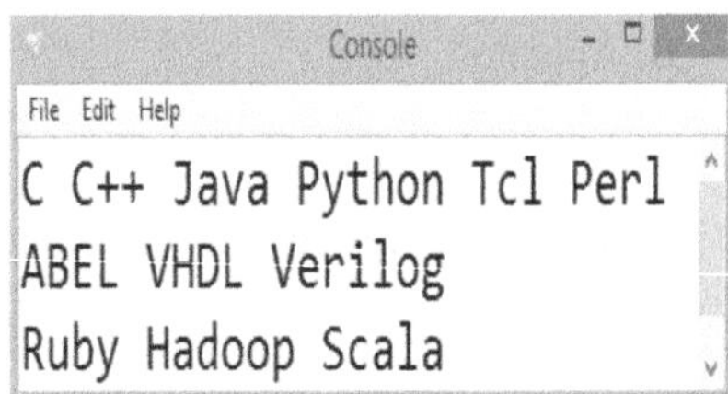

Figure 4.21 List created in Tcl console.

4.2.1 List-based Commands

The list command takes any number of arguments and returns a list of those arguments. The length of the returned list is the same as the number of arguments given to the list command. The arguments to list need not have a proper list structure: they will be automatically quoted as necessary. If any of the arguments to the list are themselves lists, the result will be a nested list structure. Table 4.3 presents the command used to manipulate the list.

Table 4.3 List-based command.

Command	Description
`[llength $listname]`	Returns the length of the list; number of elements
`[lindex $listname indexnumber]`	Returns the elements of a list appointed to an index number
`[lrange$listname index1 index2]`	Returns the elements of a list indicated through `index1` to `index2`
`[linsert $listname indexnumber newelement]`	Inserts a new element to an existing list appointed to an index number
`[lreplace $listname index1 index2 element1 element2.....elementn]`	Replaces the element indicated through `index1` to `index2` by the given new elements
`[lappend $listname newelement]`	Appends a new element at the end of an existing element
`[lassign $listname var1 var2....]`	Assigns an element to a variable individually
`[lsort $listname -switch]`	Sorts the list's element defined by switches. The switches can be ASCII / integer / real / increasing/ decreasing / dictionary / unique
`[lsearch $listname element]`	Searches for a particular element in the list. Returns the index number if found else −1

4.2.1.1 List Element Commands

Element-oriented list command is presented in Figure 4.22, where `llength` returns the length of the list but it is not necessary for the element to be a single variable, as it can be a string grouped under " " or { }. The index and command in Figure 4.23 returns the element "Tk GUI" at index 3 and `lrange` returns the {`VHDL Verilog`} {`Tk GUI`} for the range of elements 2 to 3. *Here, a string is considered as a single element.*

```
set list1 {C C++ Java
Python Tcl Perl}
puts [llength $list1]
puts [lindex
$list1 3]
puts [lrange
$list1 2 5]
```

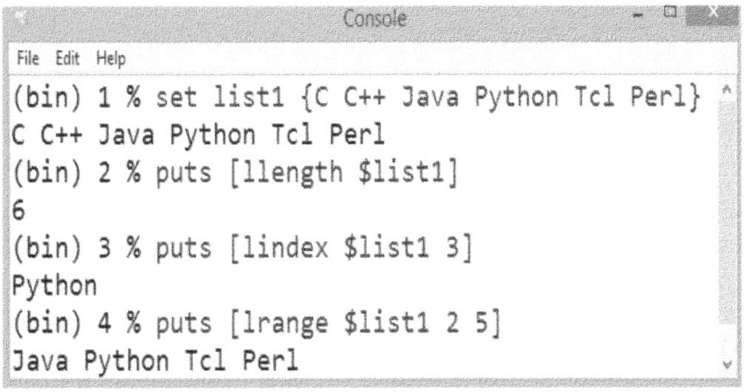

```
Console
File Edit Help
(bin) 1 % set list1 {C C++ Java Python Tcl Perl}
C C++ Java Python Tcl Perl
(bin) 2 % puts [llength $list1]
6
(bin) 3 % puts [lindex $list1 3]
Python
(bin) 4 % puts [lrange $list1 2 5]
Java Python Tcl Perl
```

Figure 4.22 Element-based list command.

```
set list2 {SQL DBMS
{VHDL Verilog}
"Tk GUI"}
puts [llength $list2]
puts [lindex
$list2 3]
puts [lrange
$list2 2 4]
```

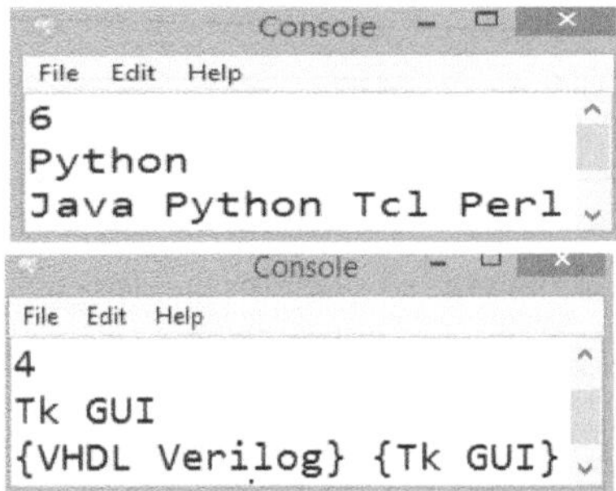

Figure 4.23 String as an element of the list.

4.2.1.2 List Modification Commands

The existing list can be modified with the `linsert` and `lreplace` commands. `linset` can insert a new element at the specified index, in the case where the index is greater than or equal to the length of the list elements appended to the end. `linsert` modifies to a new list which needs to be initialized as a new variable else the old list will be populated as shown in Figure 4.24. Figure 4.25 presents the `lreplace` which replaces the range of elements with a new element.

```
set list1 {Complier Interpreater
Debugger}
puts [linsert $list1 2
simulator]
puts $list1
puts [llength $list1]
set list2 [linsert $list1 2
simulator]
puts $list2
puts [llength $list2]
```

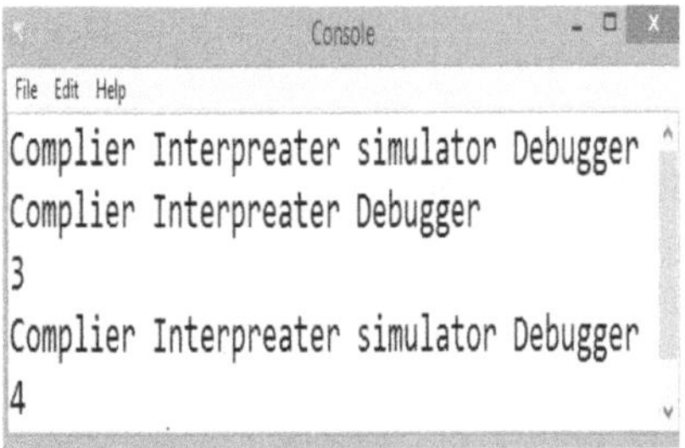

Figure 4.24 `linsert` example.

```
set list1 {Complier Interpreater
Debugger}
puts [lreplace $list1 1 2
Simulator Emulator]
puts $list1
puts [llength $list1]
```

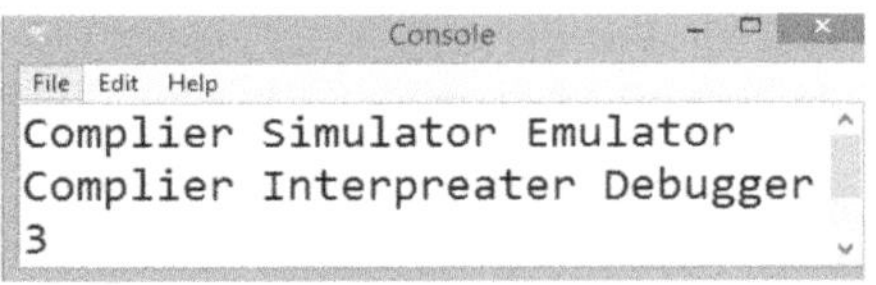

Figure 4.25 `lreplace` example.

4.2.1.3 Search and Update the List

The `lsearch` command performs a search of the element in a list and returns the index number of the first matching element (unless the options `-all` or `-inline` are specified) else it returns −1 if the specified element is found in the list. This command searches the elements of the *`list`* to see if one of them matches the *`pattern`*. Figure 4.26 describes matching the element into `list1`, and returns the index number if it matches else returns with −1.

```
set list1 {Root Trunk Stem
Fruit Flower}
puts [lsearch $list1 Fruit]
puts [lsearch $list1 Leaves]
```

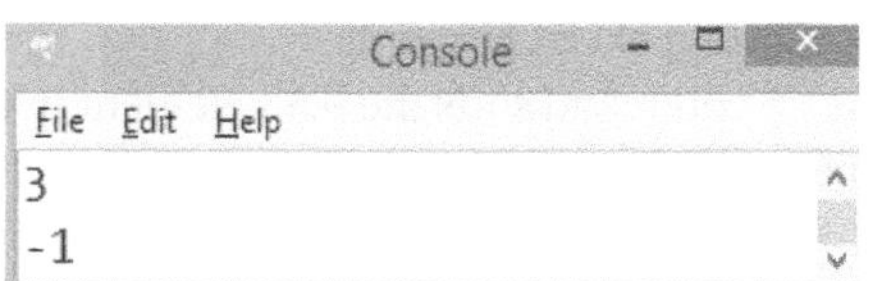

Figure 4.26 `lsearch` example.

An `-option` command with `lsearch` indicates how the element of the list is to be matched against the pattern. It must have one of the following values:

- `all` changes the result to be the list of all matching indices;
- `inline` the matching value is returned instead of its index;
- `ascii` the elements in the list are examined as a unicode string;
- `decreasing` the list elements are to be compared using a dictionary-style comparison;
- `exact` the list elements must contain the same string as the pattern;
- `glob` a glob style pattern which is matched against each list element using the string match command. It is the default style of pattern matching;
- `not` negates the sense of the match and returns the index of the first non-matching value;
- `start index`the list is searched at position index. If the index has the value end, it refers to the last element in the list, and the end-integer refers to the last element in the list minus the specified integer offset.

Example 4.1

```
lsearch {a b c d e} c => 2
lsearch -all {a b c a b c} c => 2 5
lsearch -inline {a20 b35 c47} b* => b35
lsearch -inline -not {a20 b35 c47} b* => a20
lsearch -all -inline -not {a20 b35 c47} b* => a20 c47
lsearch -all -not {a20 b35 c47} b* => 0 2
lsearch -start 3 {a b c a b c} c => 5
```

Note – If more than one of the options is specified, the option specified last takes precedence.

The example in Figure 4.27 describes each element of the list that can be assigned to a variable with the `lassign` command. A `puts` command can display each element by its index number. Similarly, by combining the elements, a new list can be formed. The curly braces do not permit variable substitution `list4` to declare with the `[list ......]` method.

```
set list3 {Cricket
Footbal Hockey}
lassign $list3 T1 T2 T3
puts $T1
puts $T2
puts $T3
set list4 [list $T1 $T2 $T3]
puts $list4
```

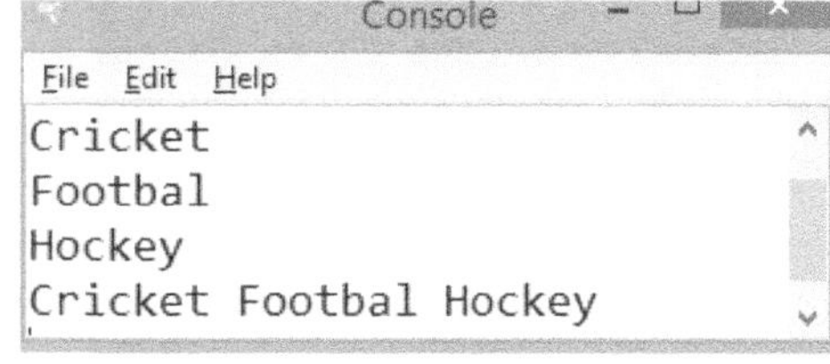

Figure 4.27 `lassign` example.

4.2.1.4 Sorting of List Elements

The `lsort` command sorts the list's element in a variety of ways and returns a new sorted list. The implementation of the `lsort` command uses the merge sort algorithm. By default, ASCII sorting is used with the result returned in increasing order. A list can be sorted by following a specified option (Figure 4.28).

- `ascii` A default sorting that returns a list in increasing order
- `dictionary` Uses a dictionary-style comparison
- `integer` Converts a list element to an integer and uses integer comparison
- `real` Converts a list element to a floating number and uses floating comparison
- `increasing` Sorts from smallest to largest
- `decreasing` Sorts from largest to smallest
- `unique` Removes duplicates

```
Console
File Edit Help
(bin) 1 % lsort -integer {1 4 9 3 5 7}
1 3 4 5 7 9
(bin) 2 % lsort -real {1 4 9 3 5 7}
1 3 4 5 7 9
(bin) 3 % lsort -real {1.1 8.7 7.5 7.6 9}
1.1 7.5 7.6 8.7 9
(bin) 4 % lsort -unique {a b c e a f e}
a b c e f
(bin) 5 % lsort -dictionary {abel c cobol python zeta}
abel c cobol python zeta
```

Figure 4.28 `lsort` example.

4.2.1.5 Split and Join

The `split` command converts a string into a list by inserting whitespace in between elements. The `Join` command are the inverse of the `split`, it takes the separated list element and reformats it as a string by the specified character (Figure 4.29).

```
Console
File Edit Help
(bin) 1 % set y [split 27/6/2021 "/"]
27 6 2021
(bin) 2 % puts "We celebrate on the [lindex $y 0]'th
day of the [lindex $y 1]'th of month"
We celebrate on the 27'th day of the 6'th of month
(bin) 3 %
(bin) 3 % set data {a b c d}
a b c d
(bin) 4 % join $data "_"
a b c d
```

Figure 4.29 Split and join example.

4.2.2 Solved Problems

1. Write Tcl script to define three variables and convert into a list by the `lappend` command.

Solution

```
set x 1
set y 2
set z 3
set output {}
foreach i {x y z} {
lappend output [set $i]}
puts $output
```

```
1 2 3
```

2. Write a Tcl script to convert a list to a string and a string to a list.

Solution

List to String

```
set list {a b c d e f}
for {set i 0} {$i<[llength
$list]} {incr i} {
    append string [lindex
$list $i]
}
puts $string
```

String to List

```
set string abcdef
set l [split abcdef {} ]
puts $l
```

---

3. Write Tcl script to swap 19 and 25 in the IP address 172.19.25.0.

Solution

```
set a 172.19.25.0
puts "Before Swap $a"
set b [ split $a . ]
set u [lindex $b 0]
set v [lindex $b 1]
set w [lindex $b 2]
set x [lindex $b 3]
set z [join "$u $w $v $x" .]
puts "After Swap $z"
```

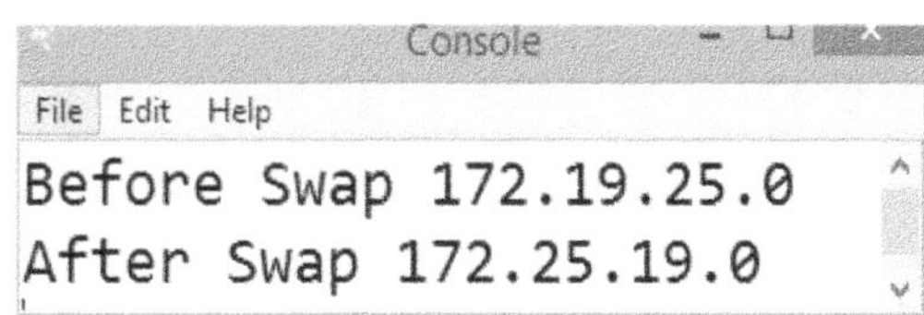

4.2.3 Review Problems

1. Practice the following problem:

```
set x {1 2}
set y "$x 3"
set y [concat $x 3]
set z [list $x 3]
puts $z
```

```
set var {orange blue red green}
set var [lreplace $var 2 3
black white]
 puts $var
```

```
set var {orange blue red green}
set var [linsert $var 3
black white]
puts $var
```

```
set var {orange blue red green}
set var [lsort $var]
puts $var
```

```
set days {Monday Tuesday Wednesday Thursday Friday Saturday Sunday}
set n [llength $days]
set i 0
while {$i < $n} {
puts [lindex $days $i]
incr i
}
```

4.2.4 MCQs on List

[1] What does the following Tcl script return?

```
set color {red blue green {orange pink} black}
puts [llength $color]
```

A 6
B 5
C 4
D 3

Solution (b)

[2] What does the `puts [lindex $listname number]` command return?

A Index number
B Variable on a specified index number
C Pair of index and variable on an index
D None of the above

Solution (b)

[3] Which statement prints out a sorted list?

A `puts [list sort {4 5 3 1}]`
B `puts [list lsort {4 5 3 1}]`
C `puts [lsort {4 5 3 1}]`
D `puts [sort {4 5 3 1}]`

Solution (c)

[4] What can be used to convert a Tcl string to a list?

A Split
B Join
C Concat
D Append

Solution (a)

[5] What does the following Tcl script return?

```
Set list1 {a e i o u}
Puts [lsearch $list1 o]
```

(a) 3,o
(b) o
(c) 4
(d) 3

Solution (d)

4.3 Arrays and their Commands

A Tcl array is the most systematic way to arrange a group of elements using indices. Each element of an array has a user-defined index. The array can be internally implemented with a hash table. The cost of accessing each element is almost the same. An array is initialized with the `set` command using either curly braces or small brackets; two popular ways to initialize a Tcl array are as follows.

Define the array by index and element.

array set arrayname {index element}

Define elements of the array separately.

set arrayname (index) element

Figure 4.30 illustrates that the initialization starts with an array where all elements need to be defined inside curly braces, that is, the index numbers and their elements need to be defined together. Each element can be accessed by the array name(index). Alternatively, array elements

```
(bin) 1 % array set lang {0 Pascal 1 Cobol 2 Fortran}
(bin) 2 % puts $lang(0)
Pascal
(bin) 3 % puts $lang(1)
Cobol
(bin) 4 % puts $lang(2)
Fortran
```

Figure 4.30 Array initialization by array command.

```
(bin) 1 % set lang(0) Pascal
Pascal
(bin) 2 % set lang(1) Cobol
Cobol
(bin) 3 % set lang(2) Fortran
Fortran
(bin) 4 % puts [array get lang]
0 Pascal 1 Cobol 2 Fortran
```

Figure 4.31 Array initialization by setting elements.

can be defined individually at the respective array index, as shown in Figure 4.31). Here the `gets` command is used to format the structure of the array.

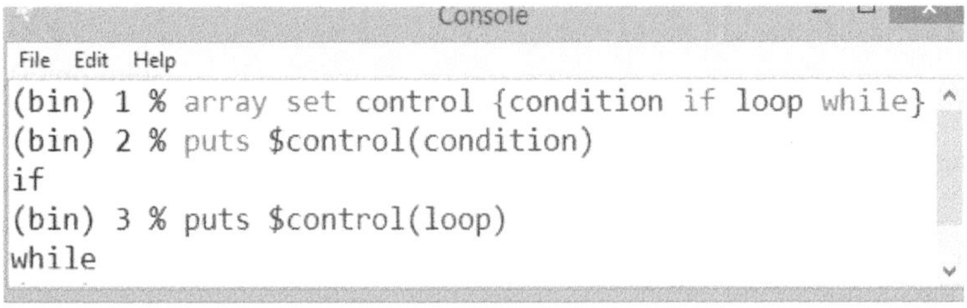

```
Console
File Edit Help
(bin) 1 % array set control {condition if loop while}
(bin) 2 % puts $control(condition)
if
(bin) 3 % puts $control(loop)
while
```

Figure 4.32 Array index as an alphanumeric character.

A Tcl array is associative. The array is sorted and retrieved without a specific order. The index does not need to be a numeric value of a string; it can be an alphanumeric character, as shown in Figure 4.32.

Table 4.4 Arrray command in Tcl.

Array Command	Description
`[array exists arrayname]`	Verifies if an array exists; returns 1 if true else 0
`[array names arrayname]`	Returns the list of indices of the array The order of the return is random
`[array size arrayname]`	Returns the size of the array, i.e., number of elements
`[array get arrayname]`	Returns the list of alternative pairs of index and element
`[parray arrayname]`	Prints only the array element
`unset arrayname/element`	Uninitializes the array or individual element

4.3.1 Array-Based Commands

An `array` command accesses the array element and returns information about the array elements through iteration. Array-based commands are given in Table 4.4.

An explanation of an array-based command is based on the following example, where the month name has been declared as an array.

```
array set month {
      1 jan       2 Feb       3 Mar
      4 Apr       5 May       6 Jun
      7 Jul       8 Aug       9 Sep
      10 Oct      11 Nov      12 Dec
      }
```

The size of an array, determined by the command `[array size month]`, provides the number of index-element pairs returned as the result. Whether the array is defined earlier or not is verified by the command `[array exist month]` that returns "1" for the true result and 0 if not refined.

```
set n [array size month]
puts "Size of array=$n"
puts "Array Exists=[array
exists month]"
```

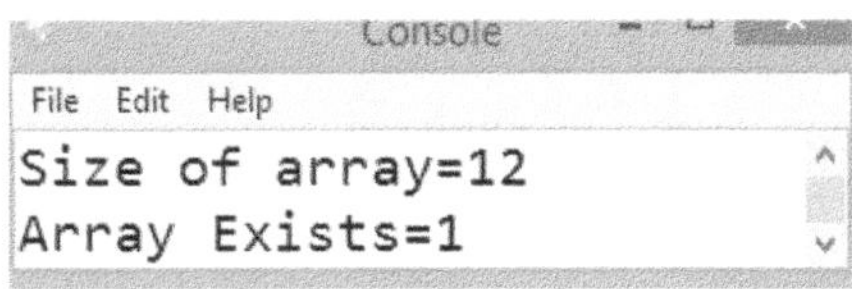

The command `parray month` simply prints the month(index) and its corresponding element in vertical order.

The command `[array get month]` prints the index-element pair horizontally.

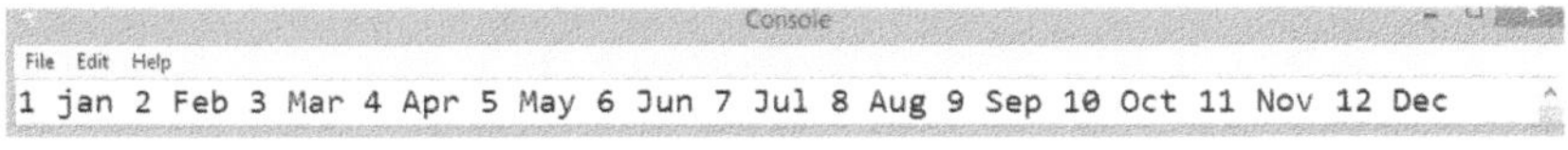

Array	List
Arrays are accessed using the index, the index can be any string.	Lists are accessed using the index, the index is an integer.
Arrays are unordered collections of values.	Lists are ordered sequences of values.

Array	List
Internally, an array is maintained by hash tables. Adding an element to an array will rearrange the elements in a "tree."	Internally list elements are stored sequentially.

"get command to convert an array to a list and array set command to convert a list to an array"

4.3.2 Solved Examples

1. Write a Tcl script to define a vowel as an array and apply the `array` command.

Solution

```
array set vowel {
0 a
1 e
2 i
3 o
4 u
}
puts [array exists vowel]
puts [array size vowel]
puts [array names vowel]
```

```
Console
File Edit Help
1
5
4 0 1 2 3
```

2. Write a Tcl script to define an array of four operating systems as variables and display using the `array` command.

Solution

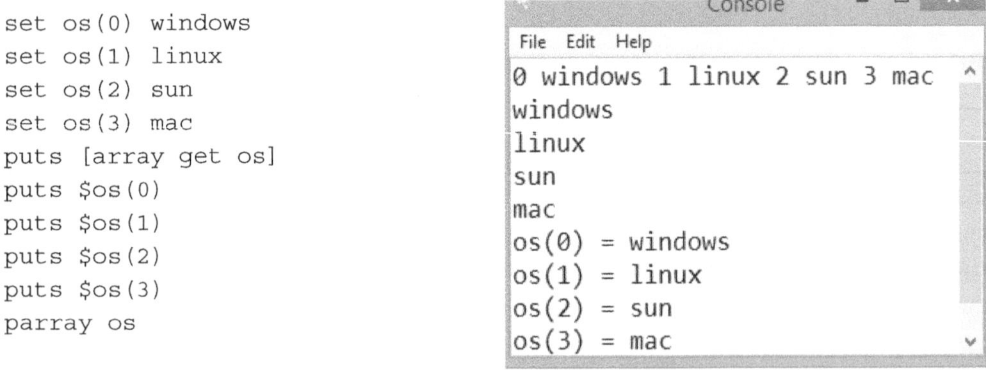

```
set os(0) windows
set os(1) linux
set os(2) sun
set os(3) mac
puts [array get os]
puts $os(0)
puts $os(1)
puts $os(2)
puts $os(3)
parray os
```

```
Console
File Edit Help
0 windows 1 linux 2 sun 3 mac
windows
linux
sun
mac
os(0) = windows
os(1) = linux
os(2) = sun
os(3) = mac
```

3. Write Tcl script to delete/remove an element from an array and display.

Solution

```
array set script {
0 tcl
1 perl
2 sql
}
parray script
unset script(1)
parray script
unset script
puts [array exist script]
```

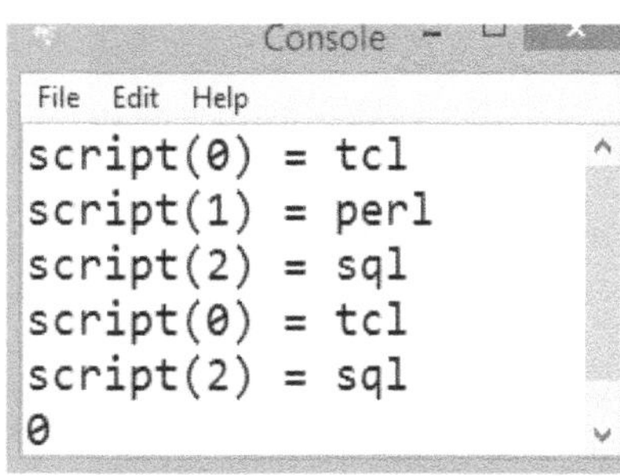

4. Write Tcl script to define a one-dimensional array.

Solution

```
for { set i 0 } { $i < 8 } { incr i } {
  set base($i) $i
  puts "base($i) = $base($i)"
}
```

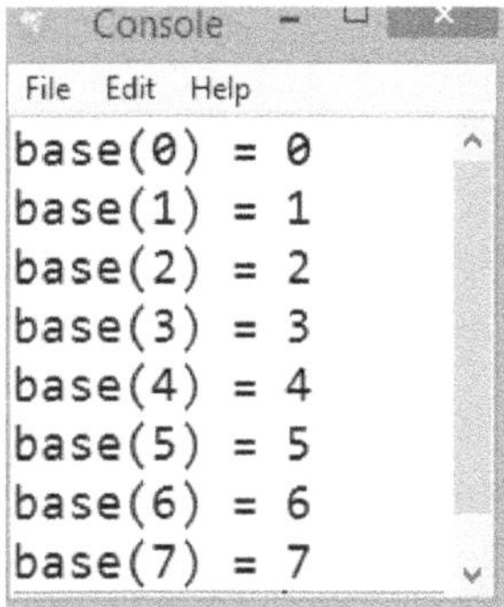

5. Write Tcl script to define a two-dimensional array.

Solution

```
for { set i 0 } { $i < 3 } { incr i } {
  for { set j 0 } { $j < 3 } { incr j } {
    set base($i,$j) $i
    puts "base($i,$j) = $base($i,$j)"
  }
}
```

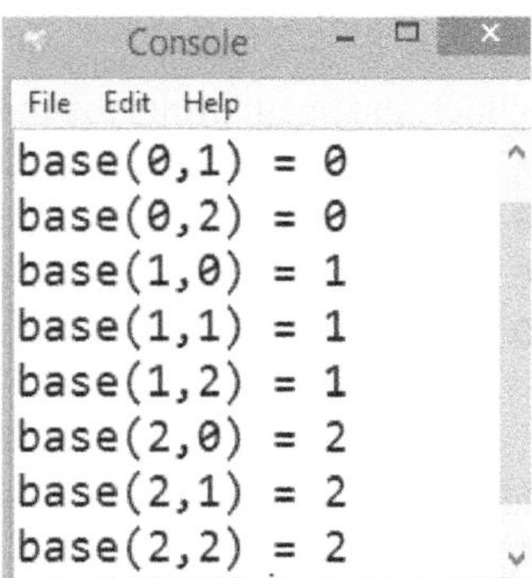

4.3.3 Review Problems

1. Execute the following program:

```
array set arr {
1 hari
2 Rajesh
3 Ram
}
if {[array exists arr]} {
puts "Array Exists"
} else {
puts "Array Does Not Exists"
}
puts "Total Array Items are : [array size arr]"
puts "Array Numbers in list are : [array names arr]"
puts "Name of persons in the arraylist are : $arr(1) $arr(2)
$arr(3)"
```

2. Practice the Tcl script shown as follows and comment on the output.

```
array set noble2020 {
Physics {Roger Penrose,Reinhard Genzel, Andrea Ghez}
Chemistry {Emmanuelle Charpentier,Jennifer A.Doudna}
Medicine {Charvey J. Alter, Michael Houghton, Charles M. Rice}
Literature {Louise Glück}
Economics {Paul R. Milgrom, Robert B. Wilson}
}
puts "Noble2020 has [array size noble2020] entries"
puts "Noble has the following entries [array names noble2020] "
puts "Prize for Medicine category goes to $noble2020(Medicine)"
puts "Prize for Chemistry category goes to $noble2020(Chemistry)"
```

4.3.4 MCQs on Arrays and their Commands

[1] Which statement prints the index of all elements in an array x?

A `puts [array elements x]`
B `puts [array elements $x]`
C `puts [array names x]`
D `puts [array names $x]`

Solution (c)

[2] Identify the command that can remove/delete an element from an array.

A set
B unset
C delete
D remove

Solution (b)

[3] Identify the command to print all elements of an array together.

A array name

B arrey get

C array exists

D parray

Solution (d)

[4] The index of an array can be

A numeric

B words

C either nuremic or words

D none of the above

Solution (c)

[5] If an array is not defined, what will `puts [array exists names]` return?

A 1

B 0

C Error

D Does not Exist

Solution (b)

References

1 https://zetcode.com/lang/tcl/arrays

2 https://www.tcl.tk/man/tcl8.4/TclCmd/array.html

3 https://www.tutorialspoint.com/tcl-tk

5

Tcl Object-Oriented Programming

The object-oriented programming concept has been introduced with Tcl 8.6. The basis of the object-oriented programming is an object. An object is represented as a real-world entity that captures the state and behavior. There are two different approaches to define a command: (i) action-oriented and (ii) object-oriented.

Action-oriented is a command for each action that can be taken as an object, and the command takes an object name as an argument. Examples are the Tcl file command. An action-oriented approach is preferred when the number of objects is large and unpredictable.

Object-oriented is a command for each object, where the name of the command is the name of an object. When the command is invoked, the first argument specifies the operation to perform on the object. The object-oriented approach prefers when the number of objects is limited to 100 and defined and exists for at least a moderate time. It is necessary to ensure object name should not conflict with the existing command [1, 2].

Tcl is flexible on which to build their system, which leads to a plethora of such systems, with diverse functionality with the following object-oriented packages.

`[incr tcl]`	The first Tcl package like C++. It duplicates the C++ model of cladding with single or multiple inheritances
`[XoTcl]`	Designed for research for into dynamic OO programming
`[Snit]`	Useful for building a Tk widget

5.1 Class

The class is a template that defines data and methods (called members) encapsulated by an object of a specific type. Creation or instantiation of the object is the primary work of the class.

5.2 Creation of a Class

In Tcl, a class can be created using the command *`oo::class create`*. A newly created class can be used to create an object. Now the class definition script defines the state for the object of the class, by adding an argument to *`oo: class create`* or *`oo: define`*.

```
oo::class create classname definitionscript
oo::define classname
```

Programming and GUI Fundamentals: Tcl-Tk for Electronic Design Automation (EDA), First Edition.
Suman Lata Tripathi, Abhishek Kumar, and Jyotirmoy Pathak.

5.3 Define a Member in a Class

Each object has associated data. Each object has its variable known as the instance variable of the data member.

```
oo::define classname {
        variable ....
}
```

The state of an object is uniquely defined by data members. A member in a class is defined through the script `oo::define`. A data member for each object variable of the class is defined by the `variable` statement. There can be multiple variable statements, defining single or multiple variables.

5.4 Define Method

An object can execute some task by defining the method. The method creates a procedure that can be evaluated within the object scope. The difference between an in-built command and a `proc` command lies in how it is invoked and how the method is executed.

```
method name argument body
```

The TclOO method has the following features:
(a) the TclOO class may have multiple methods;
(b) the method may be registered as a callback script to be evaluated when an event occurs;
(c) the object may invoke its method;
(d) everything about an object should be defined inside a class.

5.5 Constructor and Destructor

The constructor and destructor are two special methods used to create and destroy objects automatically. A constructor method runs when an object is created and a destructor method is run when an object is destroyed.

5.6 Destroying of Class

The `destroy` command will erase the definition of class; an object belonging to the class and all that is inherited from a particular class. Destroying a class is useful during interactive development and debugging, as described in Figure 5.1.

```
classname destroy
```

Figure 5.1 Destroying of class.

```
Console
File  Edit  Help
(bin) 1 % oo::class create object1 {
>     variable x
>     constructor {} {
>         set x 2
>     }
>     method increment {} {
>         return [incr x]
>     }
> }
::object1
(bin) 2 %
(bin) 2 % object1 create local              ;# Make an instance
::local
(bin) 3 % puts [local increment]        ;# Call the instance
3
(bin) 4 % puts [local increment]        ;# Call the instance
4
(bin) 5 % local destroy             ;#  Destroy the instance
(bin) 6 %
(bin) 6 % object1 destroy
```

5.7 Invoking Method

An existing command, procedure, or object can be evaluated within the body of a method. The Tcl interpreter generates an error in the case of an attempt to evaluate a procedure or object that is not defined. The method name is used as the command and the method is a subcommand within that command. Other methods can be invoked with the name of the object and the method name. TclOO provides a virtual command `my` to evaluate a method within the current object [3]. The `my` command is used in the object to invoke the method of its class. Each object has its command.

Example 5.1 Write Tcl script to invoke a class and compute locally.

Solution

```
oo::class create ascending {
    method count {} {
        my variable x
        puts "[incr x]"
    }
}
ascending create local
local count
local count
local count
local count
local count
```

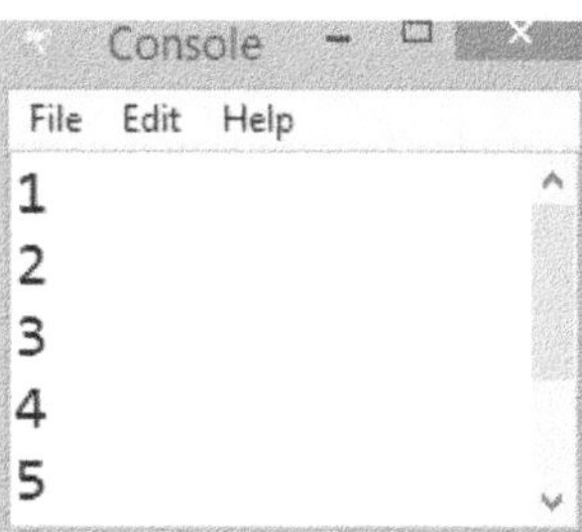

Example 5.2 Write Tcl script to create a class and evaluate via the object method.

Solution

A class is created with the following three methods to show an evaluation of the object method:

- Show   Displays the value of the object variable
- External Invokes the show method of another object
- Internal Invokes the show method of the current object

```
oo::class create withmethod {
variable var
constructor {value} {
set var $value
}
method show {} {
puts "Value is $var"
}
method external {name1} {
$name1 show
}
method internal {} {
my show
}
}

set object1 [withmethod new 1]
set object2 [withmethod new 2]

$object1 external $object2
$object1 internal
```

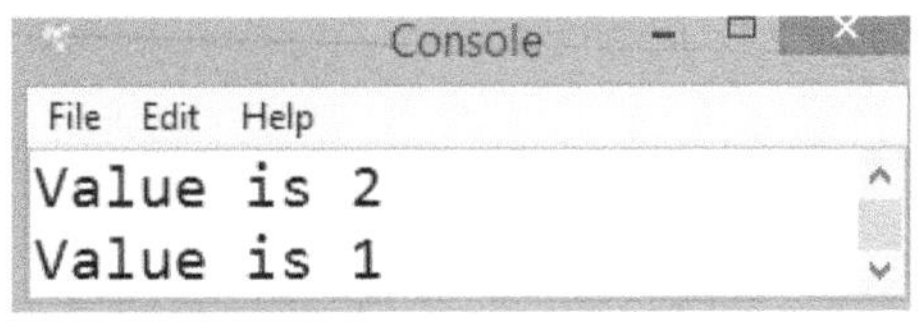

Example 5.3 Write Tcl script to compute summation with the help of class.

Solution

```
oo::class create summation {
    constructor {} {
        variable v 0
    }
    method add x {
        variable v
        incr v $x
    }
    method value {} {
        variable v
        return $v
    }
    destructor {
        variable v
        puts "Ended with value $v"
    }
}
set sum [summation new]
puts "Start with [$sum value]"
for {set i 1} {$i <= 10} {incr i} {
    puts "Add $i to get [$sum add $i]"
}
$sum destroy
```

```
Console
File Edit Help
Start with 0
Add 1 to get 1
Add 2 to get 3
Add 3 to get 6
Add 4 to get 10
Add 5 to get 15
Add 6 to get 21
Add 7 to get 28
Add 8 to get 36
Add 9 to get 45
Add 10 to get 55
Ended with value 55
```

Example 5.4 Write Tcl script to create a class and evaluate locally.

Solution

```
oo::class create method1 {
variable x y z
constructor {} {
set x 5
set y 7
set z 11
}
method show {var} {
puts "Value of var is [set $var]"
}
method bad_show {} {
puts x
puts y
puts z
}
method good_show {} {
my show x
my show y
my show z
}
}
method1 create local
puts "BAD"
local bad_show
puts "GOOD"
local good_show
local destroy
method1 destroy
```

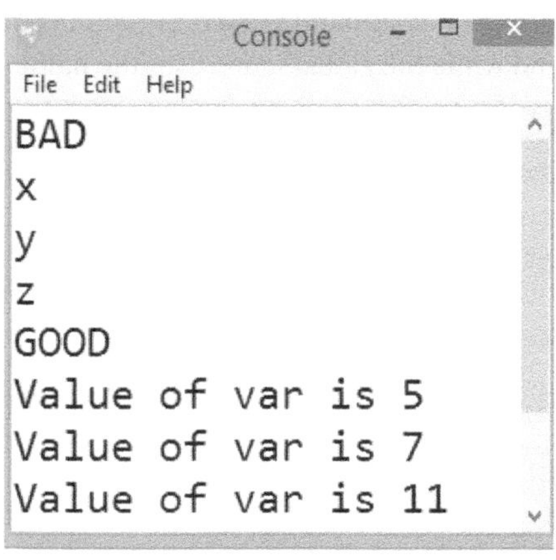

5.8 Registering Method for Callback

The Tcl/Tk mechanism is implemented via a callback. These commands require an object as a well-known method for the evaluation. The NAMESPACE package of Tcl includes the `namespace current` command to register a namespace procedure with a callback. It returns the current namespace which can be obtained with a procedure name to provide a complete path to the procedure. TclOO returns the name of the current object that can be combined with the method name and argument to register a callback [4].

Example 5.5 Write Tcl script to evaluate objects via the callback method.

Solution
The `after` command is used inside-outside an object. The method `after10` uses the self-command while the global scope uses the name of the object.

```
oo::class create delay {
variable a
constructor {var} {
set a $var
}
method show {} {
puts "a is $a at [clock seconds]"
}
method after10 {} {
after 10000 [list [self] show]
}
}

set a [delay new 2]
set b [delay new 5]
$a after10
after 5000 [list $b show]
```

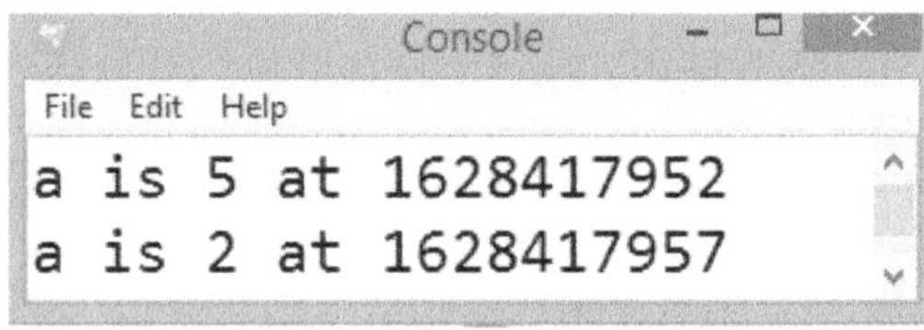

References

1 https://www.magicsplat.com/articles/oo.html
2 https://wiki.tcl-lang.org/page/TclOO
3 https://wiki.tcl-lang.org/page/TclOO+Tutorial
4 Flynt, C. (2012). *Tcl/Tk: A Developer's Guide*. Elsevier.

6

File Processing

6.1 Introduction

The file processing operation of Tcl supports accessing content to read from as well as write to a file on a disk. There are several operations on the file's attributes. The in-built command opens, gets, puts, reads, writes, and closes to read from and write to the content via a console terminal. Primarily, data enter through the command terminal; alternatively, file access is a dynamic way to interact. File systems are implemented differently for different operating systems. To support different file systems, a platform-independent interface is provided to the file system [1]. File accessing is the text-based configuration file based on the storage location. A file in Tcl is represented as a sequence of bytes that can access the data from a file in Notepad (.txt), comma-separated value (.csv), rich text format (.rtf), etc.

Data written into the file can be read on the wish terminal as the most current result can be written on the file with a given extension. Tcl supports an interface with the file system using a buffering mechanism. A temporary file ID is assigned to each of the files, and an individual file can be accessed through the given ID. File accessing activity starts with the opening of a file with the `open` command and finishes with the closing of a file with the `close` command. The intermediate section consists of reading, writing, or file manipulation activity [2]. Creating a file involves having to declare the purpose of the file (read or write); determined by `AccessMode`. A Tcl file supports six different access modes listed in Table 6.1

Table 6.1 Access mode of Tcl file.

AccessMode	Activity	Description
`r`	Only read	Opens an existing file for reading purposes. The file must exist in the working directory. It is the default access mode
`w`	Only write	Opens an existing text file for writing purposes with truncation; if the file does not exist, create a new file, start writing
`a`	Write with append	Opens a text file for writing in append mode. The file must exist and append content to the existing file content
`r+`	Read and Write	Opens a text file for both read as well as write. File must exist in the working directory
`w+`	Read and Write	Opens a text file for both reading and writing. If the file exists, start writing with truncating existing content or create a new file if it does not exist
`A+`	Read and write with append	Opens a text file for reading and writing. Read from the beginning and write in append mode. If a file exists, write after the end of the existing content or create a new file if not exist

Programming and GUI Fundamentals: Tcl-Tk for Electronic Design Automation (EDA), First Edition.
Suman Lata Tripathi, Abhishek Kumar, and Jyotirmoy Pathak.

6.2 Tcl File Command

This section describes the file-related commands of the Tcl script. Different commands are associated with reading from and writing to the file. These commands are helpful for the electronic design automation (EDA) tool to store the internal result. The Tcl file commands are `file`, `open`, `read`, `get`, `puts`, `close`, `eof`, `seek`, `tell`, and `flush`. By default, a file is accessed sequentially – the next byte is fetched after the previous byte. However, `seek`, `tell`, and `eof` can modify the accessing pattern to be non-sequential.

6.2.1 Opening a File

To open a file, Tcl uses the `open` command. The `open` command opens the file titled filename with the access type and permission provided, and returns a file pointer. The syntax of the `open` command is

```
open filename accessMode
```

The filename is chosen by the user in the assigned access mode.

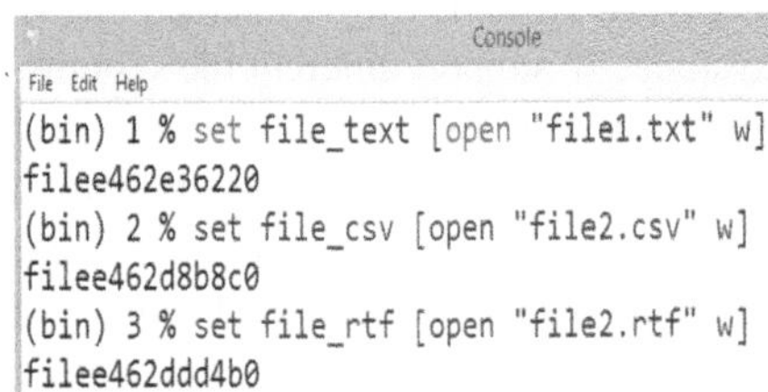

Figure 6.1 Tcl script to open a file with extension.

Figure 6.2 Result of Figure 6.1.

Figure 6.1 presents the creation of a file with the `open` command; it is possible to create multiple files where each file is assigned a unique temporary file number. Opening a file in a particular mode requires mentioning the file with an extension. Figure 6.2 shows the output of the program, where `file1` is assigned to ID "filee462w36220", `file2` is assigned to ID "filee462d8b8c0", and `file3` is assigned to ID "filee462ddd460". The `set` command has been paired to allow access to the file pointer `file1_text`, and so on. A file in write mode automatically creates the file in the "bin" directory. However, the file will be empty.

6.2.2 Closing a File

An already opened file after a programmer is finished with the access needs to closed explicitly. To close a file, Tcl uses the `close` command to flush the open channel of any pending data resulting in a writing to the disk and closing of the channel. The syntax of the `close` command is as follows, as shown in Figure 6.3.

close $filename

```
(bin) 5 % close $file_tex
(bin) 6 % close $file_csv
(bin) 7 % close $file_rtf
```

Figure 6.3 Tcl script to close a file.

```
close $filename
```

6.2.3 Writing into a File

Writing into a file is similar to writing to the console terminal. The `puts` command is used to write content into the referenced file pointer. The write activity is line-oriented or paragraph-oriented. The `puts` command is used to put the content in the opened file. In the case where multiple statements need to be written, statements must be enclosed in double quotes "……". The file must exist on the hard disk, or else the error message will state the file cannot be found.

Example 6.1 Write a few statements into a file myfile.txt, then close the file.

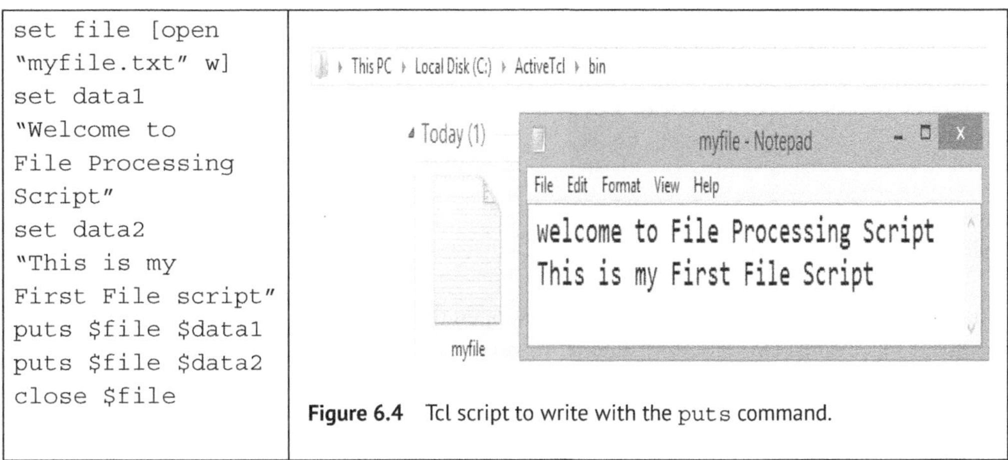

set file [open
"myfile.txt" w]
set data1
"Welcome to
File Processing
Script"
set data2
"This is my
First File script"
puts $file $data1
puts $file $data2
close $file
This PC › Local Disk (C:) › ActiveTcl › bin
Today (1)
myfile
myfile - Notepad
File Edit Format View Help
welcome to File Processing Script
This is my First File Script

Figure 6.4 Tcl script to write with the `puts` command.

Figure 6.4 shows the writing activity of content into myfile.txt with the `puts` command; here two different statements are assigned to variables `data1` and `data2`. Each statement is to be written separately. The execution results are shown in myfile.txt as a written statement. Conjunction between two statements can be added to arrange the statement like `\n` for newline `\t` for tab space etc. presented in Figure 6.5. After writing, the file must be closed else flush the channel to complete the write.

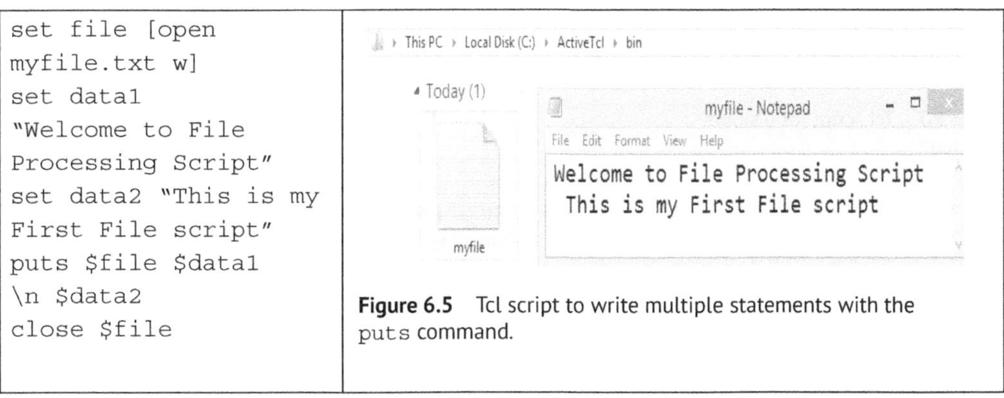

Figure 6.5 Tcl script to write multiple statements with the `puts` command.

6.2.4 Reading of the File

Reading of a file in Tcl script is supported by the `gets` command, where the content of the file is read and displayed in the console window. The `gets` command is line-oriented and can read a single line from the beginning, while the `read` command can read the complete message from the file at one time [3]. A file must exist in the bin directory of the disk titled "myfile.txt"; the content of the file is shown in Figure 6.6.

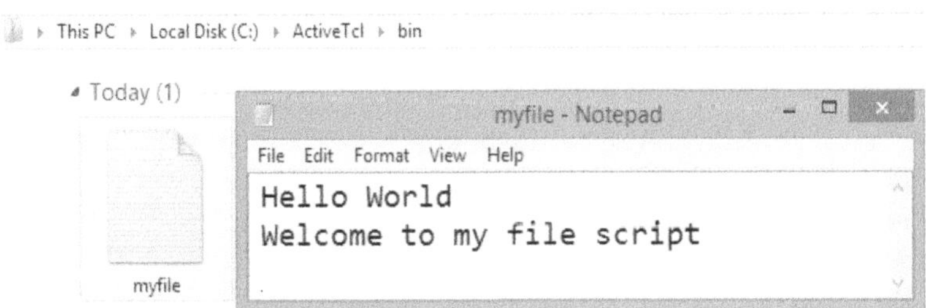

Figure 6.6 File available in the directory.

To read the content through the Tcl script, first open the file in reading mode and use the `gets` command twice since two different statements are there, as shown in Figure 6.7. While reading each statement separately, we can assign each onto two separate variables, as presented in Figure 6.8.

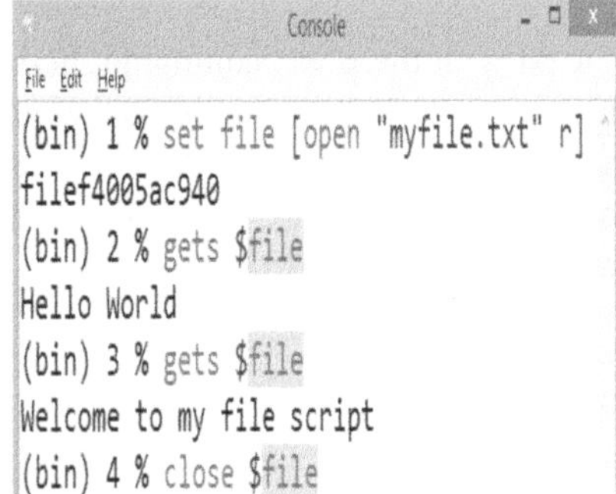

Figure 6.7 Tcl script for a single statement.

```
(bin) 5 % set file [open "myfile.txt" r]
file5530e16f90
(bin) 6 % set stat1 [gets $file]
Hello World
(bin) 7 % set stat2 [gets $file]
Welcome to my file script
(bin) 8 % puts "$stat1 \t $stat2"
Hello World    Welcome to my file script
(bin) 9 % close $file
```

Figure 6.8 © Tcl script for multiple statements.

To read multiple statements from myfile.txt, the `gets` command can be conjugated with the `while` loop, as shown in Figure 6.8. The `while` loop continues to execute until the content of the file is greater than zero and is assigned to variable data, which can be displayed even after the closing of the file. To read the multiple statements without a `while` loop, alternatively, the `read` command can be used and assigned to variables independently, as shown in Figures 6.9 and 6.10.

```
set file [open "myfile.txt" r]
while {[gets $file data] > 0} {
puts $data
}
close $file
```

```
Console
File Edit Help
(bin) 1 % set file [open "myfile.txt" r]
file2299203870
(bin) 2 % while {[gets $file data] > 0} {
> puts $data
> }
Hello World
Welcome to my file script
(bin) 3 % close $file
```

Figure 6.9 Tcl script to read the file in a loop.

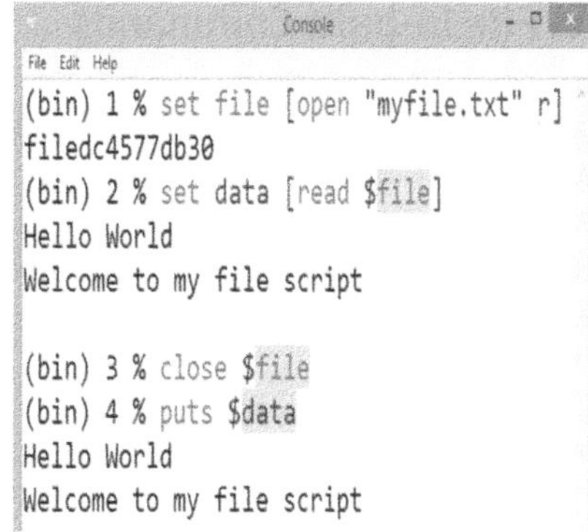

Figure 6.10 Tcl script for the `read` command.

6.2.5 Write with Append Mode

A Tcl file in append mode allows updating of the content in an existing file. This mode is used to preserve the content of the existing file and new content will be added after the previous content. Figure 6.11 shows the existing content in the file. The `foreach` command can been used to add more statements at the end of the first statement. A local variable of the `foreach` loop selects the string and appends; the result of execution is presented in Figure 6.12.

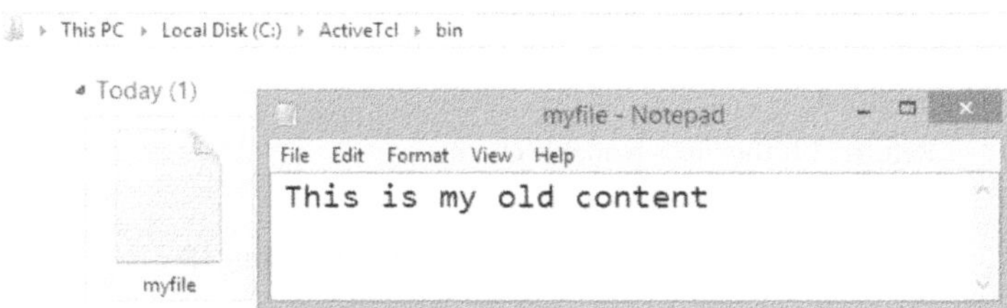

Figure 6.11 Previous content in the file.

```
set file [open "myfile.txt" a]
foreach content {"This is my new content" "I will write after
previous one"} {
puts $file $content
}
close $file
```

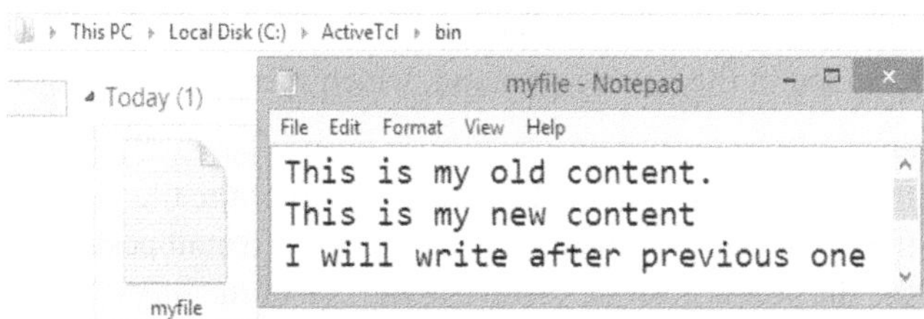

Figure 6.12 Result after appending.

6.3 Tcl File In-built Commands

In this section, the in-built commands of Tcl are listed. `File` manipulates the name and its attributes. The syntax of the file command is as follows.

file option filename arg1 arg2…….

Option indicates what to do with the file name. A list of file commands are presented in Table 6.2 [4, 5] (Figure 6.13).

Table 6.2 Tcl file in-built command.

File command	Description
`file atime filename`	Returns decimal string with which file was accessed last time
`file dirname filename`	Returns a name comprising all of the path components in the name excluding the last element. If the name is a relative file name and only contains one path element, then returns ".″ (or ":″ on a Macintosh). If the name refers to a root directory, then the root directory is returned.
`file executable name`	Returns 1 if the file is executable else 0
`file exist name`	Returns 1 if the file exists else 0
`file extension name`	Returns the extension of the existing file .xxxx
`file isdirectory name`	Returns 1 if the file is a directory else 0
`file isfile name`	Returns 1 if the file is a file else 0
`file mtime name`	Returns the decimal string with which the file name was last modified
`file readable name`	Returns 1 if the file is readable else 0
`file writable name`	Returns 1 if the file is writable else 0
`file size name`	Returns the number of bytes assigned into a file string ID
`file type name`	The return type of the file name, i.e., File, directory, characterSpecial, blockSpecial, FIFO, link, or socket.
`file tail name`	Returns all of the characters in the *name* after the last directory separator. If the *name* contains no separators, then returns the *name*

6.3.1 File Seek Command

The `seek` command changes the sequence of accessing bytes from a file. `Seek` requires two arguments, a file identifier and integer, within the file.

seek $filename 100

This change the file sequence to read or write from byte number 100.

Sometimes, a third integer can be included in the `seek` command, which specifies the integer such as start, current, end, start.

- *file.start* Measures the file access position relative to the start of the file
- *file.current* Measures the file access position relative to the file's current position
- *file.end* Measures the file access position relative to the end of the file
- *seek $filename – 100 start* Sets the file access position to 100 bytes from the start of the file

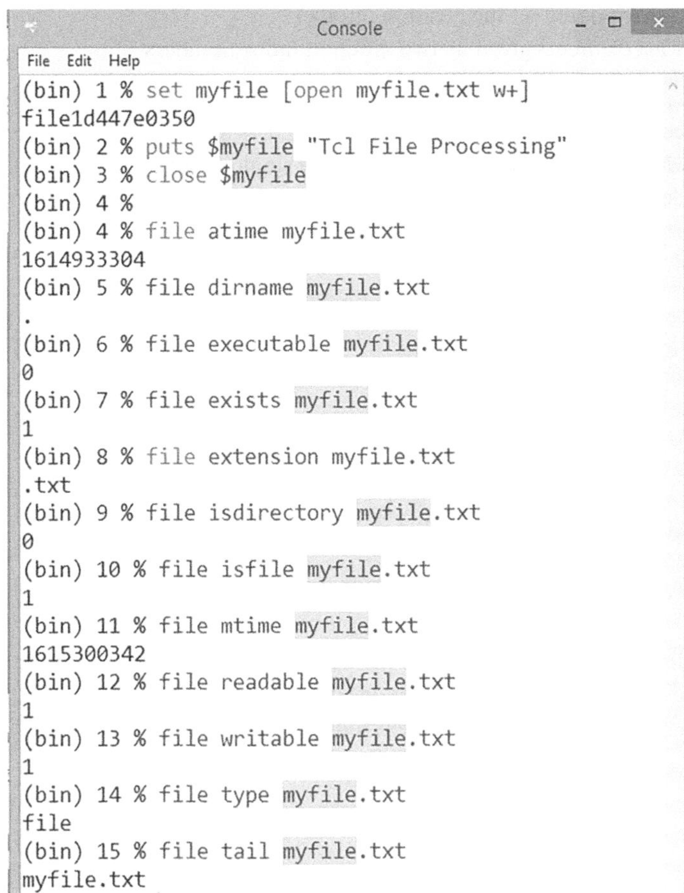

Figure 6.13 File-based in-built commands with examples.

6.3.2 File Tell Command

The `tell` command returns the file current position of a particular file identifier.

```
tell $filename 50 →returns 50
```

6.3.3 File Eof Command

The `eof` command takes a file identifier as an argument and returns 0 or 1; indicates whether a recent `gets` command for the file attempts to read past the end-of-file (EOF).

```
eof $filename→returns 0
```

6.3.4 List-based Command into the File

A list-based command starts with character "l"; the list is an ordered collection of elements separated by space assigned to an index in ascending order. A list element can be accessed through a particular index number. A few popular list commands are as follows.

- `lindex` Returns a list element based on the position number
- `lrange` Returns a set of list elements given by two different index numbers
- `linsert` Inserts a new element into the existing list

Based on this list command, accessing files can be manipulated. There is a file available in the directory shown in Figure 6.14, where the `gets` command can read a single statement, the `read` command reads the complete block of the message, while for the requirement to read a specific index or range of content from the file, `lindex` and `lrange` should be used.

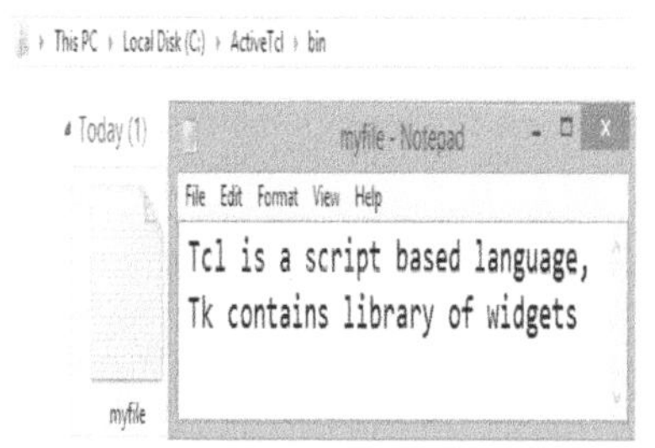

Figure 6.14 Initial content in a file.

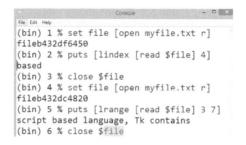

```
(bin) 1 % set file [open myfile.txt r]
fileb432df6450
(bin) 2 % puts [lindex [read $file] 4]
based
(bin) 3 % close $file
(bin) 4 % set file [open myfile.txt r]
fileb432dc4820
(bin) 5 % puts [lrange [read $file] 3 7]
script based language, Tk contains
(bin) 6 % close $file
```

Figure 6.15 Execution result of file access by the `list` command.

The execution result is shown in Figure 6.15 and explains the use of the list command with file read. The command `lindex` reads the element available at index number 4 (index starts at 0), i.e., "based" and `lrange` displays the range of elements between indexes 3 and 7, i.e., "script-based language", contained by Tk.

6.4 Solved Questions

Problem 6.1

Write a Tcl script to write multiple statements in the file and read by combining them as a single statement.

Solution

The above program says to write multiple statements and read too; the file must be writable as well readable.

- Open a file in W+ access mode.
- Write the following statements using the `puts` command:
  - Statement1: Tcl script preferred by EDA industry
  - Statement2: With the integration of the TK widget possible to create a GUI
  - Stetement3: Independent system can be developed
  - Statement4: I love the Tcl script
- Close the file
- Open the file in reading mode
- Read the individual statement assigned to a local variable
- Close the file again
- Concatenate each local variable

```
set file [open
myfile.txt w]
puts $file "Tcl
script preferred by
EDA industry"
puts $file "With
integration of TK
widget possible to
create GUI"
puts $file
"Independent system
can be developed"
puts $file "I love
Tcl script"
close $file
```

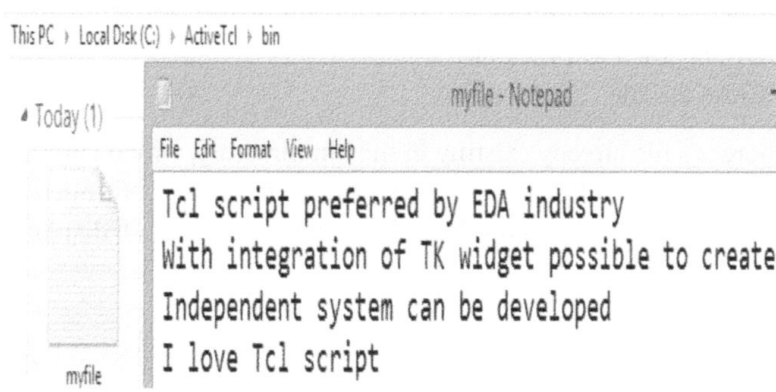

Figure 6.16 Writing with the `puts` command.

```
set file [open
myfile.txt r]
set line1
[gets $file]
set line2
[gets $file]
set line3
[gets $file]
set line4
[gets $file]
close $file
set line [con-
cat $line1,
$line2, $line3,
$line4]puts $line
```

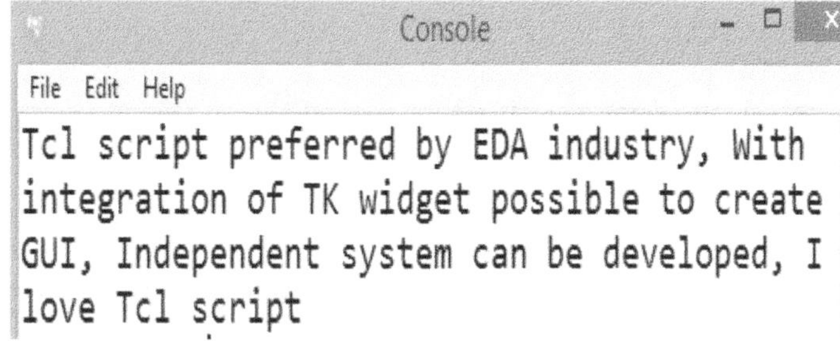

Figure 6.17 Reading with the `gets` command.

The `open` command creates myfile.txt in the bin directory, four statements have been written in the file with the `puts` command, as shown in Figure 6.16. The reading activity is completed by the `gets` command presented in Figure 6.17. Since `puts` and `gets` are line-oriented, four times are used to write and read the four statements.

Problem 6.2

Write a Tcl script to read multiple statements from an existing file using the `gets` command inside a loop.

Solution

Since the `gets` command is line-oriented, it can read a single statement. By initializing the `gets` command inside a loop, it is possible to read multiple statements until the loop is true.

- Open the file in reading mode
- Initialize a `while` loop
- Declare a local variable upon reading a statement with the `gets` command

- Check for condition EOF if reading completes; close the file
- Display the local variable
- Close the file

There is a file already existing in the bin directory, which contains the following statement. To read with loop, the following script is given. The script continues to execute until the end of the file encounter, then closes the file. The `puts "line \n"` displays each statement.

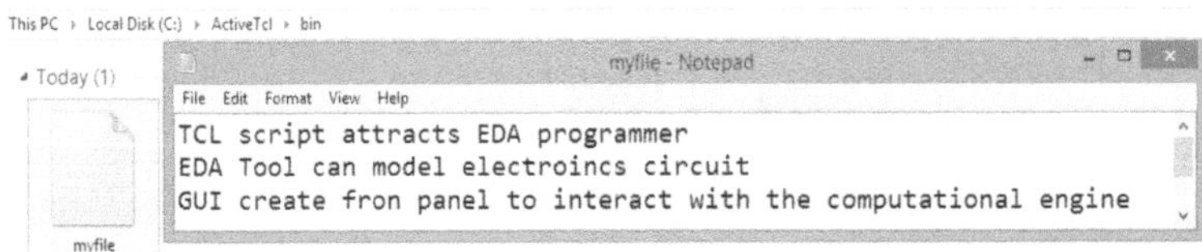

Figure 6.18 Earlier content written in the file.

```
set file [open
myfile.txt r]
 while {1} {
 set line [gets $file]
 if {[eof $file]} {
 close $file
}
 puts "$line \n"
}
}
```

```
Console
File Edit Help
Tcl script preferred by EDA industry

With integration of TK widget possible to create GUI

Independent system can be developed

I love Tcl script
```

Figure 6.19 Execution result of the `read` inside the loop.

Figure 6.18 presents the content already available in myfile.txt. The script above includes a `while` (1) loop which will continue to read the statement from the beginning of the file line by line using the `gets` command and display on the console terminal, as shown in Figure 6.19. The condition for the loop is checked with the EOF; when encountered, stop reading and close the file.

Problem 6.3

Write Tcl script to calculate the sum integer written over a file and display the result.

Solution

- Make sure the file is available in the bin directory
- Open the file in read mode
- Initialize the sum variable to zero
- Initialize a loop to each variable and add with sum variable
- Display the sum variable
- Close the file

```
set file [open myfile.txt r]
set sum 0
foreach num [read $file] {
   set sum [expr $sum + $num]
 }
puts $sum
close $file
```

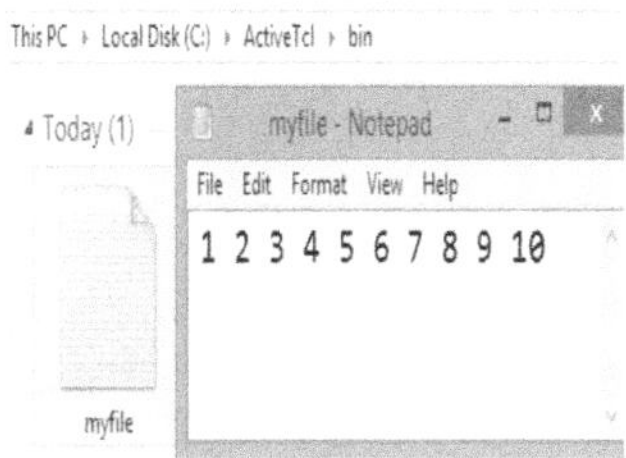

Figure 6.20 Integer already written in the file.

```
Console
File Edit Help
(bin) 1 % set file [open myfile.txt r]
filecff1b983d0
(bin) 2 % set sum 0
0
(bin) 3 % foreach num [read $file] {
>  set sum [expr $sum + $num]
> }
(bin) 4 % puts $sum
55
(bin) 5 % close $file
```

Figure 6.21 Execution result of `read` command.

In this program, the Tcl script tends to read the integer written in myfile.txt displayed in Figure 6.20. Initialize a sum variable with zero; the `foreach` loop uses a local variable and applies to each integer read from the file, which are added to the sum variable. At the end of the loop, the result of sum 55 is displayed, as shown in Figure 6.21.

Problem 6.4

Write a Tcl script to write 10 different names in a file with extension .csv and copy the content into another file with extension .csv without physically accessing the directory.

Solution

We seek to read the content of the file and write onto another file. One needs to open two independent files with the .csv extension, one file in reading mode and the other file in write mode. Read the first line from one.csv using the `gets` command and write into two.csv using the `puts` command. This read–write activity can be completed within a loop until the reading is completed.

- Open a file one.csv in reading mode and another two.csv in write mode
- Initialize a `while` loop where the condition content after reading is not zero
- Declare a local variable to hold the read name
- Write the located variable into two.csv
- Close both files

```
set file1 [open one.csv r]
set file2 [open two.csv w]
while {[gets $file1 data] > 0} {
puts $file2 $data
}
close $file1
close $file2
```

Figure 6.22 displays the 10 different names to be read from the file one.csv. Reading and writing activity is accomplished in a `while` loop based on the `gets` and `puts` commands, respectively. At the end of the loop, execution of the script generates a two.csv file in the bin directory and updates the content in the file two.csv, as displayed in Figure 6.23.

Alternatively, a similar result can be executed by the Tcl script with the `split` command. Here, the `read` command reads the entire message and updates in the local variable data. Each element from the read block is to be split; separate each state by `\n` a newline, and assign to variable lines. A `foreach` loop writes each line onto `file2`, until all lines have been read out.

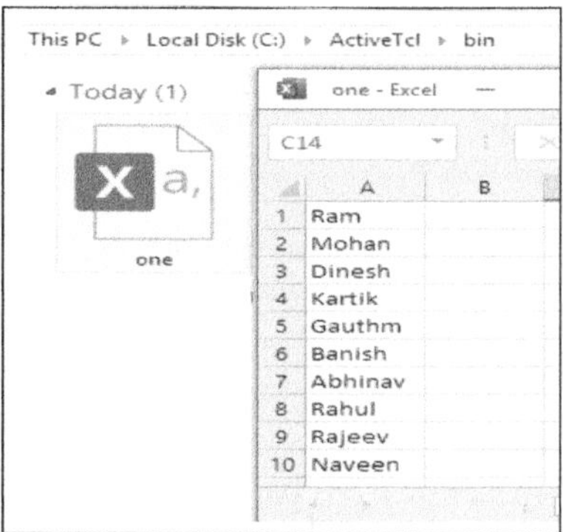

Figure 6.22 Content of file one.csv to be read.

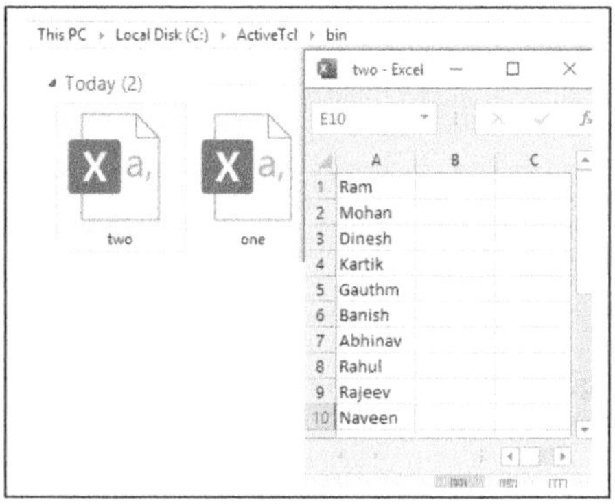

Figure 6.23 Content written in two.csv.

```
set file1 [open one.csv r]
set file2 [open two.csv w]
set data [read $file1]
set lines [split $data "\n"]
foreach line $lines {
puts $file2 $line
}
close $file2
close $file1
```

Problem 6.5

Write a Tcl script to generate 10 random numbers and write them into the file.

Solution

- Open a file in write mode (.csv extension)
- Declare a `for` loop to execute 10 times
- Initialize a local variable num to hold the variable
- Write the num in the file
- Close file

```
set file [open
myfile.csv w]
for {set i 0} {$i < 10}
{incr i} {
set num [expr
round(rand()*100)]
puts $file $num
}
close $file
```

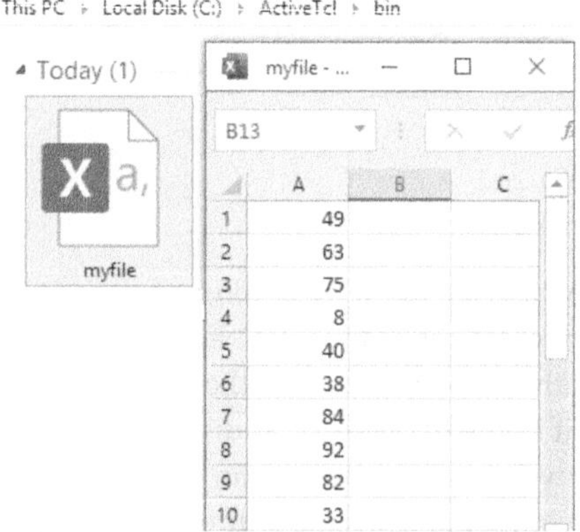

Figure 6.24 Random number written in the file.

This Tcl script generates random numbers in the range 0–100. The `rand()` function generates a random number in the range of 0 to 1 with precision bits up to 16 bits, and `round(rand())` produces only integers. The range of random numbers can be enhanced with a multiplication of 100. Here, a generated random number is written in the file myfile.csv. The generation and the `puts` activity is repeated 10 times using the `for` loop, which results in 10 random numbers, as displayed in Figure 6.24.

Problem 6.6

An experiment of testing an electronics component is performed by measuring the voltage and current through the terminal. The table in Figure 6.25 presents the component ID, voltage, and current. The results column indicates whether the component has passed the test and is suitable for usage, else it fails. Write Tcl script to pick the components that passed.

Solution

Figure 6.25 presents the data collected during the experiment. The Result column shows which component passed or failed. To following procedure locates only the components that "Pass".

- Make the file experiment.csv available in the bin directory
- Write script, open the file in the reading mode
- Read the first statement of the experiment with the `gets` command
- Look for the result (Result column) based on `lindex` or `lrange` and update in the local variable
- If the local variable matches with "Pass", display the component (Component column)
- Close file

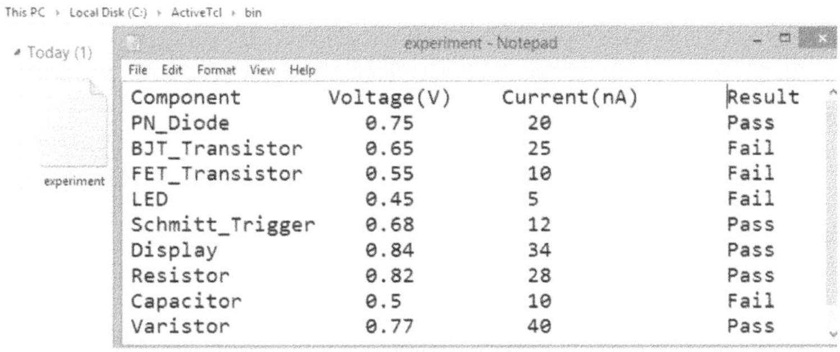

Component	Voltage(V)	Current(nA)	Result
PN_Diode	0.75	20	Pass
BJT_Transistor	0.65	25	Fail
FET_Transistor	0.55	10	Fail
LED	0.45	5	Fail
Schmitt_Trigger	0.68	12	Pass
Display	0.84	34	Pass
Resistor	0.82	28	Pass
Capacitor	0.5	10	Fail
Varistor	0.77	40	Pass

Figure 6.25 Initial measurement of experiments.

```
set file [open experiment.txt r]
while { [gets $file data] > 0} {
if {[lrange $data 3 3] == "Pass"} {
puts [lindex $data 0]
}
}
close $file
```

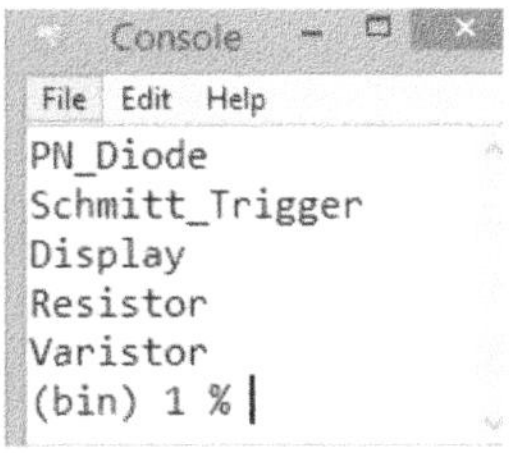

Figure 6.26 Result of the script.

Here list-based commands `lrange` and `lindex` have been used to read the selected value from the statement. A statement is read by the `gets` command; look for an element available in a range 3–3, if a match to "pass", write the content in index 0 (name of component). Repeat these activities in a `while` loop. The execution result of the script is given in Figure 6.26. The console terminal displays a list of components that passed in the experimentation.

6.5 Review Questions

1. Write a Tcl script to read the 10 integers from the file and sort the even and odd numbers.
2. Write a Tcl script to read the 10 integers from the file arranged in ascending/descending order and write into another file.

6.6 MCQs based on Tcl File Processing

1 How many different Tcl file access modes are there?
A 2
B 4
C 6
D 8

Solution (c)

2 Which default access modes provide Tcl file access?
A r
B w
C a
D r+
E w+
F a+

Solution (a)

3 Which file access modes provide permission to read?
A r
B r+
C w+
D a+
E All of above

Solution (e)

4 Which file access modes provide permission to write?
A w
B w+
C r+
D a
E a+
F All of above

Solution (f)

5 Which file access modes allow to write without losing existing content from the file?
A w
B w+
C a
D a+

Solutions (c) and (d)

6 Which file access modes write with overlap to existing content?
 A w
 B w+
 C a
 D a+

Solutions (a) and (b)

7 Which file access modes can automatically create a new file?
 A w
 B w+
 C a+
 D All of above

Solution (d)

8 Identify the incorrect statement.
 A The `puts` command can write single line onto the file
 B The `gets` command can read a single line from file
 C The `read` command reads the complete content of the file
 D None of the above

Solution (d)

9 Which of the following are line-oriented commands?
 A `set` and `reset`
 B `gets` and `puts`
 C `printf` and `scanf`
 D `seek` and `read`

Solution (b)

10 How is the content of a Tcl file accessed?
 A Sequentially
 B Concurrently
 C Parallelly
 D Randomly

Solution (a)

References

1 Welch, B.B., Jones, K., and Hobbs, J. (2003). *Practical Programming in Tcl/Tk*. Prentice Hall Professional.
2 Flynt, C. (2012). *Tcl/Tk: A Developer's Guide*. Elsevier.
3 Wheeler, B. (2011). *Tcl/Tk 8.5 Programming Cookbook*. Packt Publishing Ltd.
4 https://www.tcl.tk/man/tcl/TclCmd/file.htm
5 Ousterhout, J.K. (1993). *Tcl and the TK Toolkit*. Addison.

7

Toolkit Widgets

Toolkit (Tk) is a free and open-source cross-platform widget toolkit, which provides a library of widgets to create a graphical user interface (GUI). Tk offers a library of widgets for many programming languages. Some of the most popular widgets are button, text, label, frame, menu, canvas, etc., which provide a better mechanism to interact with the system. A widget is an integral component of a GUI that has a particular appearance and behavior, through which an end-user communicates with the application. The Tcl script is meant for a computational purpose in the background and the GUI view is developed with the widget for visual appearance. The Window Shell (WISH) [1] program provides a mechanism to run the tclsh shell in the graphical window. The Tk window acts like a frame or container into which all the widgets are placed.

7.1 Features of Tk Widgets

The following are the important features of a Tk widget [2]:

(a) platform independent – can be designed with multiple platforms;
(b) customizable – all the features of a Tk widget are customizable. Size, color, shape, and appearance can be customized as per the need;
(c) configurable – widget instances are stored in the database, which can be manipulated or read just through the configurable feature;
(d) it is open source;
(e) it provides a high level of extendibility;
(f) it can be used with other dynamic languages and not just Tcl;
(g) GUI looks identical across platforms;
(h) offers a large number of widgets;
(i) Tk provides a set of Tcl commands that create and manipulate widgets;
(j) a widget is a window in a GUI that has a particular appearance and behavior.

Tk supports the Tcl command to manipulate widgets. The Tcl computation is performed in the background, and the user can interact via the widget. Some of the widgets are dedicated to providing an input and some of them display the output of a specified widget. A simple way to invoke a widget is by its name. Each widget has its appearance and configuration options, and a set of methods that are used to access and manipulate the widget. Table 7.1 lists the available widgets in the Tk library.

Programming and GUI Fundamentals: Tcl-Tk for Electronic Design Automation (EDA), First Edition.
Suman Lata Tripathi, Abhishek Kumar, and Jyotirmoy Pathak.

Table 7.1 Tk widget command.

Command	Description
`Button`	Creates a button that is clickable and triggers an action
`Label`	Creates a single line of text (read-only)
`Entry`	Creates a single-line text-entry widget
`Message`	Creates multiple-line text (read-only)
`Frame`	Creates a frame that holds other widgets
`Radiobutton`	Creates a radio button that has a set of on/off buttons linked to a variable
`Checkbutton`	Creates a toggle button linked to a Tcl variable
`Toplevel`	Creates a frame that is a new top-level window
`Text`	Creates general-purpose text
`Frame`	Creates a container used to hold child widgets
`Menubutton`	Creates a button for displaying the menu
`Menu`	Creates a menu
`Listbox`	Creates a widget that displays a list of cells, one or more of which may be selected
`Scale`	Creates a scale to horizontally/vertically choose a numeric value through the slider
`Scrollbar`	Creates a scrollbar linked to another widget or text
`Progressbar`	Creates a widget to provide visual feedback on the progress of a long operation, like a file upload.
`Canvas`	Drawing widget for displaying graphics and images
`Spinbox`	Creates a widget that allows for selecting a value through spinning
`Treeview`	Creates a hierarchy of widgets

7.2 Geometry Manager

Each widget is under the control of the geometry manager which manipulates or optimizes the size and location on the screen. The three mostly used geometry managers are (i) Grid, (ii) Pack, and (iii) Place [3]. The geometry manager arranges the widget on the screen according to the script. A widget will not appear on the screen until the geometry manager learns about it. Tk-based programs are event driven, where events are driven by users via a mouse or keyboard. The binding feature enables the binding of the widget with the Tcl script. Eventbinding structures the hierarchy of global binding, class binding, and instance binding. A widget binds with a particular action to execute the program and displays the result on the linked widget. The geometry manager learns about the Tk widget and makes them appear on the screen. The three types of geometry manager are the following.

(i) **Grid** – arranges the widget in the 2D grid; according to either a specified row or column-wise from the top left of the screen.

```
    grid .widget_name -row x1 -column y1 -rowspan x2 -
columnspan y2
```

Here, x1 and y1 specify the position to keep the .widget_name, x2 and y2 specify the number of rows and columns required to adjust according to the following widgets.

-column number	Sets the column position for the widget.
-row number	Sets the row position for the widget.
-columnspan number	Number of columns to be used for this widget, Default 1.
-rowspan number	Number of rows to be used for this widget, Default 1.

(ii) **Pack** – are constraint-based, and packs the widget around the edge of the cavity. It packs the widget in horizontal and vertical boxes.

```
pack .widet_name  -padx x1 -pady y1
```

Here, x1 and y1 are integers, and –padx and –pady put a space between the widgets.

(iii) **Place** – places a widget at the constraint using absolute positioning.

```
place .widget_name -x x1 -y y1
```

Here, x1 and y1 specify the distance from the horizontal and vertical borders of the screen.

7.3 Widget Naming

The naming system in Tk reflects the order in the hierarchy of widgets. The root window is named with (.) and an element in the window is accessible with (.name_of_widget). A button can be named as .b and can be accessed as an element with the same name (.b) for configuration and manipulation. Each widget acts as a child of the main window, a frame is declared with .f and a button associated with frame .f.b and so on. Here, the frame acts as a parent and the button acts as a child. The drawback of the naming system is, in the case of the interface changes, the frequent updates in the widget of positioning and the need to change its name.

7.4 Widget Dimension

The default unit of the widget is the pixel, specified without dimension. Other dimensions are inches (i), millimeters (m), centimeters (cm), and points (p).

7.5 Widget Configuration

Tk treats each widget name as a command name and can perform operations on a specific widget by invoking the widget's name. Attributes to the widgets are specified by arguments. The attribute changes the appearance of the widget and beautifies the interface, starting with a dash (–) and the name for the widget specified with -text. A widget can have one or more attributes. The setting of a widget instance can change by the configuration (config) command. The syntax for config uses the same-named argument that is used to create that widget. Features of the widget can be assigned during instantiation or can be configured later in the programming.

Syntax: `.widgetname config attribute`

Table 7.2 Widget configuration.

Configuration Attribute	Description
`-background color / -bg color`	Changes the background color of the widget
`-foreground color / -fg color`	Changes the foreground color of the widget
`-borderwidth n`	Draws a border in 3D effect
`-font {Descriptor size feature}`	Changes the font of widget Description – time, ariel, caliber, etc. Size – 0–100 Feature – bold, italic, underline
`-height n`	Sets the height of a widget to be n pixels
`-width n`	Set width of widget to be n pixels
`-text "Widget_Text"`	Sets the text for the widget
`-flash`	Flashes the widget, to draw attention
`-relief feature`	Sets the 3D shape of the widget Feature – flat or raised or groove or ridged or solid or sunken
`-textvariable`	Updates the text value dynamically

Table 7.2 lists the different configurations available for GUI development.

7.6 Widget Programming

The Tk script begins with the creation of the widget, arranging with the geometry manager, and binding with the course of action.

7.6.1 Button Widget

A button is a very popular widget used in developing the GUI, A button is instanced from the name `button` followed by its name `.b`. A widget may contain one or more attribute feature. It possesses the in-built action of a left click of the mouse and generates an event whenever someone triggers and executes the bonded task.

Syntax for the button widget is *button .b -command attribute........*

```
button .b -text Hello -command {puts "Hello Tk World"}
grid .b -row 0 -column 0
```

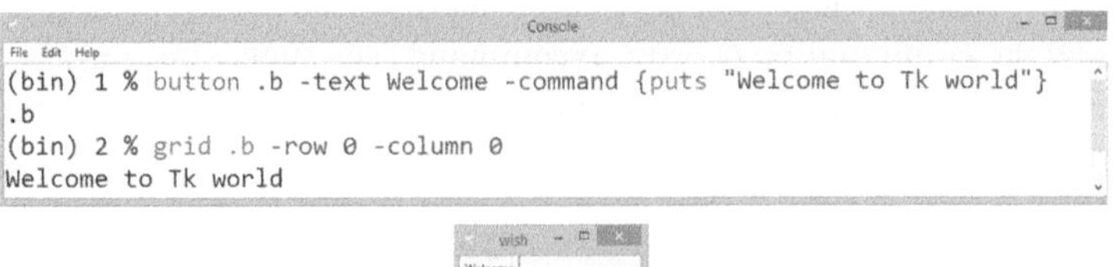

Figure 7.1 Button widget.

This script is used to create an instance of the button named `.b`, and the text printed on the button is "Welcome". The `button .b` has the default binding with the left click of the mouse. A left click of the mouse executes the Tcl command and displays the statement "Hello Tk World" on the console (Figure 7.1).

The grid manager learns to make a button appear on row 0 column 0 and maps accordingly. Similar to an object-based system, the naming of the Tk widget begins with the (`.`) dot convention. A class of the widget is a command that creates an instance of that widget.

Example 7.1 Write a Tcl script to display the widgets on the GUI screen, as shown in Figure 7.2.

Solution

The GUI presented in Figure 7.2 possesses a label that displays a single-line statement "Widget for GUI," a button titled "widgets," an entrybox, a checkbutton, a radiobutton, a horizontal scale, and a vertical scrollbar.

```
label .l -text "Widget for GUI"
button .b -text widgets
entry .e
checkbutton .c
radiobutton .r
scale .s -orien h
scrollbar .sb

grid .l -row 0 -column 3
grid .b -row 1 -column 1
grid .e -row 2 -column 2
grid .c -row 3 -column 1
grid .r -row 3 -column 3
grid .s -row 4 -column 2
grid .sb -row 5 -column 1
```

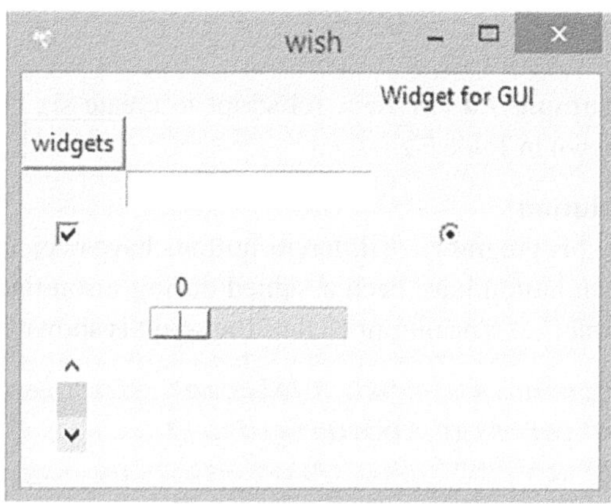

Figure 7.2 Multiple widgets on screen.

Each widget is invoked from the library by its name and needs an instance name. Finally, each widget learns with the grid manager to appear at a particular row number and column number to avoid overlap.

Example 7.2 Write a Tcl script to create a button. An event on the button displays the output as a standard output.

Solution

The following Tk script creates a button titled "Press Me," which has a default action with a click of the mouse. For each action on the button, the statement is displayed on the standard output device (Figure 7.3).

```
button .b -text "Press Me" -
command {puts "Welcome to Tk
World"}
pack .b
```

Figure 7.3 Button with the `puts` command.

Example 7.3 Write a Tcl script to create a button widget. An event on the button closes the tool.

Solution

In this example, the exit command is linked with a button, attribute `-text` labels the button "Press Me," and `-command` binds the in-built command exit with the button. Left-click action of the mouse on the button closes the tool (Figure 7.4).

```
button .b -text "Press Me" -
command exit
pack .b
```

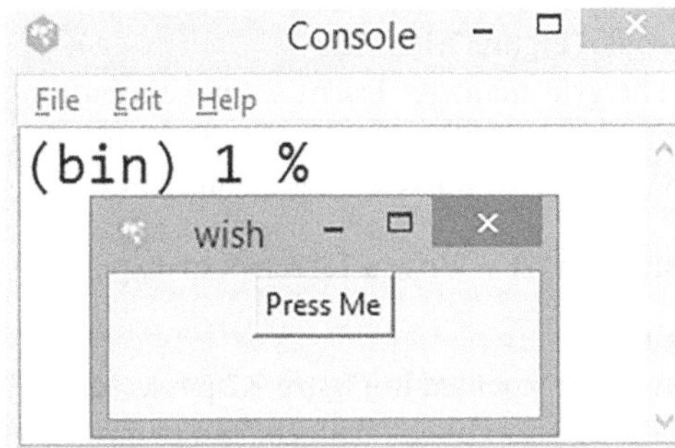

Figure 7.4 Button with the `exit` command.

Example 7.4 Write a Tcl script to create six buttons and configure with a different attribute shown in Table 7.2.

Solution

In this program, six different buttons have been created, namely (`b1......b6`). The attributes to each button have been assigned during instantiation itself (configuration attributes are given in Table 7.2). The output GUI of the script is shown in Figure 7.5

```
button .b1 -text "Welcome" -fg black -bg green -height 5 -width 10 -
relief flat -borderwidth 7
button .b2 -text "to" -fg blue -bg pink -height 5 -width 10 -relief
raised -borderwidth 7
button .b3 -text "my" -fg white -bg black -height 5 -width 10 -
relief groove -borderwidth 7
button .b4 -text "World" -fg red -bg yellow -height 5 -width 10 -
relief ridge -font {times 15 italic} -borderwidth 7
button .b5 -text "of" -fg yellow -bg pink -height 5 -width 10 -
relief solid -borderwidth 7 -font {times 15 underline}
button .b6 -text "GUI" -fg black -bg red -height 5 -width 10 -relief
sunken -font {times 15 bold} -
borderwidth 7

grid .b1 -row 0 -column 0
grid .b2 -row 0 -column 1
grid .b3 -row 0 -column 2
grid .b4 -row 1 -column 1
grid .b5 -row 2 -column 1
grid .b6 -row 3 -columnspan 3
```

Note – Each widget must be arranged in a separate row and column to avoid overlap.

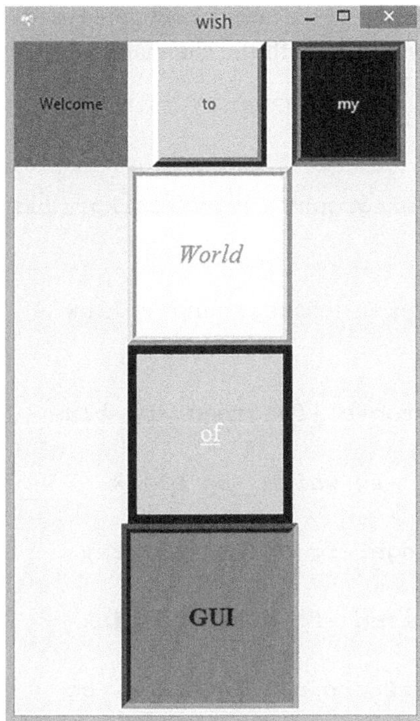

Figure 7.5 Button and different attributes.

7.6.2 Label Widget

The label widget is incorporated into almost all Tk applications that are used to display a single line of text. Here, \n displays a single line in multiple statements (Figure 7.6).

Syntax: *label .l label_name -command attribute ......*

```
label .l1 -text "A single line
statement"
pack .l1
label .l2 -text "More than one
\n statement in \n label
widget"
pack .l2
```

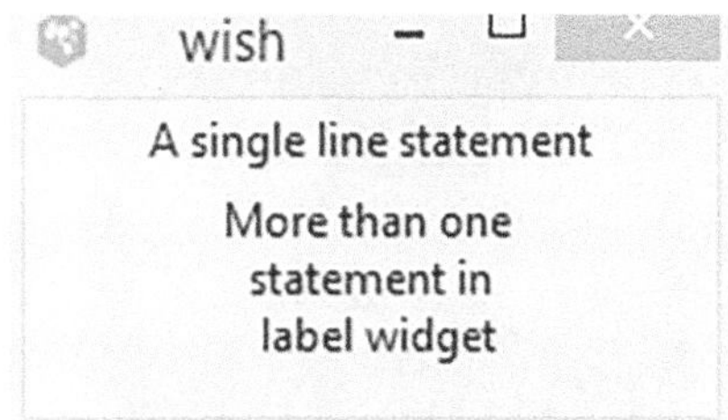

Figure 7.6 Label widget.

Example 7.5 Write a Tcl script to create different labels to configure their attributes.

Solution

In the following program, eight different labels are created. The background of the label is configured with the command `-background color`/`-bg color` according to the name of the color. Similarly, the foreground of the label is configured with the command `-foreground` `color/-fg color` according to the name of the color. The text of the label is configured as 3D with the command `-relief`. The format of the text is configured with the command `-font`, requiring a combination of {`font size style`} (Figure 7.7).

```
label .lab1 -text "This is text"
pack .lab1
label .lab2 -text "This is colored text" -foreground green -background
blue
pack .lab2
label .lab3 -text "Sunken text" -relief sunken -foreground yellow -
background black
pack .lab3
label .lab4 -text "Grooved text" -relief groove -fg green -bg blue
pack .lab4
label .lab5 -text "Flat text" -relief flat -fg white -bg black
pack .lab5
label .lab6 -text "Ridged text" -relief ridge -fg black -bg gray
pack .lab6
label .lab7 -text "Raised text" -relief raised -fg blue -bg pink
pack .lab7
label .lab8 -text "Times font" -font {times 25 bold} -fg black -bg
green
pack .lab8
```

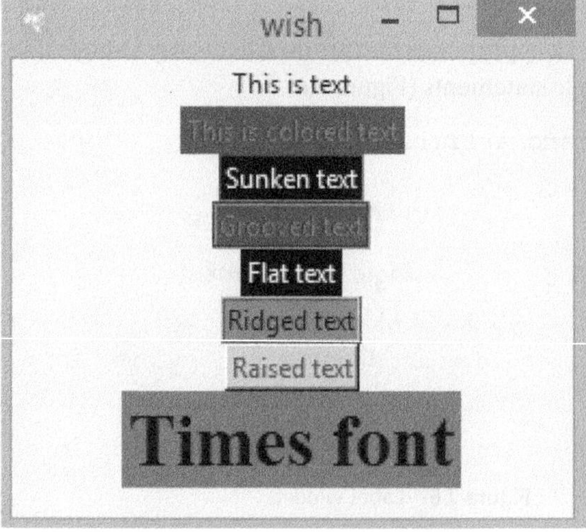

Figure 7.7 Label with different attributes.

Example 7.6 Write a Tcl script to define the button, and label the widget and change the button text with a configuration command.

Solution

In this program, a button (`.b`) has been invoked titled "Programming Language." The packer lets it be displayed on the screen. The `.b config` command adds a different feature to the button, as shown in Figure 7.8.

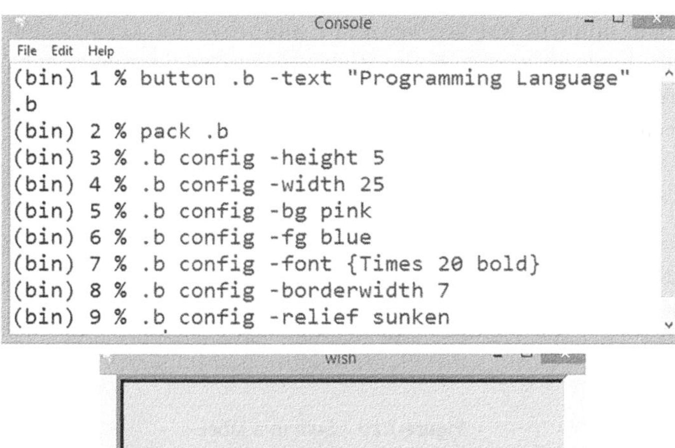

Figure 7.8 Button with config.

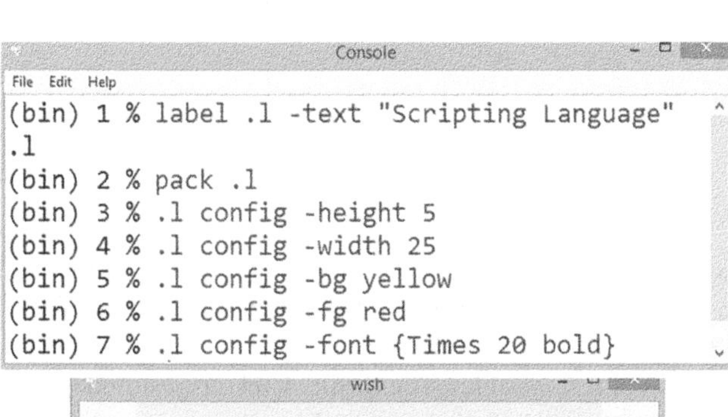

Figure 7.9 Label with config.

Similarly, the above script can be modified for other widgets too. Figure 7.9 presents the `config` command with the label. A label has an instant title `(.l)`, and the packer lets it be displayed on the screen. The `config` command adds the different features into the label.

7.6.3 Textvariable Widget Command

The textvariable dynamically updates the variable values linked to a specified widget value. Whenever the widget value changes, its content updates throughout the program. It is mostly used on entry and label widgets. A textvariable is useful to update the variable in the main program where the result is returned from a procedure.

The following script contains two different textvariables `var1` and `var2` for `input1` and `input2`, respectively. A constant value is assigned to both variables. However, the value can be updated from the console terminal or other widget links. The result of summation is updated to `var3` and will be placed on the mentioned row and column, as presented in Figure 7.10.

```
label .l1 -text "Input1="
label .l2 -textvariable var1
label .l3 -text "Input2="
label .l4 -textvariable var2
label .l5 -text "Input1 + Input2="
label .l6 -textvariable var3
set var1 25
set var2 35
set var3 [expr $var1 + $var2]
grid .l1 -row 0 -column 0
grid .l2 -row 0 -column 1
grid .l3 -row 1 -column 0
grid .l4 -row 1 -column 1
grid .l5 -row 2 -column 0
grid .l6 -row 2 -column 1
```

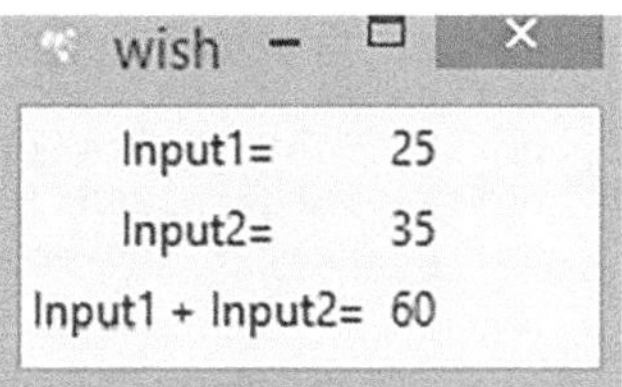

Figure 7.10 Sum in a label.

7.6.4 Entry Widget

The `entry` is the most important widget that accepts a single line of text as an input. The appearance is an `entry` widget like a space, where the user can input some value. Acceptance of the input from users is essential in every Tk application, as shown in Figure 7.11. The `-entry` supports the display of results with a combination of textvariables. The result of Tcl script stored in the textvariable gets updated and displays the value over a linked entry blank space.

Syntax: `entry .e -command attribute`

```
entry .e
pack .e
.e config -bg pink
```

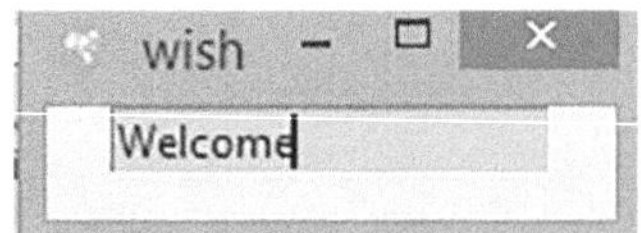

Figure 7.11 Entry for user input.

Figure 7.12 experiments with the `entry` widget and textvariable. Whenever the value of the variable class is updated, it displays the latest value of the entry space.

```
entry .e -bg red -textvariable class
set class "Online or Offline"
pack .e
```

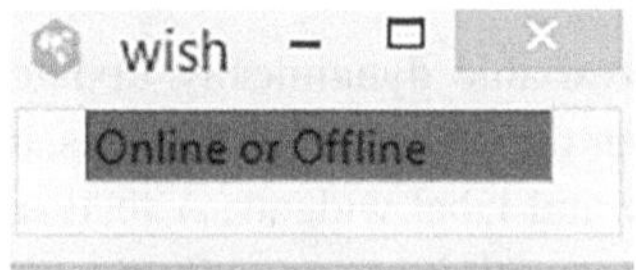

Figure 7.12 Entry with textvariable.

The above script creates an entry space, and the pack manager learns to display it. The configuration command can update the feature according to the attribute. Additional features applicable to entry widgets are given in the following.

-justify Justifies the side of text left, right, or center (default left)
-show Hides the characters for security purposes

```
entry .e -bg yellow -width 20 -
textvariable var -justify right
-show "*"
set var "GUI Application"
pack .e
```

Figure 7.13 Entry space with a hidden character.

For example, Figure 7.13 shows hiding of the characters in the entry space with a special character using `-show`. It is helpful for creating security-related applications.

7.6.5 Frame Widget

The frame widget is a rectangular container widget that groups widgets for designing the GUI. The purpose is to act as a spacer or container for complex window layouts. The frame creates a new window and makes it for the frame widget. The primary purpose of the frame widget is to act as a spacer or container for complex window layouts. The `frame` command returns the pathname of the new window. Other widgets can be arranged in the frame.

Syntax: `frame frameName options`

Where options present the feature of the frame widget, the common options are `-background`, `-height`, `-padx`, `-pady`; the `-relief` condition sets the 3D condition and `-borderwidth` the width used to draw a border with the 3D effect. Figure 7.14 shows two different frames with different attributes and packs. The default packing order is from top and center. The frame appears in the same sequence as it packed.

```
frame .myFrame1 -background red -relief ridge
-borderwidth 8 -height 100  -width 100
frame .myFrame2 -background blue  -relief
raised -borderwidth 8 -height 100 -width 50
pack .myFrame1
pack .myFrame2
```

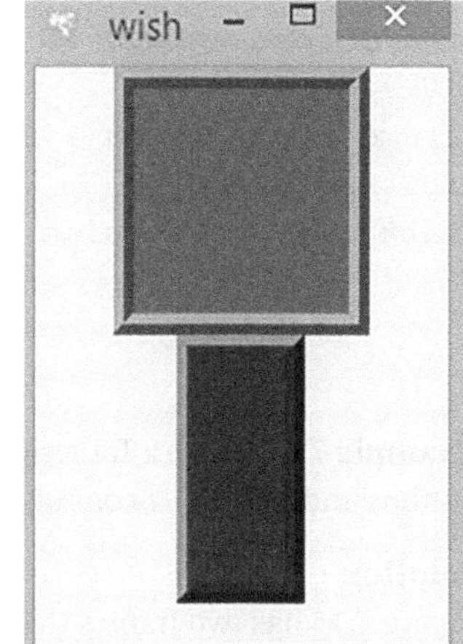

Figure 7.14 Frame widget.

A frame positioned on the window can pack along the top, bottom, right, or left sides. While packing, the `-side` direction command instructs to arrange the widget with the mentioned direction.

`pack.one.two -side bottom` → `frame. two bottom of frame.one.`

```
frame .one -width 40 -height
40 -bg red
frame .two -width 100 -height
100 -bg green
pack .one .two -side bottom
```

pack.one.two -side top ➔ frame. two top of frame.one.

```
frame .one -width 40 -height
40 -bg red
frame .two -width 100 -height
100 -bg green
pack .one .two -side top
```

pack.one.two -side left ➔ frame. two left of frame.one.

```
frame .one -width 40 -height
40 -bg red
frame .two -width 100 -height
100 -bg green
pack .one .two -side left
```

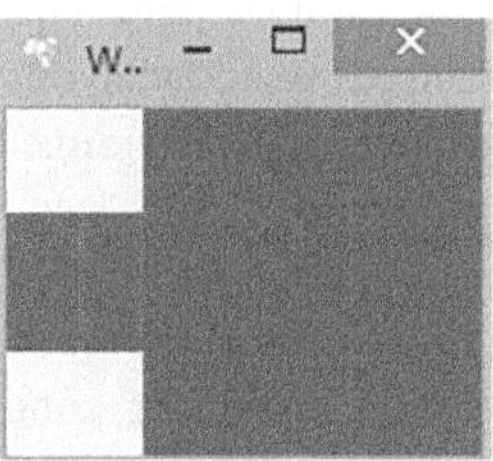

pack.one.two -side right ➔ frame. two right of frame.one.

```
frame .one -width 40 -height
40 -bg red
frame .two -width 100 -height
100 -bg green
pack .one .two -side right
```

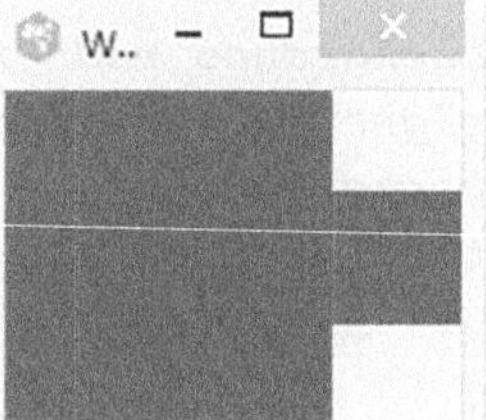

Example 7.6 Write a Tcl script to create two frames, where `frame-1` consists of three horizontal buttons and `frame-2` consists of two vertical buttons, as shown in Figure 7.15.

Solution

Figure 7.15 has two frames that need to pack with a `-side top` command. Add three buttons to `frame1` and two buttons to `frame2`.

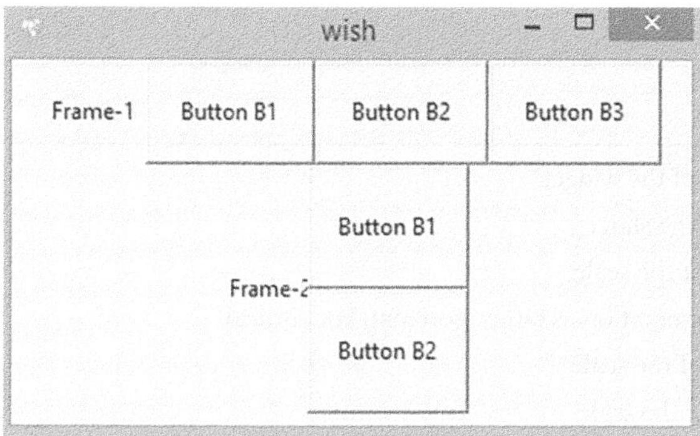

Figure 7.15 Buttons in horizontal and vertical arrangements.

```
frame .f1 -width 100 -height 60
frame .f2 -width 20 -height 50
pack .f1 .f2 -side top
label .f1.l1 -width 7 -text "Frame-1"
button .f1.b1 -padx 15 -pady 15 -text "Button B1"
button .f1.b2 -padx 15 -pady 15 -text "Button B2"
button .f1.b3 -padx 15 -pady 15 -text "Button B3"
pack .f1.l1 .f1.b1 .f1.b2 .f1.b3 -side left

label .f2.l1 -width 5 -text "Frame-2"
button .f2.b1 -padx 12 -pady 20 -text "Button B1"
button .f2.b2 -padx 12 -pady 20 -text "Button B2"
pack .f2.l1 -side left
pack .f2.b1 .f2.b2 -side top
```

7.6.6 Scale Widget

Scale is one of the widgets used to provide an input to the program. It can be either horizontal or vertical. It consists of a slider in the scale widget, the movement of the scale left–right (horizontal scale), and top–bottom (vertical scale) is used to set numeric values in the specified range. A slider above the scale points to the current value of the scale and is displayed next to the slider. Scale can be instantiated by the following syntax.

Syntax: `scale .scale_name -command attribute`

The features of the scale widget can be described by the commands in Table 7.3.

There are three major fields where the value of scale can be used:

(a) to get/set the value explicitly;
(b) scale can associate with the Tcl variable. Tcl command/procedure can synchronize with the current value of scale;
(c) Tcl command/procedure executes when the scale slider value changes (Figure 7.16).

Table 7.3 Scale commands.

Scale Command	Description
`-length number`	Sets the length of the widget
`-sliderlength`	Sets the size of the slider
`-label`	Sets the label for the scale
`-orient`	Sets the scale orientation as either horizontal or vertical
`-from`	Starting range of the scale
`-to`	Ending range of the scale
`-tickinterval`	Sets the interval for the slider over the scale
`-command`	Invokes a procedure to be executed on the binded action
`-textvariable`	Updates the variable value

```
scale .s -orient horizontal -
from 0 -to 100 -length 100 -
label "My Horizontal Scale"
pack .s
```

```
scale .s -orient vertical -from
0 -to 100 -length 100 -label
"My Vertical Scale"
pack .s
```

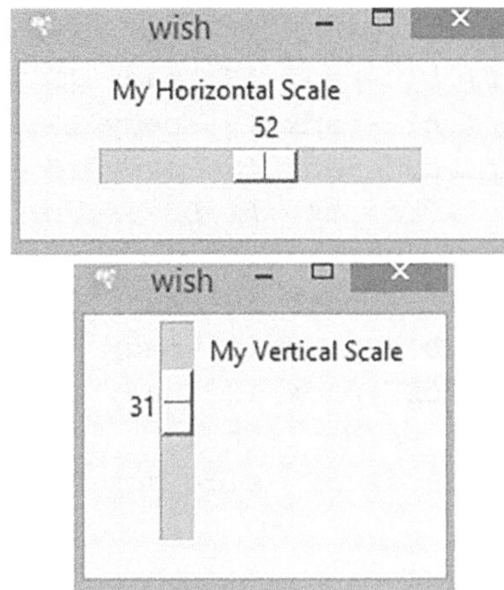

Figure 7.16 Scale orientation.

The attribute to the scale set can be instantaneous or can be updated via the `config` command.

7.6.6.1 Slider Value Synchronize to Label

The current value of scale pointed by the slider can be set as a variable. The current value of the slider can be declared as the `-variable` value updates the value of `-textvariable` of other widgets. The linking of variable to textvariable is accomplished by the same name and can update the value dynamically. The example in Figure 7.17 presents that the current value of the slider is 81, which is passed to the linked label.

```
scale .s -orient horizontal -
from 0 -to 100  -length 150  -
variable val -label "Current
Value of Scale is"
label .l -textvariable val
pack .s .l
```

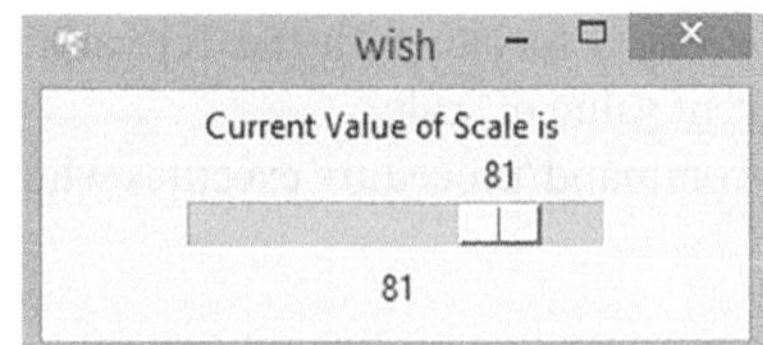

Figure 7.17 Slider on a scale.

Example 7.7 Write a Tcl script to design a horizontal scale and display the current value of the slider after moving it.

Solution

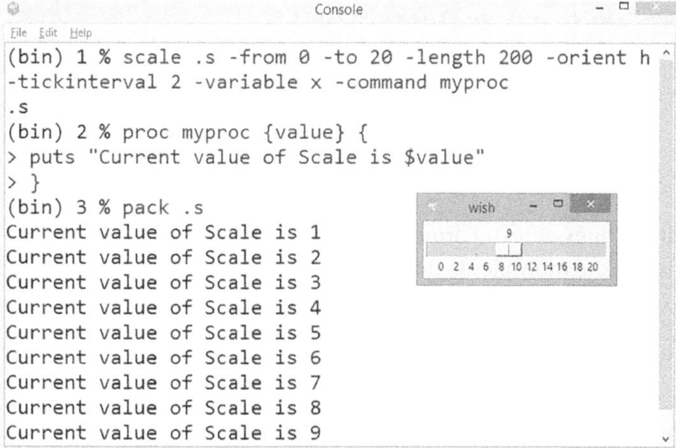

Console
File Edit Help
(bin) 1 % scale .s -from 0 -to 20 -length 200 -orient h
-tickinterval 2 -variable x -command myproc
.s
(bin) 2 % proc myproc {value} {
> puts "Current value of Scale is $value"
> }
(bin) 3 % pack .s
Current value of Scale is 1
Current value of Scale is 2
Current value of Scale is 3
Current value of Scale is 4
Current value of Scale is 5
Current value of Scale is 6
Current value of Scale is 7
Current value of Scale is 8
Current value of Scale is 9
wish
9
0 2 4 6 8 10 12 14 16 18 20

Example 7.8 Write a Tcl script to design a scale that returns the square of the current value of the slider after moving it (Figure 7.18).

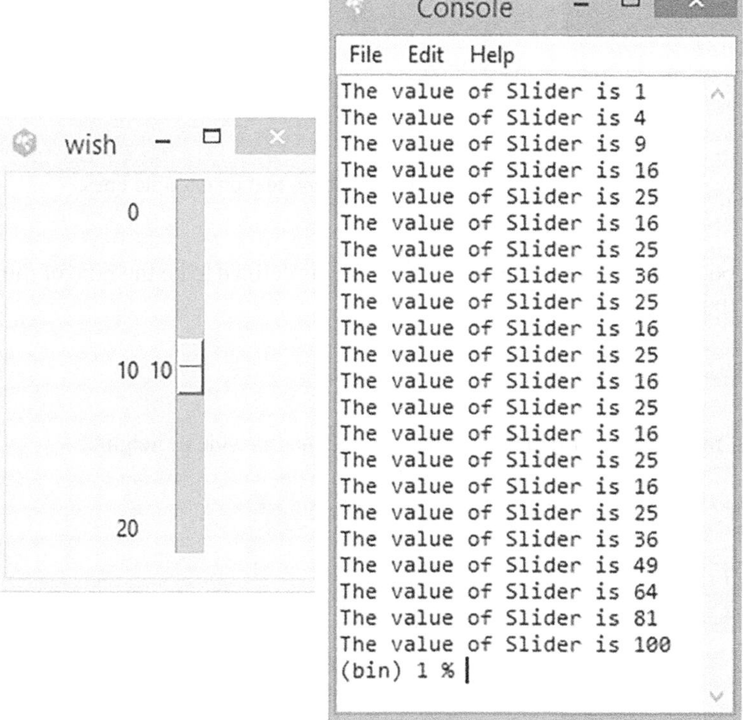

Figure 7.18 Scale with procedure.

Solution

```
scale .s -from 0 -to 20 -length 200 -tickinterval 10 -variable x -
command myproc
proc myproc {value} {
puts "The value of Slider is [expr $value*$value]"
}
pack .s
```

7.6.7 Message Widget

The message widget displays multiple lines of text. Formatting the text into multiple lines is done with "\". A backslash is used to display the multiple statements separately without embedding [4]. It is designed for use in dialog boxes. It formats the text into a box of a given width.

Syntax: `message .messagename option`

The available options for the message widget is `-font`, `-background`, `-foreground`, `-borderwidth`, etc., as given in Table 7.2. Additional options are (i) `-justify alignment`, which sets the alignment of the text, and can be left, center, or right; and (ii) `-aspect ratio`, which sets the aspect ratio in percent. Figure 7.19 shows the message formatted into multiple lines and center justified.

```
message .msg -text "Write single
statement
\ into multiple line" -jus-
tify center
pack .msg
```

Figure 7.19 Message text on multiple lines.

It formats the text into a box with a given width. The aspect ratio is defined to be the ratio of the width to the height, times 100.

$$aspect\ ratio = (width\ /\ height) * 100$$

The default is 150, which means the text will be one and a half times as wide in height.

```
message .msg -aspect 100 -jus-
tify left -text \
"this is my first line,
this is my second line"
pack .msg
```

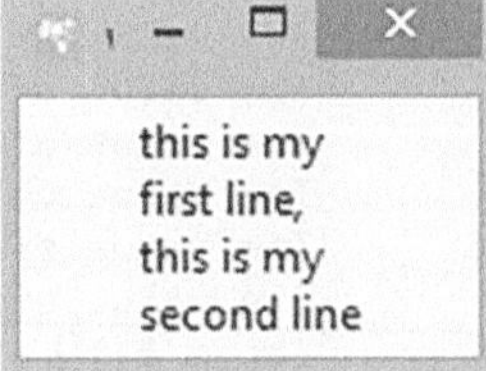

```
message .msg -aspect 300 -jus-
tify left -text \
"this is my first line,
this is my second line"
pack .msg
```

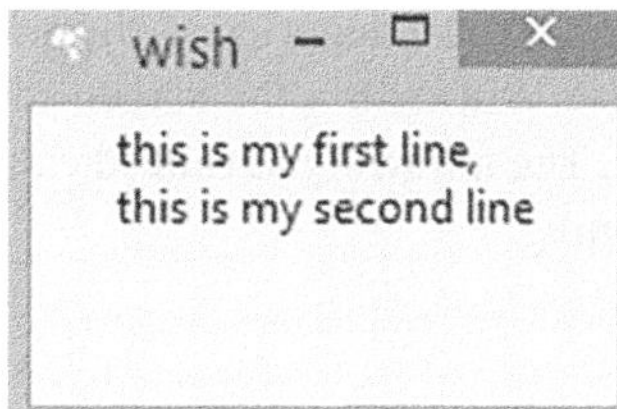

7.6.8 Spinbox Widget

Spinbox widget allows users to choose numbers or arbitrary values. It contains the option to spin the value upward or downward by defined steps actioned by a mouse left-click. Its structure possesses an entry box and an up-down arrow which increments or decrements the value with a click action (default 1). It is one graphical widget used to provide input to the Tcl script. Through spinning or direct entry into the box, the current value of the spin box is held in a defined `-textvariable` which is linked to other widgets.

Syntax: `spinbox .sp -command attribute`

Additional attributes to the spin box are

`-from num` start value of the spinbox
`-to num` end value of the spinbox
`-increment num` incremental step
`-textvariable char` variable associated with the spinbox

Example 7.9 Write a Tcl script to compute the product of two digits where the input is provided through a spinbox.

Solution

Figure 7.20 shows a GUI containing two different spinboxes, a button, and a label/input to the program is provided by textvariables `x` and `y` of `sp1` and `sp2`, respectively.

```
spinbox .sp1 -from 0 -to 100 -increment 1 -textvariable x -bg pink -
font {times 18 bold}
spinbox .sp2 -from 0 -to 100 -increment 1 -textvariable y -bg pink -
font {times 18 bold}
pack .sp1 .sp2 -side left -anchor nw
button .b -text Compute -command {set z [expr $x * $y]} -font {times
12 bold}
label .l -textvariable z -bg yellow -font {times 18 bold}
pack .b .l -side top
```

Figure 7.20 Product with a spinbox widget.

In this chapter, the basic categories of the widget are described. The configuration command beautifies the widgets and makes the screen more presentable. These configuration commands apply to all widgets. The following advanced categories of widgets are going to be discussed along with widget positioning.

7.7 Solved Problems

1. Write a Tcl script to develop a GUI for random number generation with an event on button.

Solution

There are two different frames, the first frame contains the button "Random" and the second frame contains a label that displays the random number with click action on a mouse (Figure 7.21).

```
frame .f1 -width 100 -height 100 -bg red
frame .f2 -width 100 -height 10
pack .f1 .f2 -side top
button .f1.b1 -padx 50 -pady 50 -bg yellow -text "Random" -command
{set var [expr round(rand()*100)]}
label .f1.l1 -width 10 -textvariable var
pack .f1.b1 .f1.l1 -side left

label .f2.l -width 50 -text "Script to generate Random Number"
pack .f2.l -side left
```

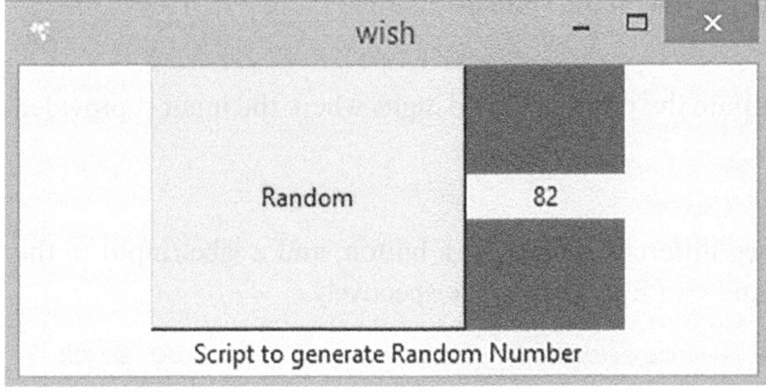

Figure 7.21 GUI for random number generation.

2. Write a Tcl script to create two different scales, with the movement of the first slider displaying the half value, and the movement of the second slider displaying the double value.

Solution

Here, two different scales red and green, linked with the Tcl procedure, return half and double of the slider value, respectively. The current value of the slider passes to the procedure and displays the half and double value on the console (Figure 7.22).

```
proc color1 {value1} {
set x1 [expr $value1 / 2]
puts "Half of red =$x1"
}
```

```
proc color2 {value2} {
set y1 [expr $value2 * 2]
puts "Twice of green=$y1"
}
scale .s1 -orient horizontal -from 0 -to 100 -tickinterval 5
-variable x -length  500 -tickinterval 5 -label Red -command color1
scale .s2 -orient horizontal -from 0 -to 100 -tickinterval
5 -variable y -length  500 -tickinterval 5 -label Green
-command color2
pack .s1 .s2 -side top
```

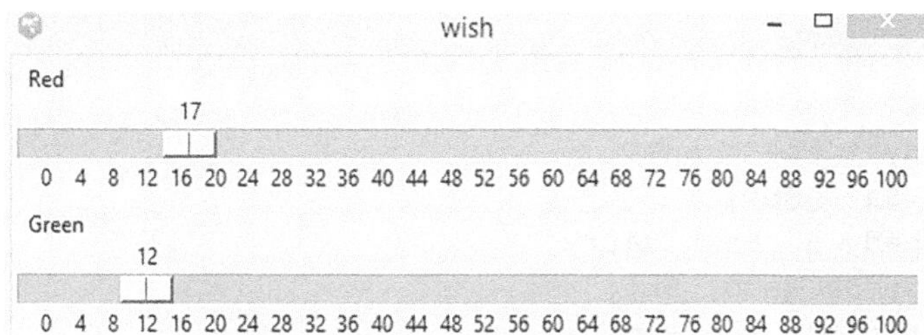

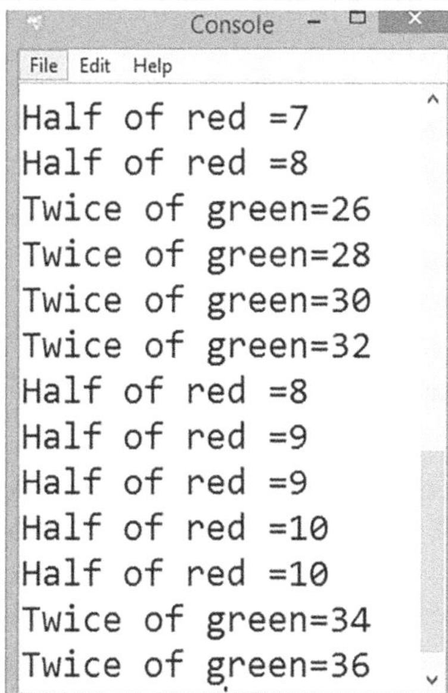

Figure 7.22 Scale with procedure.

3. Write a Tcl script to create a GUI for the half adder.

Solution

A half adder is a combinational digital circuit that accepts two inputs and results in the sum and carry. The truth table presents the relation between the input and output sum, and carry (Figure 7.23).

Input		**Output**	
A	**B**	**Sum**	**Carry**
0	0	0	0
0	1	1	0
1	0	1	0
1	1	0	1

Sum = A ^ B

Carry = A & B

```
checkbutton .a -textvariable a -width 10
-height 10
checkbutton .b -textvariable b -width 10
-height 10
grid .a -row 0 -column 0
grid .b -row 0 -column 1
button .sum -padx 5 -pady 5 -text sum
-command {set sum [expr $a ^ $b]}
button .carry -padx 5 -pady 5 -text carry
-command {set carry [expr $a &amp; $b]}
label .resultsum -textvariable sum -bg
yellow -width 5
label .resultcarry -textvariable carry
-bg yellow -width 5
grid .sum -row 1 -column 0.
a -textvariable a -width
grid .carry -row 1 -column 1
grid .resultsum -row 2 -column 0
grid .resultcarry -row 2 -column 1
```

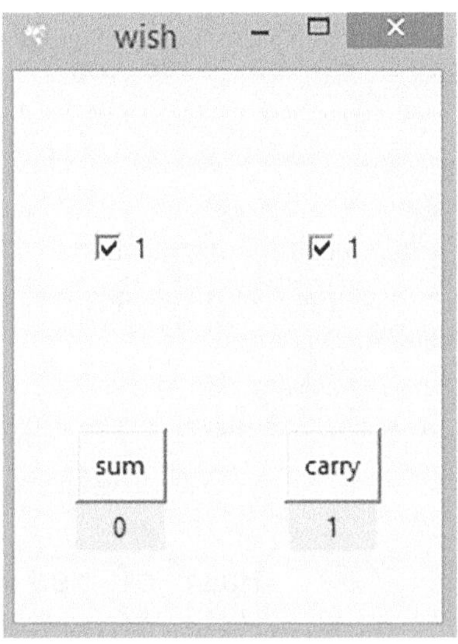

Figure 7.23 GUI of the half adder.

4. Write a Tcl script to create a GUI for the full adder.

Solution

A full adder is a combinational circuit that performs the addition of three current values and results in the sum and carry. The truth table of the full adder justifies the relation between the input and output (Figure 7.24).

Input			**Output**	
A	**B**	**C**	**Sum**	**Carry**
0	0	0	0	0
0	0	1	1	0
0	1	0	1	0
0	1	1	0	1
1	0	0	1	0
1	0	1	0	1
1	1	0	0	1
1	1	1	1	1

Sum = A ^ B ^ C

Carry = (A & B) | (A & C) | (B & C)

```
label .l -text "GUI of Full Adder" -font {times 20 bold}
checkbutton .a -textvariable a -width 10 -height 10
checkbutton .b -textvariable b -width 10 -height 10
checkbutton .c -textvariable c -width 10 -height 10
grid .l -row 0 -column 1
grid .a -row 1 -column 0
grid .b -row 1 -column 1
grid .c -row 1 -column 2

button .sum -padx 5 -pady 5 -text sum -command {set sum [expr $a ^
$b ^ $c]}
button .carry -padx 5 -pady 5 -text carry -command {set carry [expr
($a &amp; $b)|($b &amp; $c)|($a &amp; $c)]}
label .resultsum -textvariable sum -bg yellow -width 5
label .resultcarry -textvariable carry -bg yellow -width 5

grid .sum -row 2 -column 0
grid .carry -row 2 -column 2
grid .resultsum -row 3 -column 0
grid .resultcarry -row 3 -column 2
```

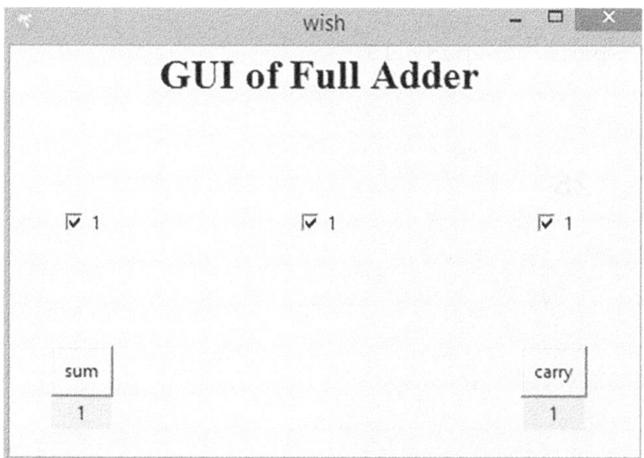

Figure 7.24 GUI of the full adder.

5. Write a Tcl script to create a GUI for an arithmetic calculator.

Solution

Two entry boxes accept the input from the user and four arithmetic operations are linked to the button, which updates the result into a textvariable result. The third entry box content is defined by the textvariable result. The result of the arithmetic operation is dynamically updated in the third entry box (Figure 7.25).

```
frame .f -width 1000 -height 1000 -bg grey
entry .f.e1 -textvariable x -width 10 -bg yellow -font {times
20 bold}
```

```
entry .f.e2 -textvariable y -width 10 -bg yellow -font {times
20 bold}
button .f.b1 -text "+" -command {set result [expr $x + $y]} -relief
groove -font {times 20 bold}
button .f.b2 -text "-" -command {set result [expr $x - $y]} -relief
raised -font {times 20 bold}
button .f.b3 -text "*" -command {set result [expr $x * $y]} -relief
ridge -font {times 20 bold}
button .f.b4 -text "/" -command {set result [expr $x / $y]} -relief
sunken -font {times 20 bold}
button .f.b5 -text "%" -command {set result [expr $x % $y]} -relief
raised -font {times 20 bold}
entry .f.e3 -textvariable result -width 10 -bg yellow -font {times
20 bold}
grid .f -rowspan 3 -columnspan 5
grid .f.e1 -row 0 -column 1 -padx 10 -pady 10
grid .f.e2 -row 0 -column 3 -padx 10 -pady 10
grid .f.b1 -row 1 -column 0 -padx 10 -pady 10
grid .f.b2 -row 1 -column 1 -padx 10 -pady 10
grid .f.b3 -row 1 -column 2 -padx 10 -pady 10
grid .f.b4 -row 1 -column 3 -padx 10 -pady 10
grid .f.b5 -row 1 -column 4 -padx 10 -pady 10
grid .f.e3 -row 2 -column 2 -padx 10 -pady 10
```

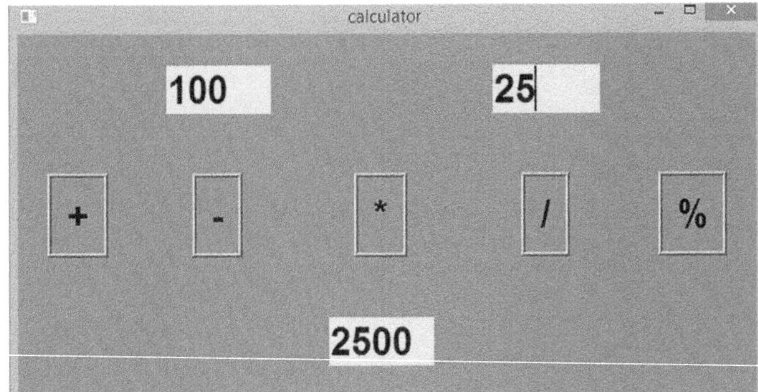

Figure 7.25 GUI of a calculator.

6. Write a Tcl script to create a simple GUI to develop the power of a number.

Solution

Two user-defined inputs are assigned to the entry box and the button titled "=" computes the power of them and updates the result into the third entry box. It is necessary to declare the result of the button and the content of the entry space with the same textvariable (Figure 7.26).

```
entry .e1 -textvariable x
label .l -text "to power"
entry .e2 -textvariable y
```

```
button .b -text = -borderwidth 7 -command {set result [expr
$x ** $y]}
entry .e3 -textvariable result
pack .e1 .l .e2 .b .e3 -side left
```

Figure 7.26 GUI of a power calculation.

7. Write a Tcl script to display the message statement justified on four different sides with aspect ratios of 10, 50, 100, and 500.

Solution

The aspect ratio arranges the message test according to the specified height and width (Figure 7.27).

```
message .msg1 -aspect 50 -justify left -text "This is online class
of Tcl Tk"
pack .msg1 -side left
message .msg2 -aspect 100 -justify right -text "This is online class
of Tcl Tk"
pack .msg2 -side right
message .msg3 -aspect 500 -justify center -text "This is online
class of Tcl Tk"
pack .msg3 -side top
message .msg4 -aspect 10 -justify center -text "This is online class
of Tcl Tk"
pack .msg4 -side bottom
```

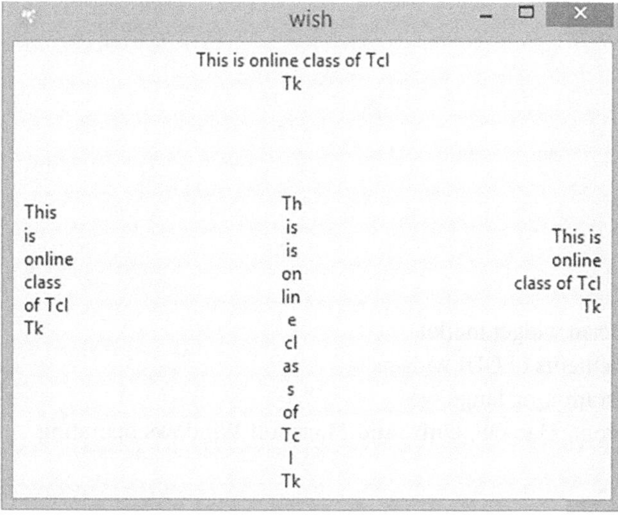

Figure 7.27 Message justified with the aspect ratio.

7.8 Unsolved Problems

1. Write a Tcl script to create the shown screen containing a label and button widget. The title of the label is Welcome and the title of the button Exit. Action on the button closes the tool.

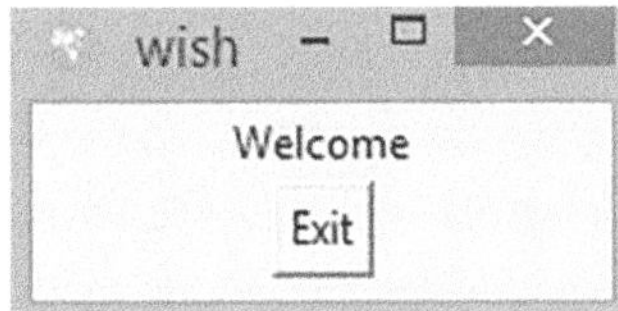

2. Write a Tcl script to create a simple GUI for the following arithmetic operation.

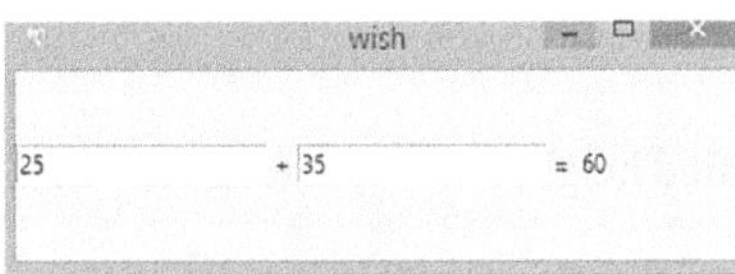

3. Write a Tcl script to create the following simple GUI.

4. Write a Tcl script to create the following frame and position the widget.

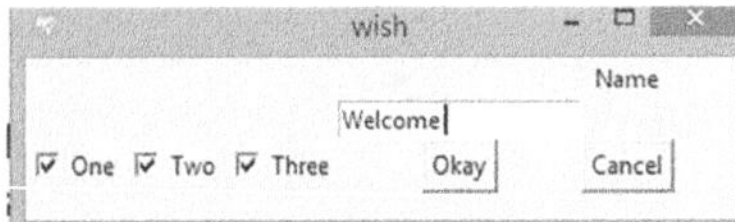

7.9 MCQs on Tk Widgets

[1] Select the correct statement.

- **A** Tk is an open-source, cross-platform widget toolkit
- **B** A library provides of the basic elements of GUI widgets
- **C** A GUI can be built in many programming languages
- **D** Tk widgets are supported by Linux, Mac OS, Unix, and Microsoft Windows operating systems
- **E** All of the above

[Solution (e)]

[2] Is Tk is an extension of Tcl?

A No
B Maybe
C Yes
D None of the above

[Solution (c)]

[3] Which describe(s) the use of a widget?

A To create a widget
B To manipulate a widget
C To rearrange a widget
D All of the above

[Solution (d)]

[4] What is the distance between widgets measured in?

A Millimeters
B Centimeters
C Inches
D Pixels

[Solution (d)]

[5] Which widget accepts input from a user?

A Entry
B Checkbutton
C Scale
D Spinbox
E All of the above

[Solution (e)]

[6] Which widget can display output results?

A Entry
B Label
C Both
D None

[Solution (d)]

[7] With what can two widget values be communicated?

A Text
B Textvariable
C Variable
D All of above

[Solution (b)]

[8] Which command is used to determine the orientation of the scale widget?

A `-orien h`
B `-orient h`
C `-orient v`
D All of the above

[Solution (d)]

[9] What command is given to name a widget?
- **A** `-text`
- **B** `-textvariable`
- **C** All of the above
- **D** None of the above

[Solution (a)]

[10] What command is given to associate a variable with a widget?
- **A** `-text`
- **B** `-textvariable`
- **C** All of the above
- **D** None of the above

[Solution (b)]

[11] Which are types of geometry managers?
- **A** Pack
- **B** Place
- **C** Grid
- **D** All of the above

[Solution (d)]

[12] What is/are the primary objective(s) of a geometry manager?
- **A** To plan the layout for the GUI
- **B** To keep the widget at a given coordinate location
- **C** To keep the widget horizontally or vertically or at the corner
- **D** All of the above

[Solution (a)]

[13] Which is the correct statement?
- **A** A label widget can display a single line
- **B** A message widget displays more than one line
- **C** A label with `\n` is equivalent to a message
- **D** All of the above

[Solution (d)]

[14] What is/are necessary to use to make the widget appear on the GUI screen?
- **A** Pack geometry manager
- **B** Place geometry manager
- **C** Grid geometry manager
- **D** Any one of the above

[Solution (d)]

[15] Which command can be used to manipulate a widget even after making the widget appear on the GUI screen?
- **A** `.config`
- **B** `.configure`
- **C** Either (a) or (b)
- **D** None of the above

[Solution (c)]

[16] Which command(s) causes a different 3D shape of the widget?

A `-relief raised`
B `-relief groove`
C `-relief ridge`
D `-relief sunken`
E All of the above

[Solution (e)]

[17] What is `-command` used for?

A Bind an in-built Tcl command with a specific widget
B Bind a procedure with a particular widget
C Both (a) and (b)
D Neither (a) nor (b)

[Solution (c)]

[18] What will the following program display?

```
proc color2 {value2} {
set y1 [expr $value2 * $value2]
puts "$y1"
}
scale .s2 -orient horizontal -from 0 -to 100 -tickinterval 5
-variable y -length  500 -command color2
pack .s2 -side top
```

A Factorial of the variable pointed by a slider over a horizontal scale
B Factorial of the variable pointed by a slider over a vertical scale
C Square of the variable pointed by a slider over a horizontal scale
D Square of the variable pointed by a slider over a vertical scale

[Solution (c)]

[19] Which widgets comprise the following GUI?

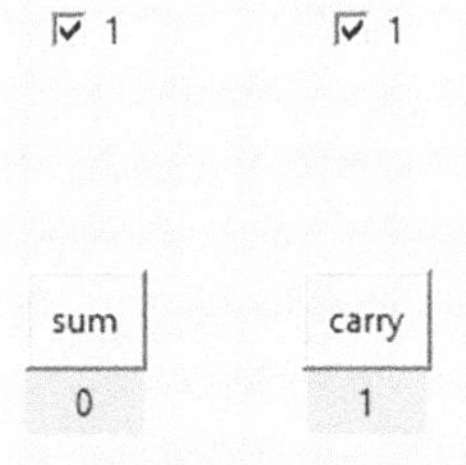

A Input radiobutton, function button, and result on label
B Input button, function button, and result on entry
C Input checkbutton, function button, and result on entry
D Input checkbutton, function button, and result on label

[Solution (d)]

[20] What will the following script display?

```
entry .e1 -textvariable x
entry .e2 -textvariable y
button .b -text = -borderwidth 7 -command {set result [expr
$x ** $y]}
entry .e3 -textvariable result
pack .e1 .e2 .b .e3 -side left
```

A X*Y
B X^Y
C X + Y
D X/Y

[Solution (b)]

References

1 Welch, B.B., Jones, K., and Hobbs, J. (2003). Practical Programming in Tcl/Tk. Prentice Hall Professional.
2 https://www.tutorialspoint.com/tcl-tk/index.htm
3 https://www.tcl.tk/man/tcl/UserCmd/wish.html
4 https://zetcode.com/gui/tcltktutorial/dialogs/

8

Binding Commands and Other Widgets

The `bind` commands bind the Tcl commands with an event on the Tk widget. Tk widgets are event-driven and execute the in-built Tcl command or user-defined procedure whenever a bonded action triggers. The keyboard and mouse are two inputs to trigger an action of events. The different events are key press, key release, button press, button release, mouse enter, mouse leave, focus in, focus out, destroy, window change size, window open, and window close. A `bind` command associates X events with the Tcl script and to be executed in sequence [1].

Syntax: *bind .widgetName < eventSpecification > TclCommand*

Three components of the `bind` command are (a) widget name of a particular widget on which an event is triggered, (b) event specification specifying the action of an event applied through a mouse or keyboard, and (c) Tcl command executing an in-built or user-defined procedure in sequence and returning the result on the specified label or console window.

```
proc display {a} {
 puts "Bind is working"
}
button .btn -text "press me" -textvariable a
label .l -textvariable result
pack .btn .l -side left
bind .btn <Button-1> {set result [display $a]}
```

This program binds `<Button-1>` (featuring a click of the mouse) with the button “press me”. On event, it calls a procedure `display` and returns the result (Figures 8.1 and 8.2).

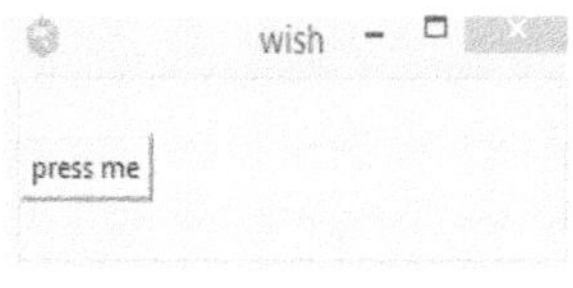

Figure 8.1 Before event.

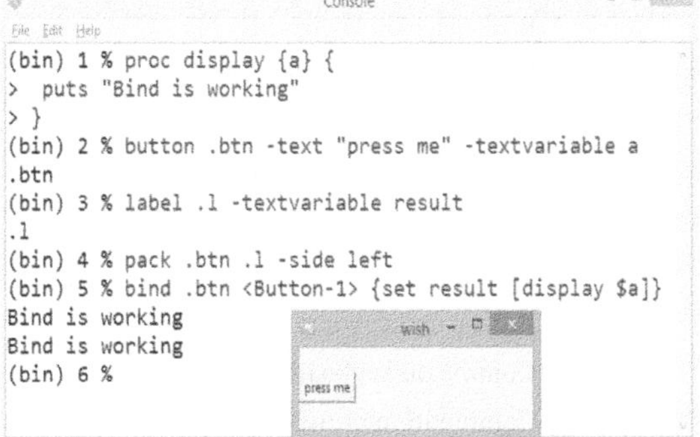

Figure 8.2 After event.

Programming and GUI Fundamentals: Tcl-Tk for Electronic Design Automation (EDA), First Edition.
Suman Lata Tripathi, Abhishek Kumar, and Jyotirmoy Pathak.

8.1 Class and Widget Binding

The `bind` command determines the next step on the occurrence of an event. The default widget follows the class binding. Table 8.1 list the different events available for Tcl. An event must be enclosed within < >. The angle brackets delimit the single event. The `bind` command allows a binding to a sequence of events. If no brackets are included, the event defaults to a KeyPress event, and all the characters specify keys in a sequence. Three different bindings are found in application: (i) global binding defined with word keyboard "all"; (ii) class binding derived with the widget name, like canvas has a class of Canvas, etc.; and (iii) instance name to a specified instance of the widget. The order of the binding is as follows: global binding; class binding; instance binding.

8.1.1 Bindtag Command

The `bind` commands are associated with a particular window, class, keyword, or other string. All of these are called bindtags [2]. Each window contains a list of bindtags that determine how events are processed for the window. Whenever an event occurs in a window (applied to the window's tag in order), for each tag, the most specified binding matches the given tag and event executed.

Table 8.1 List of event generation.

Event	Description
`<Return>`	Press Enter on keyboard
`<ButtonPress>` / `<Button>`	Button pressed on mouse
`<ButtonRelease>`	Button released on mouse
`<KeyPress>`	Focussed key pressed
`<KeyRelease>`	Focussed key released
`<Motion>`	Mouse pointer movement
`<Bi-Motion>`	Mouse motion event, a user drags the mouse with the left button pressed
`<Leave>`	Mouse leaves the widget
`<Enter>`	Mouse enters to widget
`<BackSpace>`	Backspace on keyboard
`<Down>`	Down arrow on keyboard
`<Up>`	Up arrow on keyboard
`<Left>`	Left arrow on keyboard
`<Right>`	Right arrow on keyboard
`<Tab>`	Tab on keyboard
`<Escape>`	Escape on keyboard
`<Comma>`	Comma on keyboard
`<Control-c>`	Combination of two keys

The bindtag determines which bindings apply to a window and the order of evaluation. The bindtag argument selects the window to which binding applies. A tag begins with a dot (.) or a pathname for a window else an arbitrary string. Each window has its associated list of tags and bindings that apply to a particular window.

The bindtag

- provides the name of the internal window
- provides the name of the top-level window
- provides the name of the class of a widget
- of "all" means that binding applies to all windows

8.1.2 Event Pattern

The argument sequence of one or more event patterns is separated by whitespace. Each event can take one of three forms of ASCII character, (.), or < >. The first format of the event pattern uses the ASCII character's keysym. The second format of the event pattern is longer but more general. Event patterns are enclosed by angle brackets, and may contain more modifiers, event types, and button identifications. Shift and Control are two popular modifiers. The third format of the event pattern specifies a user-defined event known as a virtual event. Binding to a virtual event created before the virtual event is defined, in the case where the event changes, the window dynamically bound to the virtual event will respond immediately to the definition.

8.1.3 Event Type

Event types are standard or nonstandard X event types that describe when an event is generated and sent to the window [3, 4].

i) Activate – sent to all sub-windows in a top-level when it changes from deactivating to activate
ii) Deactivate – sent when a window's state changes from active to deactivate
iii) MouseWheel – for a scrolling feature; by rolling the wheel, an event gets generated. Once the event is received, the movement of the wheel is substituted by delta field %D, which describes the movement of the mouse wheel. For Windows 95 and 98 machines, the minimum movement is 120; however, a higher resolution device's value of "1" corresponds to one text line. The value determines the direction your widget should scroll. Positive value Up/Left and negative value Down/Right.
iv) Configure – sent to the window when the size, position, or borderwidth changes
v) Map – top-level mapping when a transition to normal starts
vi) Unmap – top-level unmapping in a withdrawn state
vii) Visibility – when the window obscurity changes, (%s) specifies a new state
viii) Expose -- whenever all or part of a window is to be redrawn
ix) Destroy – when the window is destroyed
x) FocusIn – when the target acquires focus
xi) FocusOut – focus changed to outside of the target
xii) Enter – mouse pointer enters the window
xiii) Leave – mouse window leaves the window
xiv) Colormap – color map associated with window changes

8.1.4 Bind with Mouse Button

All three buttons of the mouse are capable of binding with the widget and executing the linked Tcl script. The default bind with the button is the left click of the mouse. Binding with pressing and releasing of a mouse button can be distinguished. Additionally, the motion of the mouse button can execute an event, whenever the mouse cursor enters or leaves the widget. KeyPress can be abbreviated as Key and since it is a special case of an event, the angle brackets can be left out. The following are four equivalent event specifications.

```
<KeyPress-1>          <Key-1>          <1>          1
```

Key is nothing but the keysym printed on the key of the keyboard, and the commonly used keysyms are listed in Table 8.1. It includes all alphanumeric ASCII characters and non-alphanumeric ASCII characters like Shift_L for the left shift key.

`<Button-1> / <ButtonPress-1 >`	Left-click press on mousc button
`<ButtonRelease-1 >`	Left-click release on mouse button
`<MouseWheel>`	Center button of mouse
`<Button-3> / <ButtonPress-3 >`	Right-click press on mouse button
`<ButtonRelease-3 >`	Right-click release on mouse button

Example 8.1 Write a Tcl script to create a GUI for arithmetic addition which executes the result upon pressing the ENTER button.

Solution

The following script develops a GUI for arithmetic addition composed of two entry boxes to accept inputs the from the user and the result of addition appears at the label. The second entry (`in2`) has been bonded with the event `<Return>` (Enter on keyboard). On pressing, the specified event occurs, executes the Tcl script (procedure to calculate the sum), and returns the result on the label (result). Here it is necessary to set the Tcl script result and label the result with the same textvariable, thus their values can be updated dynamically (Figures 8.3 and 8.4).

```
proc sum {x y} {
   set result [expr $x + $y]
  return $result
}
entry .in1 -width 6 -text-
variable in1
label .l1 -text +
entry .in2 -width 6 -text-
variable in2
label .result -textvari-
able result
pack .in1 .l1 .in2 .result -
side left
bind .in2 <Return> {set result
[sum $in1 $in2]}
```

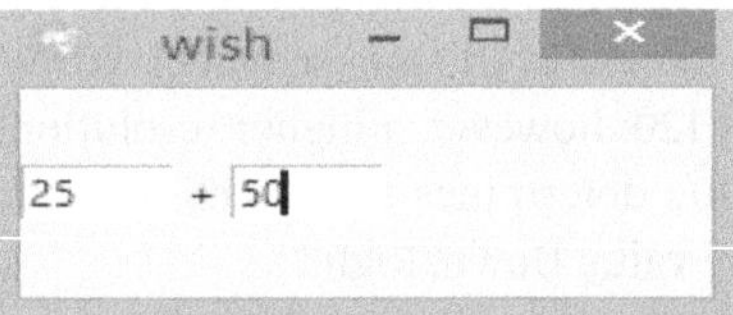

Figure 8.3 Before event.

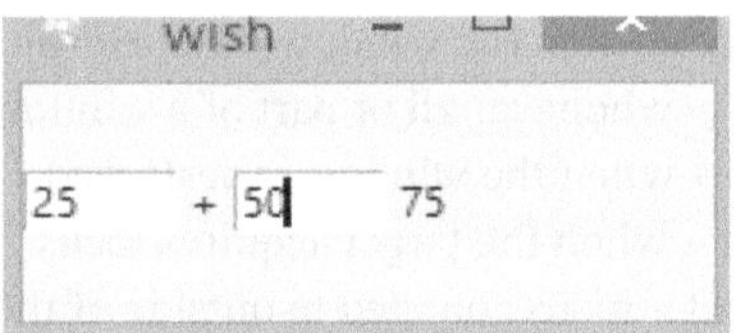

Figure 8.4 After event.

Example 8.2 Write a Tcl script to create a GUI for factorial calculation, where the result appears upon pressing the ENTER button.

Solution

The following script develops a GUI to calculate the factorial of a user-defined value, and is composed of a label and entry box. The user inserts the value to the entry space which is bonded with the event `<Return>` (Enter on keyboard). Whenever a specified event occurs, the Tcl script is executed (calling a procedure of factorial) and returns the result on the specified label result. The label result must be defined with the textvariable result to update the value (Figures 8.5 and 8.6).

```
proc factorial {num} {
if {$num <=1} {
return 1
} else {
return [expr $num * [factorial
[expr $num -1]]]
}
}
label .l1 -text
"Factorial of   "
entry .e -textvariable x
label .l2 -textvariable result
pack .l1 .e .l2 -side left
bind .e <Return> {set result
[factorial $x]}
```

Figure 8.5 Before event.

Figure 8.6 After event.

8.1.5 Bind with Mouse Motion

Tcl script supports the additional feature of event bindings with the motion of the mouse wheel. The keyword presented with `%x` and `%y` dynamically updates with the current coordinate on the mouse wheel event relative to the screen on the console window. Enter, Leave, and Motion are three commonly used events to update the coordinate value. Enter and Leave are triggered when the mouse cursor is close or away from the widget, while Motion is generated when the mouse cursor moves within the widget. The % substitution performs the command bound to the event and %% is used to display a single % symbol.

Syntax: `bind. <Motion > {puts "pointer at %x,%y"}`

`<Enter>`	Mouse cursor moves toward widget
`<Leave>`	Mouse cursor moves away from widget
`<Motion>`	Mouse cursor moves within widget

`%x` is replaced with the pointer's x-coordinate and `%y` is replaced with the pointer's y-coordinate.

Example 8.3 Write script to develop a GUI for random number generation with a mouse event.

Solution

The following script develops a GUI for a random number generator composed of a label. The first label title start is bonded with the event <Enter> (motion of mouse cursor) (mouse cursor moves toward label), generates a random number in the range of 0–100 according to the script and displays on the second label (Figures 8.7 and 8.8).

```
label .l1 -text "Generate a Random Number"
label .l2 -textvariable result -bg pink
pack .l1 .l2 -side left
bind .l1 <Enter> {set result [expr round(rand()*100)]}
```

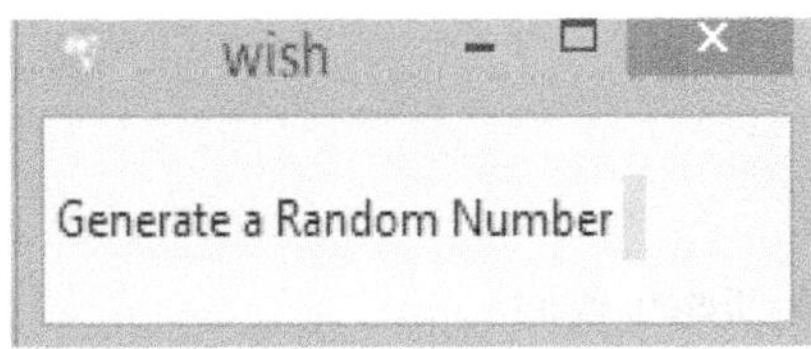

Figure 8.7 Before event.

Figure 8.8 After event.

Example 8.4 Write a Tcl script for a scale widget whose scrolling feature is controlled by the left and right keys on the keyboard.

Solution

The following Tcl script instances a horizontal scale whose scrollbar movement is performed by a key <Left>/<Down> and <Right>/<Up> event. The event generate command expands with %, and focus %W specifies the *focus* field for the event and creates a surrounding on the focused scale. The scale is bonded with the <MouseWheel> event. *Delta (%D)* refers to the MouseWheel direction and magnitude that the mouse wheel was rotated. The value is not the screen distance but is in units of motion of the mouse wheel; in multiples of 120. The field corresponds to the %D substitution for binding scripts. The variable increment maps the increment value to the <Left> key and the decrement value to the <Right> key (Figure 8.9).

```
scale .s -orient horizontal -from 0 -to 100
pack .s
bind .s <Enter> {focus %W}
bind .s <MouseWheel> {set increment [expr (%D/360)]
                  if {$increment == 1} {
                 event generate %W <Left>
                 } else {
                 event generate %W <Right>}
                                         }
```

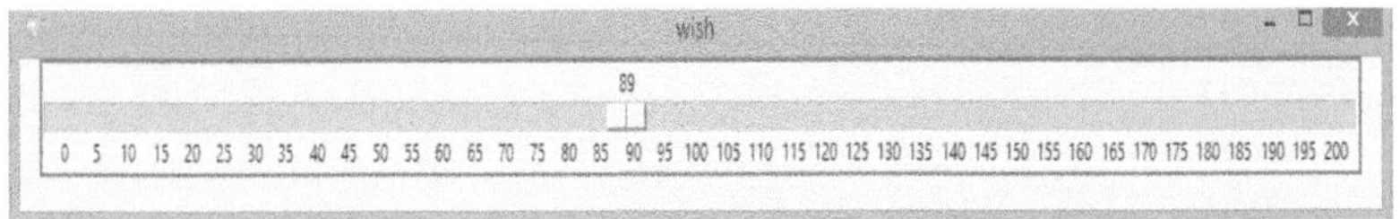

Figure 8.9 Horizontal scale scrollbar movement maps of keysym.

8.2 Widget Characteristic Commands

8.2.1 Unpack Command

The `pack` command makes the widget appear on the screen. To remove the mapped widget, one may use the *`pack forget`* command. The mapped specified widget gets removed. If more than one widget is mapped on a frame and `pack forget` is applied to the frame, the whole widget along with the frame get unmapped.

Syntax: *`pack forget .widget_name`*

Example 8.10 Write a Tcl script to create a group of labels and buttons and two different frames, and delete the button from both frames and later delete one of the frames.

Solution

```
frame .f1 -bg red -width 100
-height 100
button .f1.b1 -text Button-1
label .f1.l1 -text Label-1
pack .f1
pack .f1.b1 .f1.l1 -side left
```

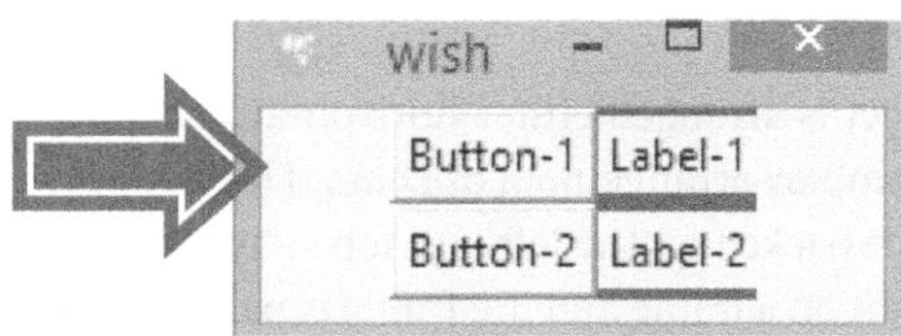

Figure 8.10 Button-label on Frame-1.

```
frame .f2 -bg green -width
100 -height 100
button .f2.b2 -text Button-2
label .f2.l2 -text Label-2
pack .f2
pack .f2.b2 .f2.l2 -side left
```

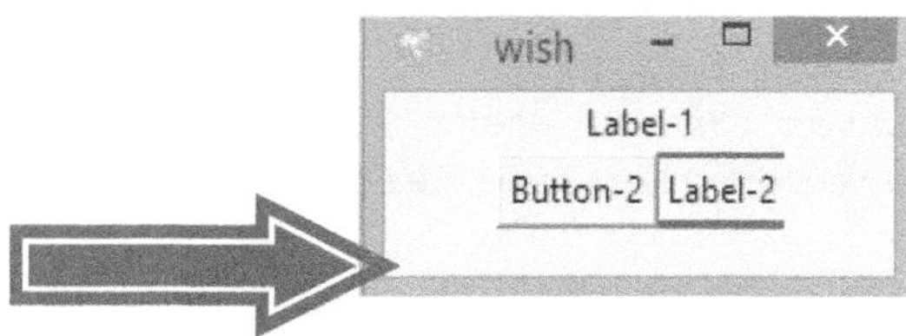

Figure 8.11 Button-label on Frame-2.

```
pack forget .f1.b1
```

Figure 8.12 Remove button from Frame-1.

```
pack forget .f2.l2
```

Figure 8.13 Remove label from Frame-2.

```
pack forget .f1
```


Figure 8.14 Remove Frame-1.

Figures 8.10 and 8.11 show the creation of a button and label on `frame-1` and `frame-2`. Removal of an individual widget with the `pack forget` command is shown in Figures 8.12 and 8.13 and deletion of the frame is shown in Figure 8.14.

8.2.2 Arranging on Side

The instantiated widget can arrange on four possible sides: top; bottom; left; and right. The default side is the top. During packing of the widget, the command `-side` directs the widget to pack in the specified side. In the case where more than one widget is packed together, the order of packing follows the instantaneous order and follows the side concerning the first widget in sequence. Figure 8.15 presents the ordering of three button widgets from the right side.

```
button .b1 -text B1
button .b2 -text B2
button .b3 -text B3
pack .b1 .b2 .b3 -side right
```

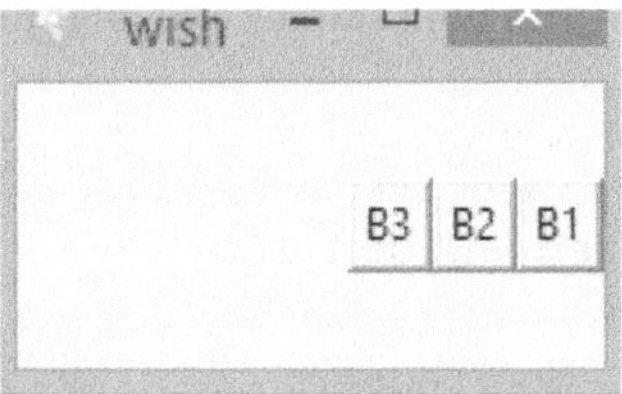

Figure 8.15 Arrange a button on the right side.

8.2.3 Stacking

The widget is arranged either horizontally or vertically. If widgets are stacked on more than one side, a complex arrangement appears. The example below shows the horizontal and vertical stack of buttons packed on the left and top sides. In the first example, two buttons are stacked from the left to right on a frame and the frame is packed on the left side. In the second example, two buttons are framed from left to right and the frame is packed on the top side (Figure 8.16 and 8.17).

```
frame .one -bg pink
foreach i {x y} {
button .one.$i -text $i
pack .one.$i -side left
}
pack .one -side left
```

Figure 8.16 Horizontal stack.

```
frame .two -bg grey
foreach i {x y} {
button .two.$i -text $i
pack .two.$i -side top
}
pack .two -side top
```

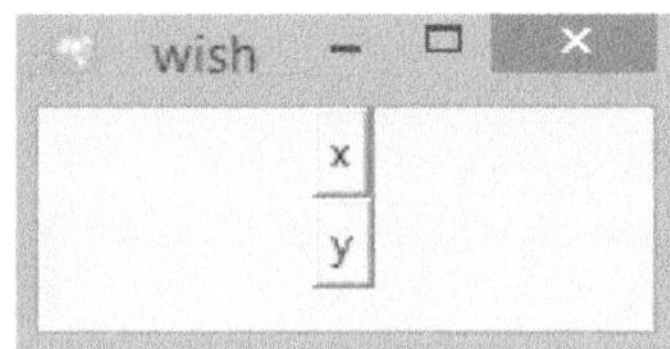

Figure 8.17 Vertical stack.

8.2.4 Cavity Model

The cavity model presents the available free space on the frame. In the example shown below, four frames have been placed in the main window with a different dimension, but there is free space leftover where more widgets can be placed. The packing is based on the cavity. Packing on another side does not stack on the side of the existing frame because the frame is packed along with the mainframe (Figure 8.18).

```
frame .one -width 50 -height 50
-bg grey
frame .two -width 100 -height
100 -bg yellow
frame .three -width 30 -height
20 -bg green
frame .four -width 60 -height
200 -bg red
pack .one -side left
 pack .two -side right
pack .three -side top
pack .four -side bottom
```

Figure 8.18 Remove button from Frame-1.

8.2.5 Packing and Display Space (the -fill and -expand commands)

The display space is the area requested by a widget to paint itself while the packing space is the area allowed by the packer for the placement of the widget. Within geometry constraints, a widget may be allocated more (or less) packing space than it needs to display itself, causing a cavity space. The `-fill` command allows the widget to stretch on the side and fill the space. A widget can fill horizontally, vertically, or in both directions to the blank background of the main window (Figures 8.19 and 8.20).

```
frame .one -width 10 -
height 20 -bg red
frame .two -width 40 -
height 60 -bg yellow
frame .three -width 30 -
height 25 -bg green
pack .one -side bottom
pack .two -side top
pack .three -side left
```

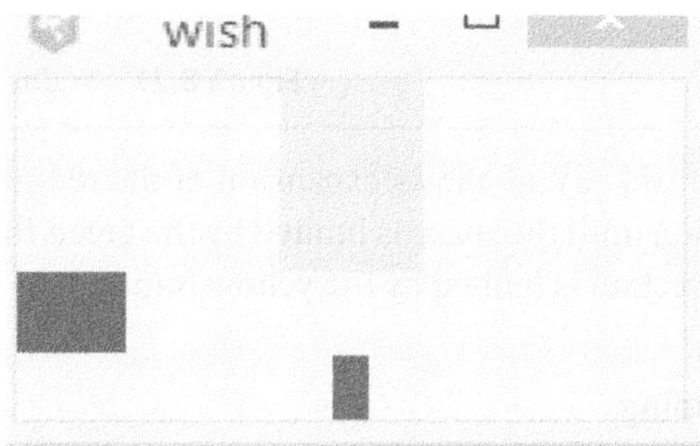

Figure 8.19 Widget showing cavity on frame.

```
pack .one -side bot-
tom -fill x
pack .two -side top -fill y
pack .three -side left -
fill both
```

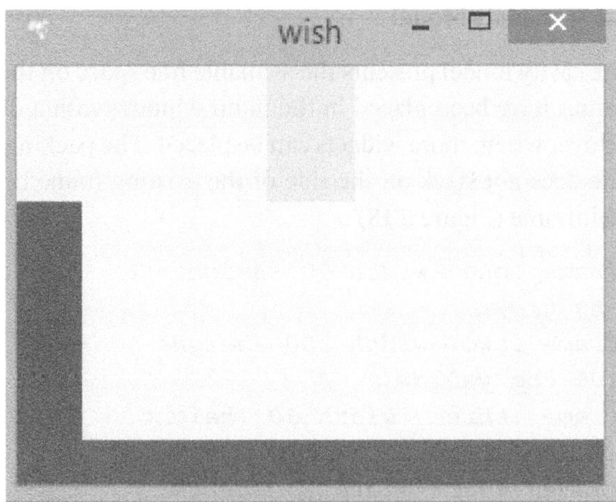

Figure 8.20 Widget with -fill command.

The -fill command stretches the side of the frame in a specified detection. The red frame can be expanded horizontally but resists expanding vertically due to the green frame. The yellow frames do not expand in the vertical cavity since the vertical space is occupied by a green frame. The -expand true command allows the widget to expand its packing space into any unclaimed space in the packing cavity. It uses its extra packing space for its display (Figure 8.21).

```
pack .one -side bottom
-fill x -expand true
pack .two -side top -
fill y -expand true
pack .three -side
left -fill both -
expand true
```

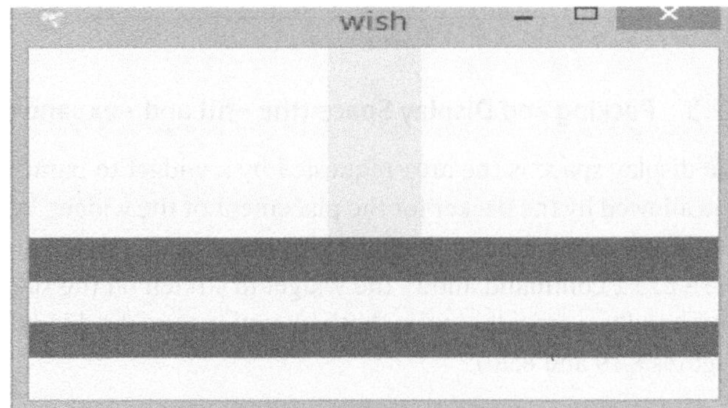

Figure 8.21 Widget with -expand command.

The -expand true allows expansion of the red frame in the x-direction, the yellow frame in the y-direction until the space is limited by the green frame, and the green frame in the x-direction but the y-direction is limited by the yellow frame.

8.2.6 Padding

Padding is an alternative way to fill the blank space. The two types of padding are external and internal. Internal padding -ipadx and -ipady allocate more display space in the x and y direction, respectively, inside the border. To add some space around each frame, the padding of each cell needs to be set. Padding is some blank space that surrounds a widget and separates it visually from its content.

-ipadx n Specifies how much horizontal internal padding to leave on each side of the content, defaults to 0.

-ipady n Specifies how much vertical internal padding to leave on each side of the content, defaults to 0.

```
frame .f -width 100 -height 100
-bg pink
pack .f
button .f.b1 -text PAD1
button .f.b2 -text PAD2
pack .f.b1
pack .f.b2 -ipadx 10 -ipady 10
```

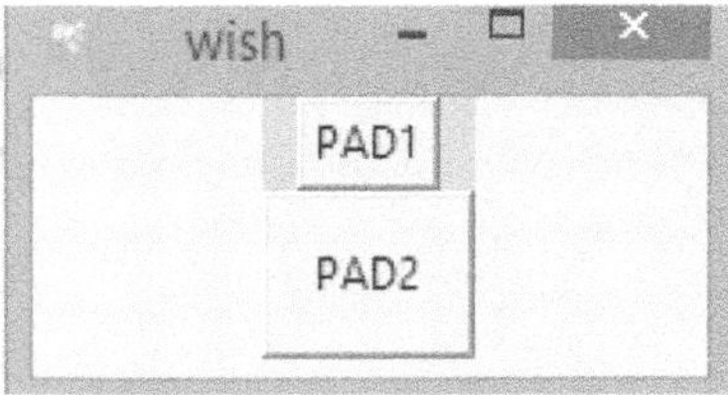

Figure 8.22 Button with ipad.

The example shows a place frame of size 100*100, button PAD1 without internal padding, and PAD2 with internal padding. Extra internal space is provided in the x and y directions, as presented in Figure 8.22.

External padding adds some space around the outside of a grid cell: (i) `padx` adds padding in the horizontal direction and (ii) `pady` adds padding in the vertical direction. Both `padx` and `pady` are measured in pixels, not in units, so setting both of them to the same value will create the same amount of padding in both directions. In a button widget, `-padx` and `-pady` provide more display space outside the border, giving them more space to keep the button text away from the edge of the button.

8.2.7 Anchoring

In an earlier section, we described packing of the widget by side, expanding, and filling; still, there is space left at the corner. A widget can be placed at a particular position mentioned as `n, ne, e, se, s, sw, w, nw,` and `center`, as shown in Figure 8.23. Default anchoring is `-anchor center`.

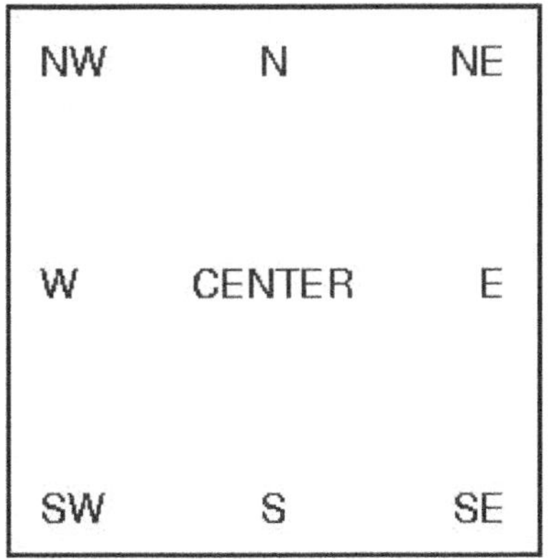

Figure 8.23 Direction with anchoring.

```
label .l1 -text Foo1
label .l2 -text Foo2
label .l3 -text Foo3
label .l4 -text Foo4
label .l5 -text Foo5
label .l6 -text Foo6
label .l7 -text Foo7
label .l8 -text Foo8
label .l9 -text Foo9
```

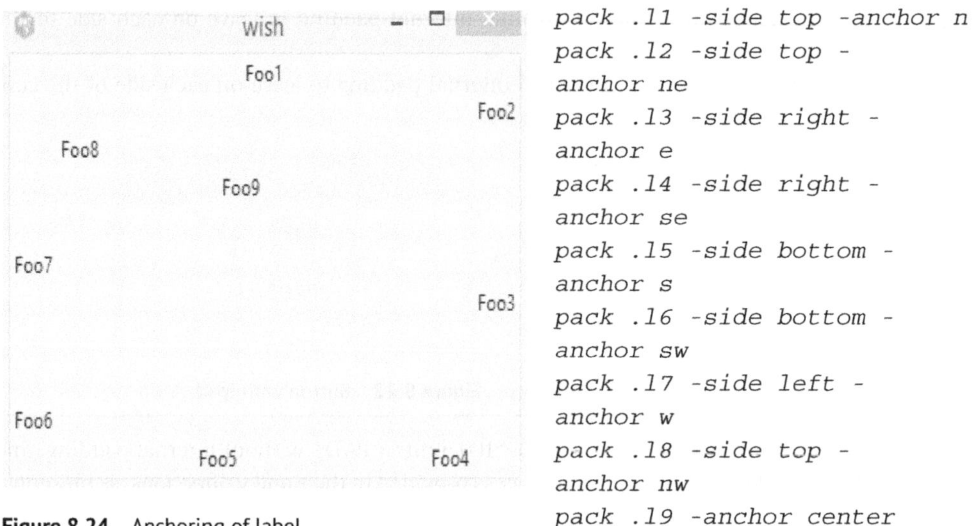


```
pack .l1 -side top -anchor n
pack .l2 -side top -
anchor ne
pack .l3 -side right -
anchor e
pack .l4 -side right -
anchor se
pack .l5 -side bottom -
anchor s
pack .l6 -side bottom -
anchor sw
pack .l7 -side left -
anchor w
pack .l8 -side top -
anchor nw
pack .l9 -anchor center
```

Figure 8.24 Anchoring of label.

The example above contains nine labels; four of them are packed in the north, east, west, and south directions, four are packed on north-east, south-east, south-west, and north-west corners, and one is at the center, presented in Figure 8.24.

Note: `-side` chooses the side direction and `-anchor` chooses the corner between two sides.

8.3 Menubar-Menu-Menubutton

The menu is composed of a set of button-like entries. Users can create a menu and then insert entries into it, as shown in the example. Entries into the menu include a radiobutton, checkbutton, button, and command. Between two entries, there is the provision of a separator to maintain the distance and set entries apart. It displays a collection of one-line entries arranged in columns. There are two special characteristics of a cascaded menu, which are to post a submenu and tearoff to detach the many child menus from the parent and make them dockable.

A menubutton is a button that posts the menu on a click. It acts as a contatiner for the menu. When a user clicks on the menubutton, a menu appears and remains till the user clicks outside the menu to dismiss it. If the user selects, presses, and holds the menubutton, the menu remains unposted. When the mouse is released over the menu, the entries to it can be selected as pointed by the mouse cursor.

Syntax for `menubutton`: `menubutton .menubuttonName options`

Syntax for `menu`: `menu .menuName options`

Syntax for adding `menu` to `menubutton`:

```
        .menuName add radio/check -label name -command
Tcl command
```

```
menubutton .mb -menu .mb.menu -
text "Select Me"
menu .mb.menu
.mb.menu add check -label Yes
.mb.menu add radio -label No
pack .mb
```

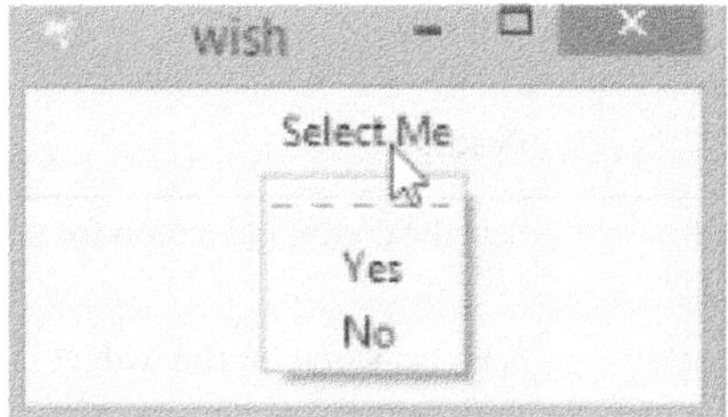

Figure 8.25 Creation of menu for menubutton.

The example in Figure 8.25 creates a menubutton labeled "Select Me." A click of the mouse over it displays a menu containing two entries, Yes and No.

8.3.1 Entries to a Menu

The menu is a child of the menubutton, similarly, a cascaded menu acts as child to the menu and so on. The first menu entry is represented by the dashed line. It is necessary to implement the `tearoff` command. Entries for the menu command, check, and radio are similar to the corresponding button types. The main difference is that the text string in the menu entry is defined by `-label` not by `-text`. The string to display on the right side of the menu entry is `-accel`. The accelerator keystroke describes a sequence that may be used to invoke the same function as the menu entry. It is a display option and does not set the corresponding binding (which can be achieved using the bind command). This option is not available for the separator or tearoff entries (Figure 8.26).

```
menubutton .mb -text File -menu
.mb.menu
pack .mb -padx 5 -pady 5
menu .mb.menu
.mb.menu add radio -label New
.mb.menu add radio -label Open
-accel "clrl+O"
.mb.menu add radio -label Save
-accel "clrl+S"
.mb.menu add radio -label "Save
As" -accel "clrl+A"
.mb.menu add radio -label Close
-accel "clrl+W"
.mb.menu add separator
```

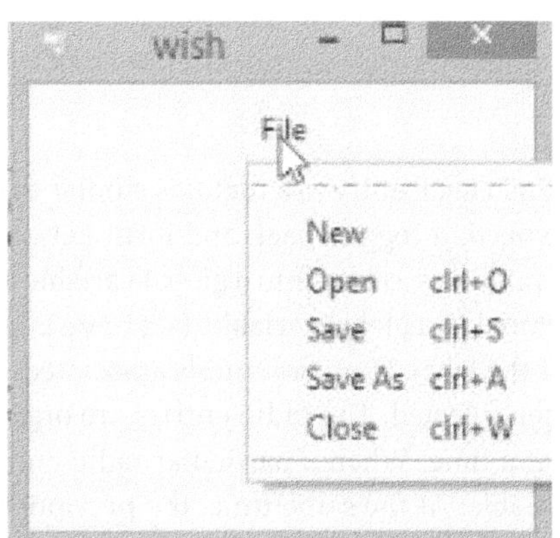

Figure 8.26 Adding entries to menu.

Entries to a menu are numbered as an index starting from 0. There are several mechanisms to add entries to the menu, the most popular are add. Name to entries is given by `-label` command. Accelerator command to the menu entry added with `-accel` command act as a shortcut to access. Each radio entry can be linked to a system-defined Tcl script to a user-defined procedure. While selecting a particular label, a tick appears on left. Tables 8.2 and 8.3 present the feature of the menubutton and menu, respectively.

Table 8.2 Attributes to menu.

Command	Description
`-command action`	Sets the command action for a button
`-text Name`	Sets the Name for the widget.
`-textvariable varname`	Variable associated with the widget. When the text of the widget changes, the variable is set to the text of the widget.
`-width number`	Sets the width for the widget.
`-menu menuName`	Specifies the name of the associated menu widget.
`-underline charPosition`	Sets the position for hotkey.

Table 8.3 Attributes to menubutton.

Command	Description
`-font descriptor`	Used to set the font for a widget.
`-menu menuName`	Specifies the name of the associated submenu widget.
`-tearoff Boolean`	Allows or disallows a menu to be removed from menubutton and displayed in a permanent window. Default is enabled.
`-command action`	Sets the command action to be done before a menu is posted.

Radio and check entry to a menu is similar to radiobutton and checkbutton widget, respectively. When invoked, it toggles back and forth between the select and deselect state. When an entry is selected, values are stored into a global variable (`-onvalue` option) and when deselected, another value is stored in a global variable (`-offvalue`). A checkbutton shows the checkbox indicator to the left of the label. If `-command` is associated with a checkbutton entry, the Tcl command is executed when selected. The radio entries are organized into groups of which only one entry may be selected at a time. When a particular radio entry is selected, it is stored in a particular value in a global variable. At the same time, the previously selected entry is automatically deselected. Each radio entry displays an indicator on the left side. If a `-command` option is specified for a radiobutton entry, then its value is evaluated as a Tcl command each time the entry is invoked; this happens after selecting the entry.

Example 8.11 Write a script to design and GUI containing a menubar menu and add entries with a separator.

Solution

The following script creates a menubutton named engineering, under which it contains menu entries, as shown in Figure 8.27.

```
menubutton .mb -text Engineering -
menu .mb.menu
pack .mb -padx 10 -pady 10
menu .mb.menu
.mb.menu add radio -label electrical
.mb.menu add radio -label electronics
.mb.menu add separator
.mb.menu add checkbutton -label CSE
.mb.menu add checkbutton -label IT
```

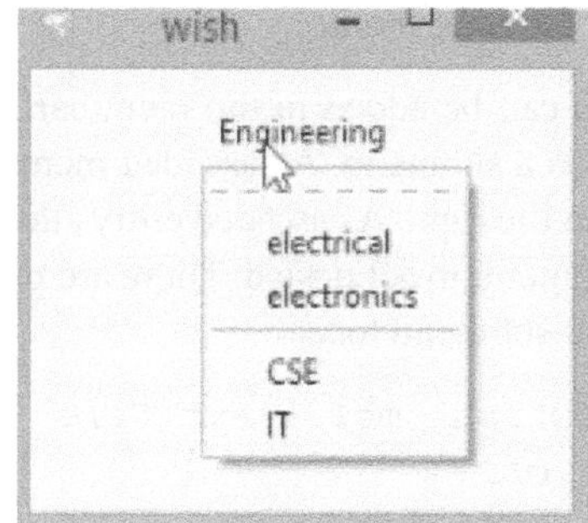

Figure 8.27 Menu with separator.

Example 8.12 Write Tcl script to develop a GUI for menubar-menu along with an accelerator and execute the procedure on each radio entry.

Solution

The following script creates a menubutton that posts a menu, five entries to the menu, and a separator. Each radio entry is linked to a Tcl command, which calls a Tcl procedure/command. Here, an in-built command and messageBox have been used to implement the procedure execution, as shown in Figure 8.28.

```
menubutton .mb -text File -menu .mb.menu
menu .mb.menu
.mb.menu add radio -label New -accel "ctrl+N" -command filecmd
.mb.menu add radio -label Open -accel "ctrl+O" -command opencmd
.mb.menu add radio -label Save -accel "ctrl+S" -command savecmd
.mb.menu add radio -label "Save As" -accel "ctrl+A"
.mb.menu add radio -label Close -accel "ctrl+W" -command exit
.mb.menu add separator
proc filecmd {} {tk_messageBox -message Filing!}
proc searchcmd {} {tk_messageBox -message Searching!}
proc savecmd {} {tk_messageBox -message Saving!}
pack .mb -padx 5 -pady 5 -side left -anchor nw
```

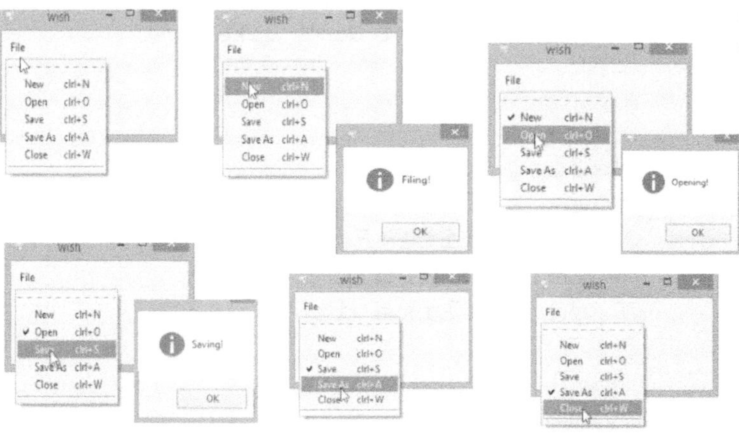

Figure 8.28 Tcl command associated with menu entry.

8.3.2 Cascade Menu

A menu can be added to the menubar and a menu added to one of the entries in the menu is known as a submenu. A cascaded menu entry associated with the menu is presented as a small arrow on the right. A cascaded entry allows the construction of a submenu when the user selects a new submenu to get posted. There are provisions to add multiple entries to the submenu and create a sub-submenu too.

```
menubutton .mb1 -text File -menu .mb1.file
pack .mb1
menu .mb1.file
.mb1.file add cascade -label New -menu
.mb1.file.fnew
.mb1.file add separator
.mb1.file add radio -label Quit
menu .mb1.file.fnew
.mb1.file.fnew add radio -label Bookmark
.mb1.file.fnew add radio -label Import
```

.mb1
.mb1.file.fnew
.mb1.file

Figure 8.29 Creation of submenu.

The example shown in Figure 8.29 shows a submenu associated with the menu entry "New." The submenu remains posted or un-posted as the submenu is controlled by New. Entries to the menu and submenu can be linked to Tcl script shown in the example to the menu entries "Hello!" and "Open." A cascaded submenu to the entry "Fruit" contains the entries "apple," "orange," and "kiwi," as shown in Figure 8.30. Each entry linked to the `puts` command displays a statement in the console window on selecting each radio entry.

```
menubutton .mb -text Sampler -menu .mb.menu
pack .mb -padx 10 -pady 10
set m [menu .mb.menu]
$m add command -label Hello! -command {puts "Hello, World!"}
$m add check -label Open -command {puts "open a file"}
$m add separator
$m add cascade -label Fruit -menu $m.sub1
set m2 [menu $m.sub1]
$m2 add radio -label apple -command {puts "My favorite Fruit"}
$m2 add radio -label orange -command {puts "A Yellow Fruit"}
$m2 add radio -label kiwi -command {puts "I don't like it"}
```

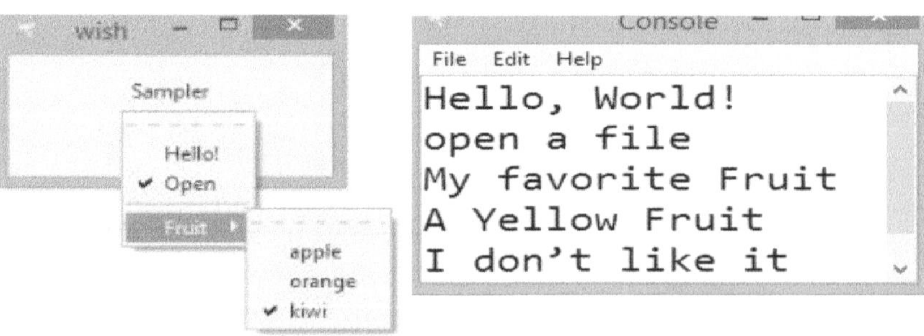

Figure 8.30 Command link to menu and submenu.

In the earlier example, while defining entries, all the features have been included, but this is not necessary after adding the remaining feature as it can be added with the configuration (`.configure`) command.

Syntax: `.configure -menu .menubar`

Example 8.13 Write a script to develop a GUI and change the configuration of entries (Figure 8.31).

Solution

```
menu .m
.m add cascade -menu .m.file      -label File
.m add command -command searchcmd -label Search
.m add command -command helpcmd   -label Help
menu .m.file
.m.file add cascade -label New
.m.file add cascade -label Open
.m.file add cascade -label Save
. configure -menu .m
proc filecmd {} {tk_messageBox -message Filing!}
proc searchcmd {} {tk_messageBox -message Searching!}
proc helpcmd {} {tk_messageBox -message Helping!}
```

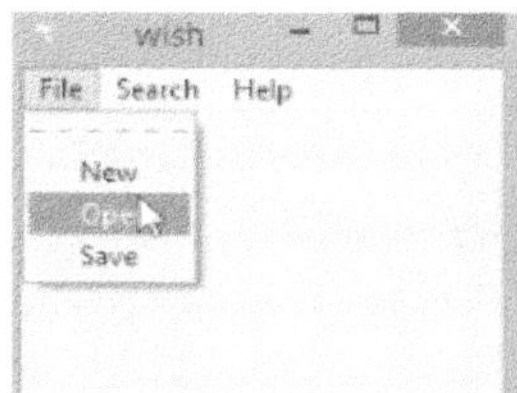

Figure 8.31 Configuring menu entries.

8.4 Tearoff Command

A tearoff entry appears at the top of the menu, enabled with the tearoff option. When a tearoff entry is created, it appears as a dashed line at the top of the menu. Under the default bindings, invoking the tearoff entry causes a tornoff copy to be made of the menu and all of its submenus. One of the applications of the tearoff command is the pop-up menu. A pop-up menu not associated with menubutton appears at the event.

`tk_popup` posts a pop-up menu. First, creating a menu followed by `$x $y` presents the x and y coordinates. It posts a menu in the screen at a defined coordinate position and configures Tk so that the menu and its cascaded children can be traversed with the mouse or the keyboard.

Syntax: `tk_popup $menu $x $y`

Example 8.14 Write a Tcl script to bind a pop-up menu with a mouse right-click.

Solution:

A pop-up menu is created with the `tk_popup` command, which appears on the provided x and y co-ordinates. Figure 8.32 shows the x and y coordinates are bound with `Button-3` (right-click of the mouse).

```
menu .m -tearoff 0
.m add command -label Beep -command bell
.m add command -label Exit -command exit
bind . <Button-3> {showMenu %X %Y}
proc showMenu {x y} {
    tk_popup .m $x $y
}
```

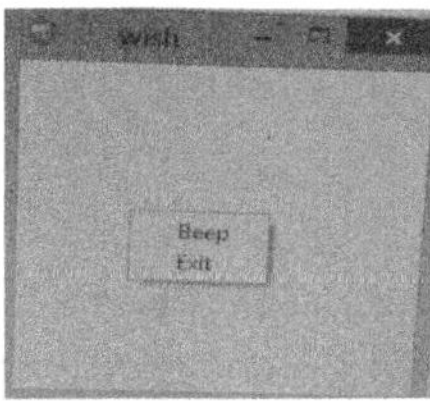

Figure 8.32 Creation of pop-up menu.

8.5 Listbox Widget

The listbox widget displays one text per line with a scrolling feature. First, the listbox is blank. There are operations to insert, select, or delete, but not modify. A listbox is always associated with a scrollbar, having the feature to scroll in both directions via `-xscrollcommand` and `-yscrollcommand`. The content in the list box is inserted starting from index 0. The content of interest can be selected with a double click of the mouse (Figure 8.33).

Syntax: `listbox .listbox_name -command attribute`

```
listbox .lstb -bg pink
.lstb insert 0 Option1
Option2 Option3
pack .lstb
```

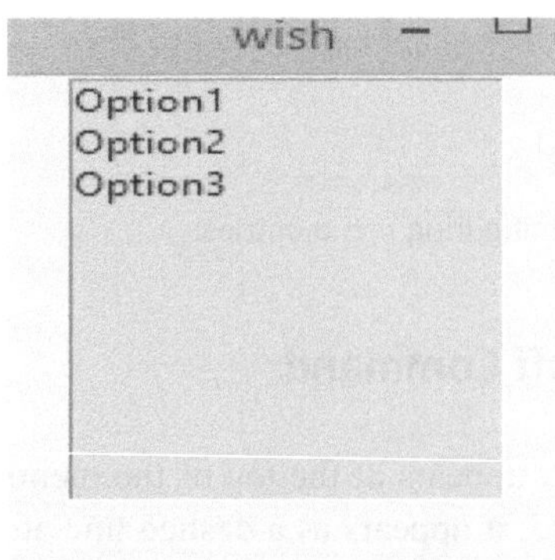

Figure 8.33 Creation of listbox.

Tk automatically creates class bindings for listboxes. The behavior of a listbox is determined by its `-select mode` option.

a) **Single/browse** at most one element can be selected in the listbox at once. Clicking button 1 on an element selects it and deselects any other selected item.
b) **Multiple/extended** any number of elements may be selected at once. Any time the set of selected item(s) in the listbox is updated by the user through the keyboard or mouse, the virtual event `<<ListboxSelect>>` will be generated.

Example 8.15 Write a Tcl script to bind a procedure with listbox content (Figure 8.34).

Solution

```
proc setlabel {text} {
.l configure -text $text
}
listbox .lstb
.lstb insert 0 choice0 choice1 cloice2
pack .lstb
label .l -text "No choice selected"
pack .l
bind .lstb <<ListboxSelect>> {setlabel
[.lstb get active]}
```

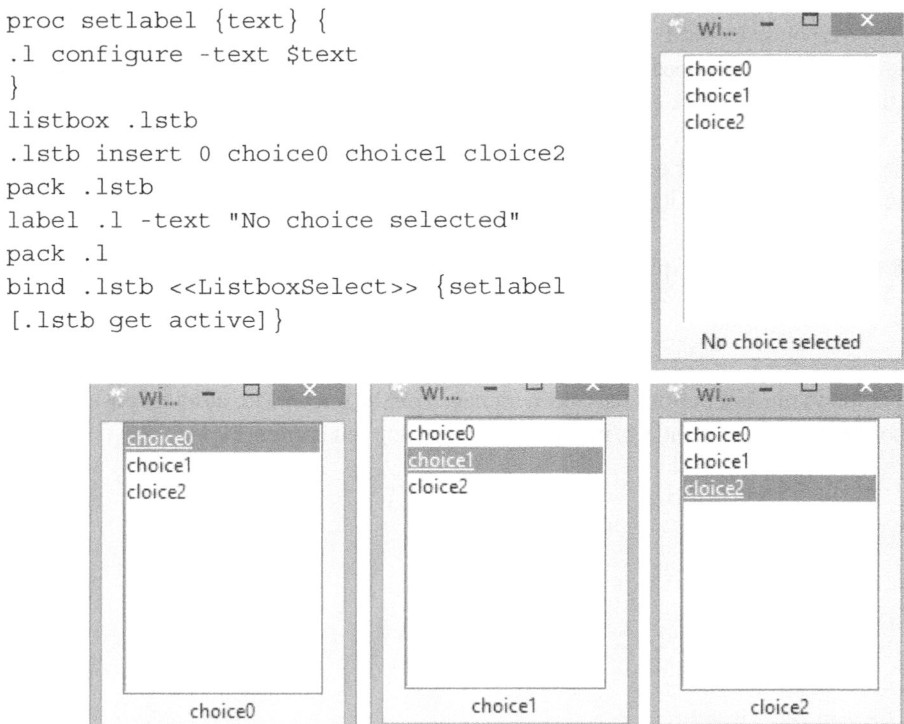

Figure 8.34 Listbox with select mode.

8.6 Place Manager

Place managers follow the absolute position or relative position for layout management based on the size. In absolute positioning, the programmer needs to specify the position and the size of each widget in pixels. The size and the position of a widget do not change even after resizing the window [1].

Syntax: `place .widget_name -x x_loc -y y_loc`

`place .widget_name -relx x_loc -rely y_loc`

`-x x_loc` Sets the absolute x position for the widget
`-y y_loc` Sets the absolute y position for the widget
`-relx x_Frac` Sets the relative x position as a fraction of the parent widget
`-rely y_Frac` Sets the relative y position as a fraction of the parent widget

The location specified in terms of screen units allows for the widgets to resize themselves when the master changes size. Preserving the relative configuration place command enables positioning of a widget at a fixed location. The relative location presents the ratio of child/parent, `relx/rely`, which is specified relatively as the floating number. Presented in Figure 8.35, 0.0 corresponds to the top-left edge of the master and 1.0 corresponds to the bottom-right edge of the master. The relative location need not be in the range of 0.0–1.0. In the case where both `x` and `-relx` are specified, then their values are summed, `-relx` 0.5 `x` −2 corresponds to a position on the left edge of the content, two pixels to the left of the center of its container.

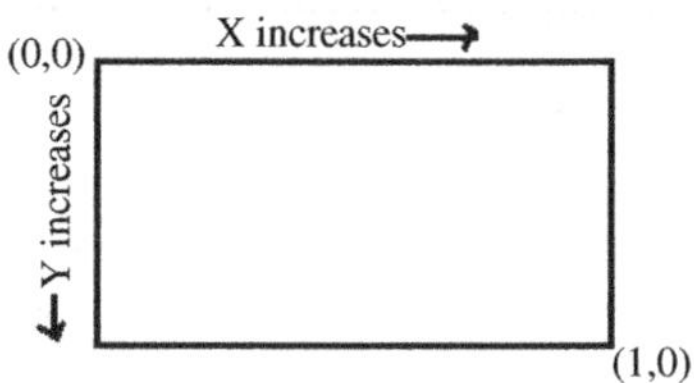

Figure 8.35 Relation position range.

Example 8.16 Write a script to place four buttons with place geometry management via absolute location.

Solution

This example shows the four buttons have been managed on the screen with absolute position. The absolute coordinate value of x and y is measured from the top-left corner (Figure 8.36).

```
button .b1 -text M
button .b2 -text E
button .b3 -text E
button .b4 -text T
place .b1 -x 0 -y 0
place .b2 -x 50 -y 0
place .b3 -x 0 -y 50
place .b4 -x 50 -y 50
```

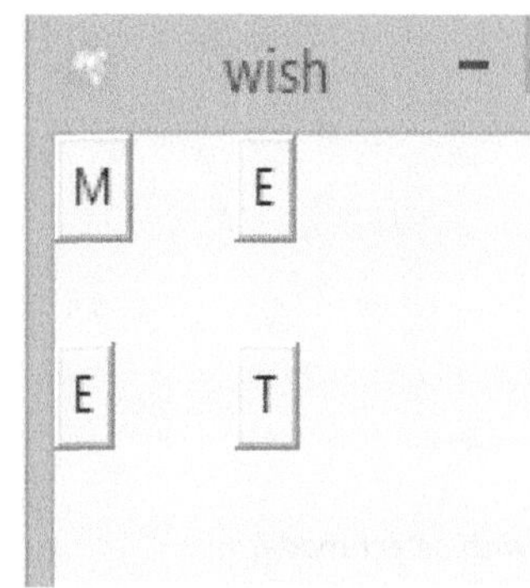

Figure 8.36 Absolute positioning with place manager.

Example 8.17 Write a Tcl script to place four buttons with place geometry management via relative location (Figure 8.37).

Solution

```
button .b1 -text M
button .b2 -text E
button .b3 -text E
button .b4 -text T
place .b1 -relx 0.0 -rely 0.0
place .b2 -relx 0.25 -rely 0.25
place .b3 -relx 0.5 -rely 0.4
place .b4 -relx 0.8 -rely 0.9
```

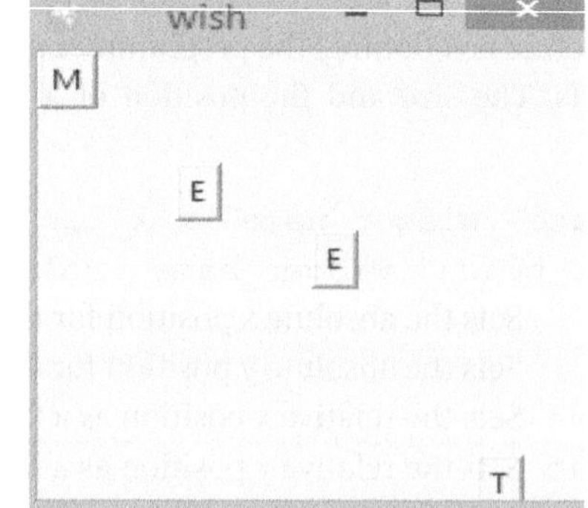

Figure 8.37 Relative positioning with place manager.

8.7 Solved Problems

1. Write a Tcl script to develop a GUI for number base conversion.

Solution

The following script develops a GUI for base conversion, composed of an entry, checkbutton, and label. The entry button is dedicated to accepting an input from a user in decimal format. Three check buttons (binary, octal, and hexadecimal) are bonded to the Tcl script and return the converted result in the specified format. Since the checkbutton is default bound with a mouse left-click, <Button-1> need not to be specified. Clicking on a specified checkbutton returns the result on the label output. To update the value dynamically, the label and checkbutton textvariable must have the same name (Figures 8.38–8.41).

```
label .l1 -text "Input"
entry .e1 -textvariable x
label .l2 -text "Select Function"
checkbutton .c1 -text Binary -command {set result [format %b $x]}
checkbutton .c2 -text Octal -command {set result [format %o $x]}
checkbutton .c3 -text Hexa -command {set result [format %x $x]}
label .l3 -text "Output"
entry .e2 -textvariable result
grid .l1 -row 0 -column 0
grid .e1 -row 0 -column 1 -columnspan 3
grid .l2 -row 1 -column 0
grid .c1 -row 1 -column 1
grid .c2 -row 1 -column 2
grid .c3 -row 1 -column 3
grid .l3 -row 2 -column 0
grid .e2 -row 2 -column 1 -columnspan 3
```

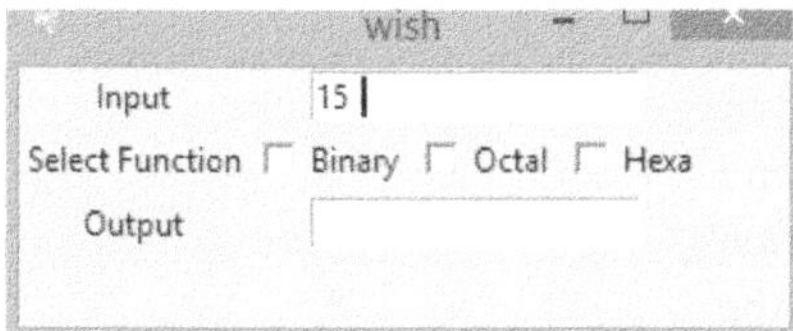

Figure 8.38 Before event.

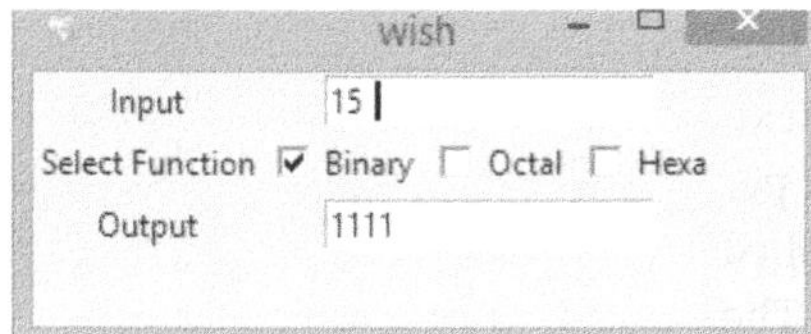

Figure 8.39 Event on binary.

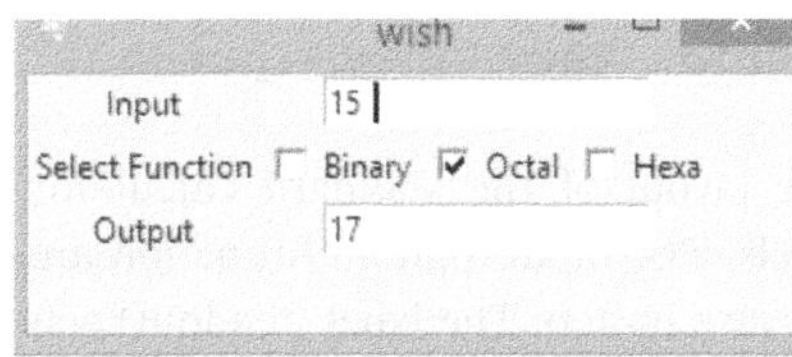

Figure 8.40 Event on octal.

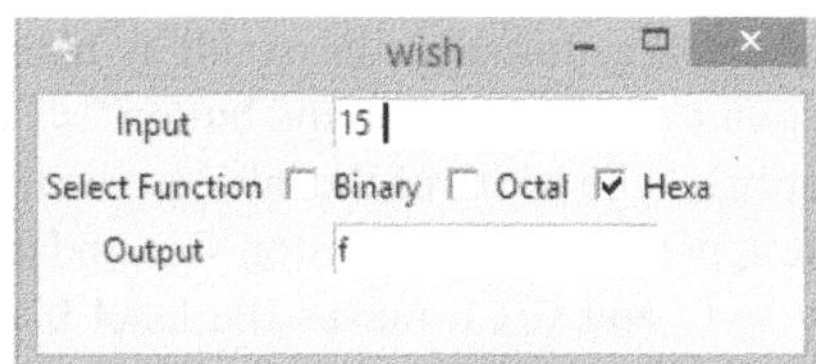

Figure 8.41 Event on hexadecimal.

2. Write a Tcl script to develop a standard calculator.

Solution

```
button .quit   -text "Off" -fg red -command exit
  label .readout -textvariable result -bg white
  set result " "
  button .key0  -text "0"    -width 3 -command {append result 0}
  button .key1  -text "1"    -width 3 -command {append result 1}
  button .key2  -text "2"    -width 3 -command {append result 2}
  button .key3  -text "3"    -width 3 -command {append result 3}
  button .key4  -text "4"    -width 3 -command {append result 4}
  button .key5  -text "5"    -width 3 -command {append result 5}
  button .key6  -text "6"    -width 3 -command {append result 6}
  button .key7  -text "7"    -width 3 -command {append result 7}
  button .key8  -text "8"    -width 3 -command {append result 8}
  button .key9  -text "9"    -width 3 -command {append result 9}
  button .point -text "."    -width 3 -command {append result .}
  button .plus  -text "+"    -width 3 -command {append result +}
  button .minus -text "-"    -width 3 -command {append result -}
  button .times -text "*"    -width 3 -command {append result *}
  button .div   -text "/"    -width 3 -command {append result /}
  button .equal -text "="    -width 3 -command {append result =
[expr $result]}
  button .sign  -text "+/-"  -width 3 -command {set result [expr
$result*-1]}
  button .clear -text "C/CE" -width 3 -command {set result ""}
  grid .quit .readout -sticky nsew
  grid .key7 .key8 .key9 .times .clear
  grid .key4 .key5 .key6 .minus .div
  grid .key1 .key2 .key3 .plus  .equal
  grid .key0 .sign .point            -
```

The layout of the standard calculator contains buttons and labels. The input digit and function are selected by a specified key as a button. The label (readout) acts as a space to show the result. Here, the same textvariable is used for the label and button to be updated dynamically. Each key (except off, C/CE, and sign) is linked to an `append` command, to write in the next right space. Initially, the result is blank. The default mouse action `<Button-1>` on the button "=" updates the result textvaribale. The width of the label (screen) is auto-adjusted as per the appended text. The button sign updates the result multiplied by "−1" and C/CE makes the label blank (clear screen). The OFF button executes the command exit which closes the tool (Figures 8.42 and 8.43).

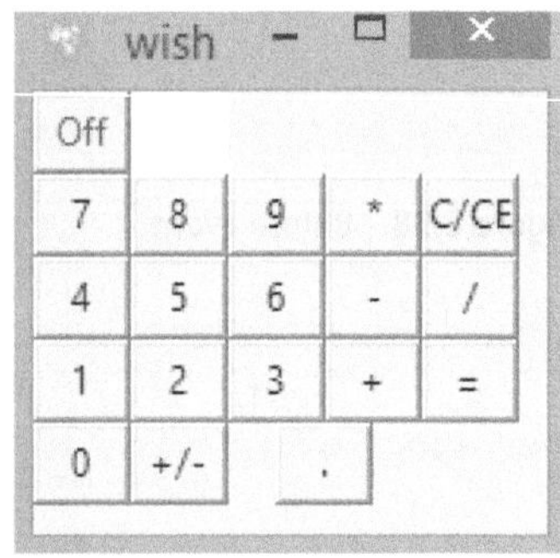

Figure 8.42 Calculator before input.

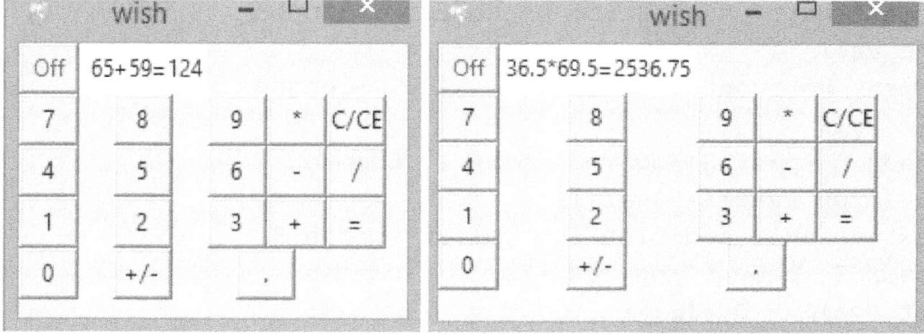

Figure 8.43 Calculator with the result.

3. Write a Tcl script to generate a five button widget with a for loop.

Solution

The following `for` loop is executed five times and on each iteration, generates a button widget whose instant number and label update with the loop counting variable (Figure 8.44).

```
for {set k 1} {$k < 6}
{incr k} {
    button .x$k -text
"Button $k"
    pack .x$k
     }
```

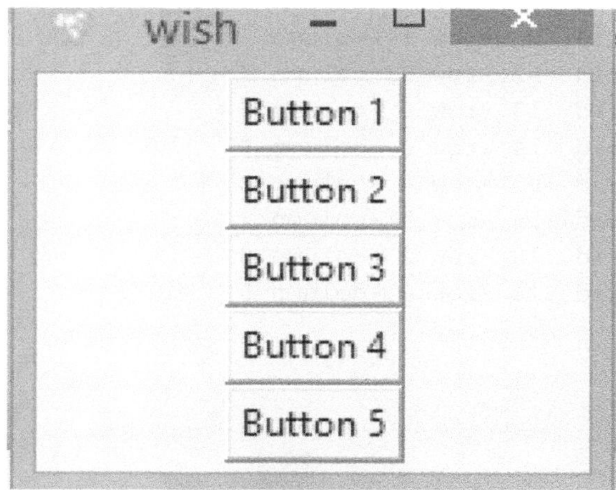

Figure 8.44 Creation of button with `for` loop.

---

4. Write a Tcl script to develop a graphical interface to compute arithmetic functions where the input is provided through scale.

Solution

The example shows two horizontal scale scrollbar values to set the input to the calculator. At the center, the button displays the function to be chosen, and the corresponding result is displayed on the provided label (Figure 8.45).

```
scale .s1 -orient horizontal -from 0 -to 100  -length
150  -variable val1
scale .s2 -orient horizontal -from 0 -to 100  -length
150  -variable val2
button .b1 -padx 5 -pady 5 -bg red -text + -command
{set addition [expr $val1 + $val2]}
label .l3 -textvariable addition -bg yellow -width 5
button .b2 -padx 5 -pady 5 -bg red -text - -command
{set sub [expr $val1 - $val2]}
label .l4 -textvariable sub -bg yellow -width 5
button .b3 -padx 5 -pady 5 -bg red -text * -command
{set Mul [expr $val1 * $val2]}
label .l5 -textvariable Mul -bg yellow -width 5
button .b4 -padx 5 -pady 5 -bg red -text / -command
{set div [expr $val1 / $val2]}
label .l6 -textvariable div -bg yellow -width 5
grid .s1 -row 2 -column 0
grid .b1 -row 0 -column 2
grid .b2 -row 1 -column 2
grid .s2 -row 2 -column 3
grid .l3 -row 0 -column 5
grid .l4 -row 1 -column 5
grid .b3 -row 2 -column 2
grid .b4 -row 3 -column 2
grid .l5 -row 2 -column 5
grid .l6 -row 3 -column 5
```

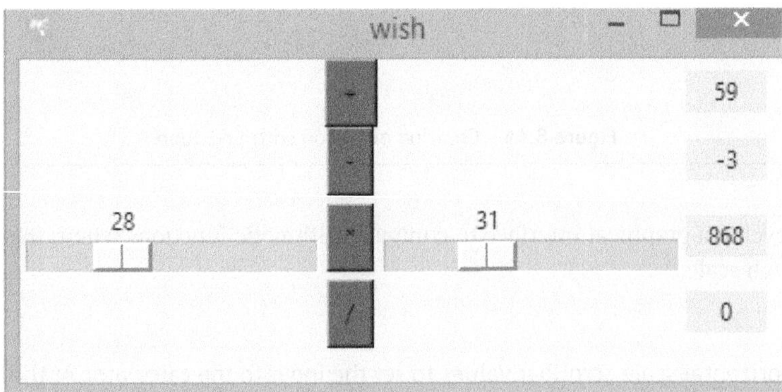

Figure 8.45 GUI of the calculator with scale input.

5. Write a Tcl script to develop a GUI containing two different menus and add entries to each menu.

Solution

The following example shows two menubuttons "File" and "Edit." Each menubutton contains separate menu entries (Figures 8.46–8.48).

```
menubutton .mb1 -text File -menu
.mb1.file
menubutton .mb2 -text Edit -menu
.mb2.edit
pack .mb1 .mb2 -side left -anchor nw
menu .mb1.file
.mb1.file add command -label Open
.mb1.file add command -label Save
.mb1.file add command -label Save As
.mb1.file add command -label Quit
```

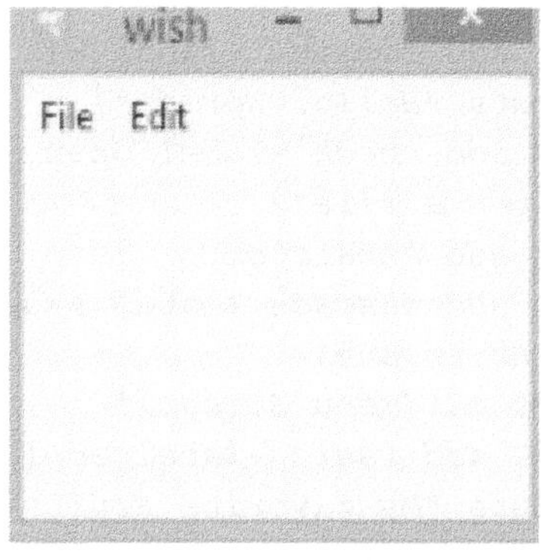

Figure 8.46 Two menubuttons.

```
menu .mb2.edit
.mb2.edit add command -label Cut
.mb2.edit add command -label Paste
.mb2.edit add command -label Copy
.mb2.edit add command -label Clear
```

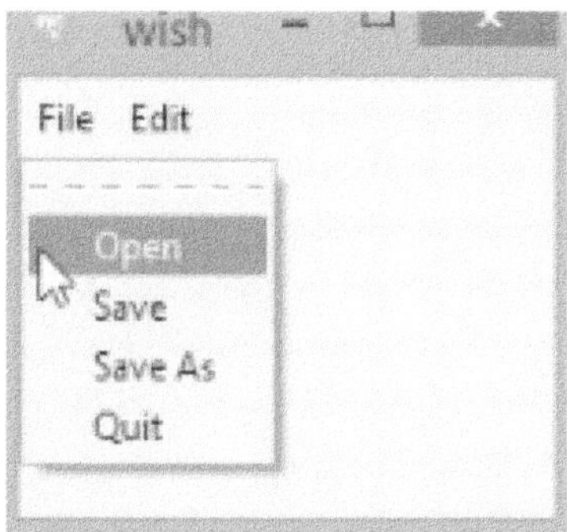

Figure 8.47 Menu of menubutton-1.

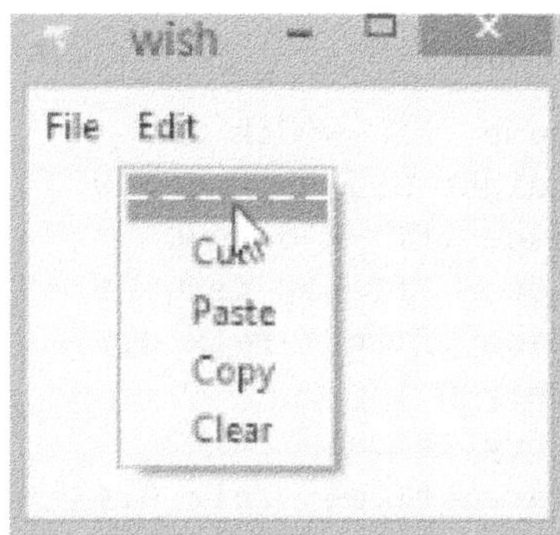

Figure 8.48 Menu of menubutton-2.

6. Write a Tcl script to develop a GUI for a submenu (Figure 8.49).

Solution

```
menubutton .mb -text Sampler -menu
.mb.menu
pack .mb -padx 10 -pady 10
set m [menu .mb.menu]
$m add command -label Hello! -command
{puts "Hello, World!"}
$m add check -label Open -command {puts
"open a file"}
$m add separator
$m add cascade -label Fruit -
menu $m.sub1
set m2 [menu $m.sub1]
$m2 add radio -label apple -command
{puts "My favorite Fruit"}
$m2 add radio -label orange -command
{puts "A Yellow Fruit"}
$m2 add radio -label kiwi -command
{puts "I like it"}
```

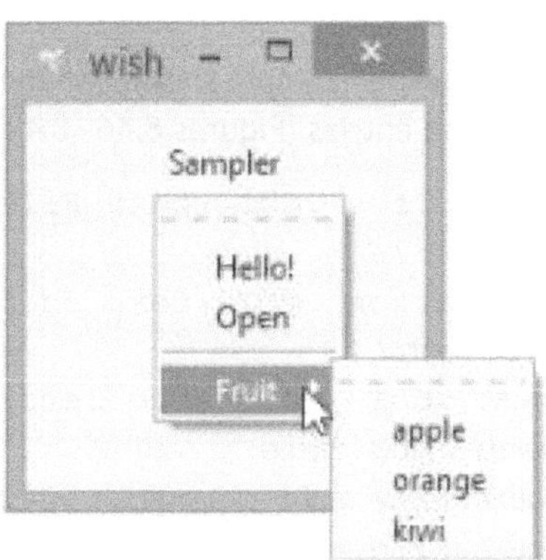

Figure 8.49 Submenu.

7. Write a Tcl script to develop a GUI that contains two frames each having a button and an entry. The layout of the GUI should be managed by the relative positioning (Figure 8.50).

Solution

```
frame .f1 -width 250
-height 250 -bg yellow
place .f1 -x 0 -y 0
button .f1.b1 -text B1
place .f1.b1 -relx 0.1
-rely 0.1
entry .f1.e1
place .f1.e1 -relx 0.4
-rely 0.2
frame .f2 -width 250
-height 250 -bg green
place .f2 -x 300 -y 300
button .f2.b2 -text B2
place .f2.b2 -relx 0.5
-rely 0.5
entry .f2.e2
place .f2.e2 -relx 0.2
-rely 0.6
```

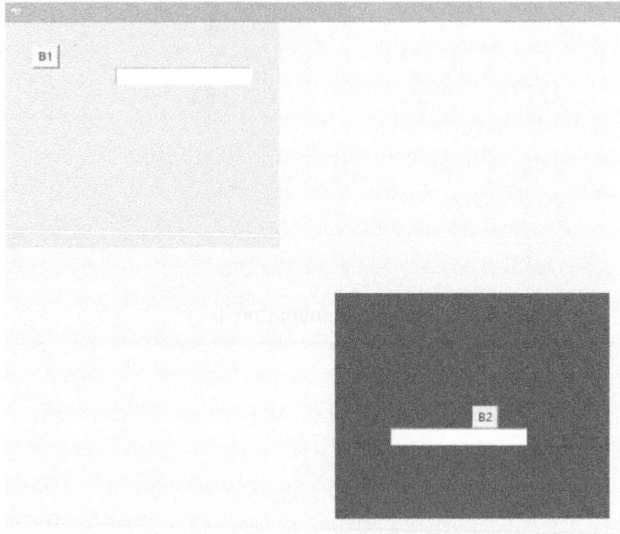

Figure 8.50 Place manager with relation position.

8.8 MCQs on Bind, Menu, and Place Manager

[1] Which is/are the correct statement(s)?

- **A** A mouse click on the menubutton displays the menu
- **B** Press and hold the mouse on a menubutton continues to display the menu
- **C** A mouse click outside to dismiss the menu
- **D** All of the above

[Solution (d)]

[2] What is/are the objective(s) of the geometry manager?

- **A** To plan the layout for a GUI
- **B** To keep the widget at the given coordinate location
- **C** To position the widget horizontally, vertically, or at the corner
- **D** All of the above

[Solution (d)]

[3] Which is the correct format of the bind command?

- **A** bind .b ButtonPress-1 {gets "Button Pressed"}
- **B** bind .b {ButtonPress-1} {gets "Button Pressed"}
- **C** bind .b <ButtonPress-1> {puts "Button Pressed"}

[Solution (b)]

[4] Place manager with the -relx and -rely commands displays the widget with relative distance to what?

- **A** Another widget
- **B** Reference widget
- **C** First widget with pack
- **D** Frame

[Solution (d)]

[5] What does button .b.f indicate?

- **A** A button b over-frame f
- **B** A-frame f over button b
- **C** A button f over frame b
- **D** A frame b over button f

[Solution (a)]

[6] With what can a widget be expanded horizontally or vertically?

- **A** -command
- **B** -anchor
- **C** -pad
- **D** -fill

[Solution (d)]

[7] With what can a widget be removed/deleted from a GUI screen?

A pack forget .widgetname
B destroy .widgetname
C Both of the above
D None of the above

[Solution (c)]

[8] What is the syntax to bind an event to a button widget with a Tcl command?

A Bind .b ButtonPress-1 {puts "Button Pressed"}
B Bind .b {ButtonPress-1} {puts "Button Pressed"}
C Bind .b {ButtonPress-1} {gets "Button Pressed"}
D Bind .b < ButtonPress-1 > {puts "Button Pressed"}

[Solution (d)]

[9] What will bind. <Motion> {puts "pointer at %x,%y"} display?

A Nothing
B x coordinate of the mouse coordinates
C y coordinate of the mouse coordinates
D x,y coordinates of the mouse coordinates

[Solution (d)]

[10] What orientation will the following Tcl script generate six buttons?

```
for {set k 1} {$k < 6} {incr k} {
        button .x$k -text "Button $k"
              pack .x$k
              }
```

A Top to bottom
B Left to right
C Right to left
D Bottom to top

[Solution (a)]

[11] What is the statement "menu is a child of the menubutton"?

A True
B False

[Solution (a)]

[12] Which of the following statements is/are correct?

A Press and hold the mouse on the menubutton will continue to display the menu
B Mouse click outside the menubutton will dismiss the menu
C Both are correct

[Solution (c)]

[13] What will the `-tearoff` command of the menu widget do?

A Invoke a Tcl command
B Delete a Tcl command
C Destroy a Tcl command
D Deactivate a Tcl command

[Solution (a)]

[14] What will the following script generate?

```
menubutton .mb -text File -menu .mb.menu
pack .mb
menu .mb.menu
.mb.menu add radio -label New
```

A A menu titled "File" and menubar titled "New"
B A menubar titled "New" and menu titled "File"
C A menu titled "File" and a menu titled "New"
D A menubar titled "File" and menu titled "New"

[Solution (d)]

[15] What will `button .b -command exit` do?

A Bind the mouse left buttonpress with a button
B Bind the mouse left buttonrelease with a button
C Bind the mouse right buttonpress with a button
D Bind the mouse right buttonrelease with a button

[Solution (d)]

References

1 https://zetcode.com/gui/tcltktutorial/layout/
2 https://www.tutorialspoint.com/tcl-tk/
3 Welch, B.B., Jones, K., and Hobbs, J. (2003). *Practical Programming in Tcl/Tk*. Prentice Hall Professional.
4 https://www.tcl.tk/man/

9

Canvas Widgets and Tk Commands

Canvas is a flexible widget that provides drawing areas. Similar to the MS-Paint feature, the user can place an object such as a line, image, polygon, rectangle, etc. and can be programmed to respond according to an input. A canvas displays any number of objects on the canvas which can be manipulated. Objects can be bonded with user action and can be animated. The `bind` command, which was discussed in Chapter 8, lets the canvas object behave according to the Tcl script.

Syntax for canvas widget:

```
canvas .canvasName attribute
```

`Canvas` creates a window and makes it into a canvas widget. Attributes to the canvas change the appearance. Table 9.1 lists the attributes to the canvas widget defined on the command line during instantiating [1].

Table 9.1 Attributes to the canvas.

Command	Description
`-background-color`	Sets the background color
`-height number`	Sets the height of the widget
`-width number`	Sets the width of the widget
`-closeenough distance`	Sets the closeness of the mouse cursor to an object over the canvas. Defaul1.0 pixel
`-scrollregion boundingbox`	Sets the bounding box of the total area of the canvas
`-xscrollincrement size`	Sets the amount to scroll horizontally for scrolling
`-yscrollincrement size`	Sets the amount to scroll vertically for scrolling

Note – The geometry manager must be applied to make the canvas appear over the interface.

Example 9.1 Write a Tcl script to create a canvas widget with a red background.

Solution

The example in Figure 9.1 creates canvas `.c`. The command line attributes to the canvas `-bg`, `-width`, and `-height` set the background color, width, and height, respectively.

Programming and GUI Fundamentals: Tcl-Tk for Electronic Design Automation (EDA), First Edition.
Suman Lata Tripathi, Abhishek Kumar, and Jyotirmoy Pathak.

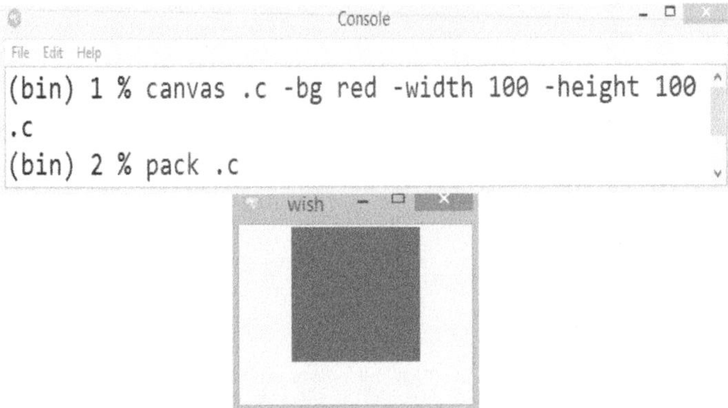

Figure 9.1 Canvas with background color.

9.1 Canvas Coordinate

The placing of the widget over the canvas is specified by the coordinate. Different objects are characterized by different set of coordinates [2, 3]. Coordinates are defined into set (x, y) values that specify their anchor point. An object like a line, rectangle, or polygon require multiple set of coordinates to draw a joining line at the end point. All coordinates over a canvas are stored as floating-point numbers. The coordinate and distance are specified in the screen unit. By default, coordinates are measured in pixels; however, it can change by suffixing the following.

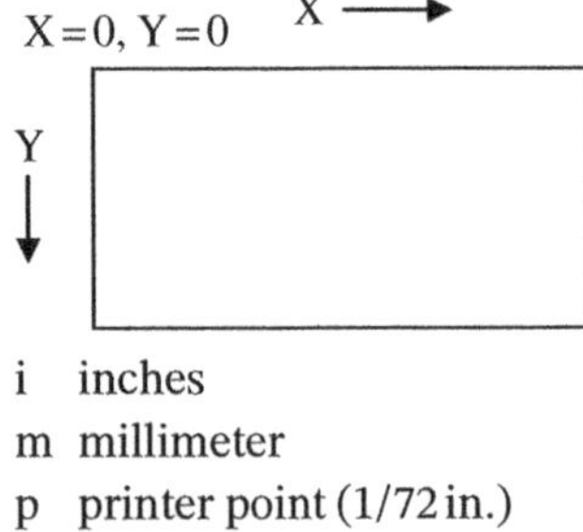

i inches
m millimeter
p printer point (1/72 in.)

The coordinates at canvas position (0, 0) define on the top left corner, and the x-coordinate value increases toward the right and the y-coordinate value increases downward. When objects are created, they occupy specified coordinates on the canvas; they can be updated with the `coords` command.

- -x position specifies the x-coordinate on the left edge of the area over the canvas
- -y position specifies the y-coordinate on the top edge of the area over the canvas

9.2 Drawing over Canvas

The following are the list of widgets for drawing over the canvas. The `create` command places the following object over the canvas widget.

Syntax for drawing an object over a canvas: `.c create object`

9.2.1 Arc

The arc widget draws an arc over the drawing area of the canvas. The dimension is set by the 4-coordinate points in the bounding box. The arc is determined by the commands `-start angle` and `-extent angle`. The *chord style* connects two endpoints of the arc and *arc style* fills the arc itself without the outline. The `-fill color` command set the color of the arc.

```
.canvasname create arc x1 y1 x2 y2
```

```
canvas .c -bg red -width 100 -height 100
pack .c
.c create arc 10 20 50 100 -fill yellow -start 45 -extent 90
```

The above script creates a canvas with a red background along with the pack manager. For the arc over the canvas in Figure 9.2, the attributes to the arc are explained as follows.

`-start degree`	Starting angle of arc
`-extent degree`	Length of arc in counterclockwise
`-fill color`	Fill color into the arc
`-outline color`	Color of the arc itself
`-stipple bitmap`	Stipple pattern for the fill
`-style style`	Set style of arc pieslice, chord
`-width number`	Set width in a specified coordinate
`-tag taglist`	Lists the tags for the arc

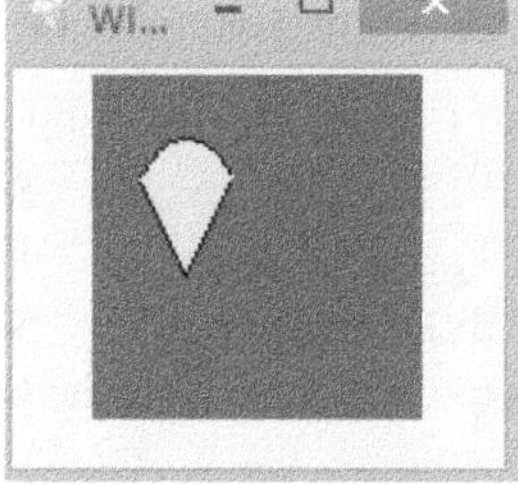

Figure 9.2 Arc on the canvas.

9.2.2 Line

The line widget draws a line over the canvas, defined by two or more sets of coordinates, where each set of coordinates define an endpoint to the line.

```
.canvasname create line x1 x2
x3 x4 ......xn yn
```

```
canvas .c -bg red -width 100
-height 100
pack .c
.c create line 10 30 50 80
-fill yellow -arrow both -width 7
```

Figure 9.3 Line on the canvas.

This example creates a line over the canvas, as shown in Figure 9.3. The following are the commands to set a feature to a line.

`-fill color`	Sets color to the line
`-arrow where`	Sets an arrow to line none, first, last, or both
`-arrowshape {a b c}`	Sets the shape of the arrow; a-length of part touching the line, b- overall length, and c- width
`-width number`	Sets the width of the line
`-capstyle what`	Sets the end style of the line as butt, projecting, or round
`-joinstyle what`	Sets the joining style of the line as bevel, miter, or round
`-smooth Boolean`	1-spline, 0-straight line
`-stipple bitmap`	Pattern for filling the line
`-tag taglist`	Lists the tags for the line item

9.2.3 Rectangle

The rectangle widget draws a rectangle over the canvas specified by the coordinates of the opposite corners. The rectangle can have the `-fill color` and `-fill outline` commands.

```
.canvasname create rectangle x1
y1 x2 y2
```

```
canvas .c -bg red -width 200 -
height 200
pack .c
.c create rectangle 20 100 70
150 -fill yellow -outline white
```

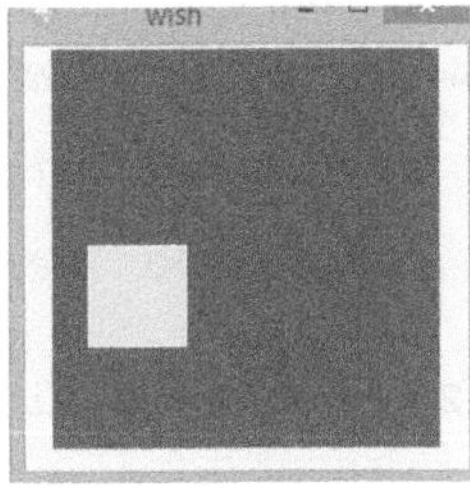

Figure 9.4 Rectangle on the canvas.

The example above creates a rectangle over canvas shown in Figure 9.4. The following commands set the feature to the rectangle.

`-fill color` Sets color to the interior of the rectangle
`-outline color` Sets color to the outline of the rectangle
`-stipple bitmap` Pattern for filling the rectangle
`-width number` Sets the thickness of the outline
`-tag taglist` Lists the tags for the rectangle

9.2.4 Polygon

A polygon widget creates a closed-shape polygon specified by several coordinate points. Each point indicates the vertex of the polygon either smoothly or straightly connected. There is no outline option for a polygon.

```
canvas .c -bg red -width 200
-height 200
pack .c
.c create polygon 60 60 80 100
120 140 80 140 20 120 \
40 120 40 100 40 100  -fill yellow
        .canvasname create
polygon x1 y1 x2 y2 .......xn yn
```

Figure 9.5 Polygon on the canvas.

This example creates a polygon over the canvas, as shown in Figure 9.5. Following commands set the features to the polygon.

`-fill color`	Sets color to the interior of the rectangle
`-smooth boolean`	Sets 1 spline curve around the points
`-splinessteps number`	Sets the line segment approximate design
`-stipple bitmap`	Sets a stipple pattern for filling
`-tag taglist`	Lists the tags for the rectangle

9.2.5 Oval

The oval widget creates an oval shape defined by two sets of coordinates, which define its bounding box. If the coordinates define a rectangle shape, a circle will be drawn. Color to interior and outline is set accordingly.

```
                .c oval create
oval x1 y1 x2 y2
canvas .c -bg red -width 200 -
height 200
pack .c
.c create oval 20 120 80 180 -
fill yellow
.c create oval 10 100 30 50 -
fill yellow
```

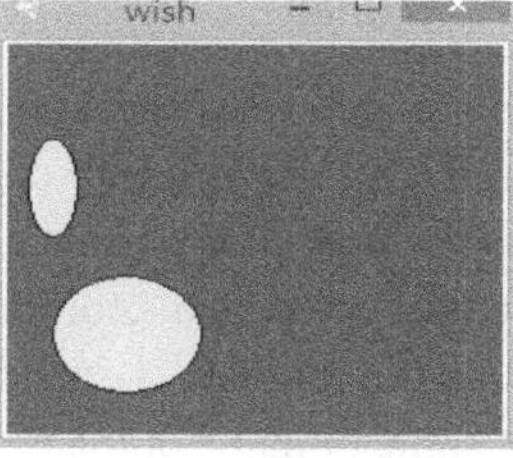

Figure 9.6 Oval on the canvas.

This example creates an oval on the canvas, as shown in Figure 9.6. The following commands set the features to the oval.

`-fill color`	Sets color to the interior of the oval
`-outline color`	Sets color to the outline of the oval
`-stipple bitmap`	Sets the pattern for filling the oval
`-width number`	Sets the thickness of the outline
`-tag taglist`	Lists the tags for the rectangle

9.2.6 Text

The `text` command creates text on the canvas having a display and edit feature. The coordinate or position of the text is specified by one set of coordinate and anchor positions. The size of the text is determined by the number of lines and length of each line. In the case where the line is longer than the specified width, then the text is wrapped onto multiple lines. The `text` command supports selection, editing, and can extend onto multiple lines.

```
 .canvasname create text
x y -text
canvas .c -bg red -width 100
-height 100
pack .c
.c create text 25 25 -text
"Canvas" -fill yellow
```

Figure 9.7 Text on the canvas.

This example creates the text "Canvas," as presented in Figure 9.7 and the following are the operations that can be applied to manipulate the canvas text.

`dchar`	Deletes a character
`focus`	Focuses on a specified index
`icursor`	Inserts a cursor before
`index`	Returns the index value
`insert`	Inserts before a specified index

`select adjust`	Moves the boundary of selection
`select clear`	Clears the section
`select from`	Starts a selection
`select to`	Extends the selection to a specified index

9.2.7 Bitmap

A bitmap refers to the graphics with background and foreground color selected by 1-bit per pixel (see Figure 9.8). A bitmap is positioned with two coordinate and anchor positions. A bitmap is specified by its symbolic name or name of the file and contains its definition beginning with @. The available bitmaps are info, error, warning, question, questhead, hourglass, gray12, gray25, gray50, gray75.

Figure 9.8 Bitmap.

```
.canvasname create bitmap x y option
```

```
canvas .c -bg red -width 120 -
height 120
pack .c
.c create bitmap 10 10 -bitmap
info
.c create bitmap 10 20 -bitmap
warning
.c create bitmap 30 50 -bitmap
question
.c create bitmap 30 80 -bitmap
questhead
.c create bitmap 50 10 -bitmap
error
.c create bitmap 80 90 -bitmap
hourglass
.c create bitmap 70 20 -bitmap
gray12
.c create bitmap 70 60 -bitmap
gray25
.c create bitmap 90 30 -bitmap
gray50
.c create bitmap 90 70 -bitmap
gray75
```

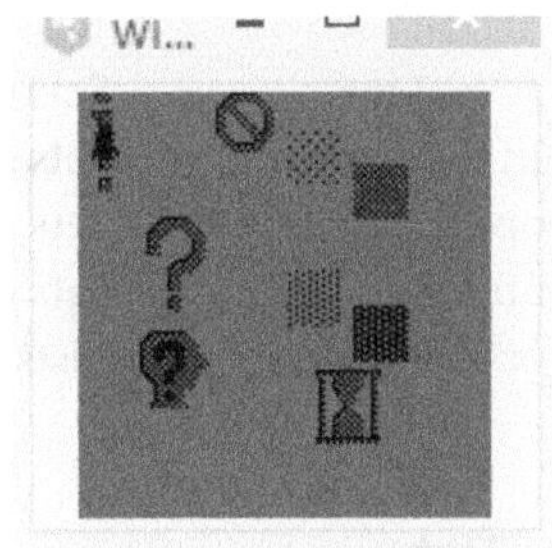

Figure 9.9 Bitmap on the canvas.

Figure 9.9 presents the addition of a bitmap on the canvas. The following commands are used to set the features to the bitmap.

`-anchor position`	Sets the anchor to c, n, ne, e, se, s, sw, w, nw
`-background color`	Sets the background color (zero bits)
`-foreground color`	Sets the foreground color (1 bit)

`-bitmap name`	Sets the built-in bitmap symbol
`-bitmap @file`	Sets the bitmap defined in a file
`-tag taglist`	Lists the tags for the bitmap

9.2.8 Image Widget

The image widgets create a displayable image on the canvas. First, images that need to be defined in the directory should be in the supported formats of GIF, PNG, PPM, PGM, JPG, JPEG, BMP, and read via the `-file` command. An image is created with the `image` command, which is a two-step process.

image create command

```
image create photo imagename -file xxxx.png
```

image display command

```
.canvasName create image x y -option
```

Here, the options are *image imageName* , which presents a variable that holds the image to the display.

Once an image is defined, one needs to specify its position on the canvas with a coordinate value, anchor point, or tag. Size and color are defined when the image is created and in the case of redefining, the image automatically gets updated.

The following commands set the features to the image.

`-image name`	Sets the name of an image
`-anchor position`	Sets the anchor to c, n, ne, e, se, s, sw, w, nw
`-tag taglist`	Lists the tags for the image

Example 9.2 Write a script to create an image of AND logic gate over the canvas.

Solution

The following command reads an image with a supported extension available in the bin directory; see Figure 9.10. It reads the and.png file, creates an image and makes the image appear over the specified coordinate, and displays on the canvas, as shown in Figure 9.11.

```
image create photo img -file
"and.png"
canvas .c -height 100 -width
200
.c create image 50 50  -image
img
pack .c
```

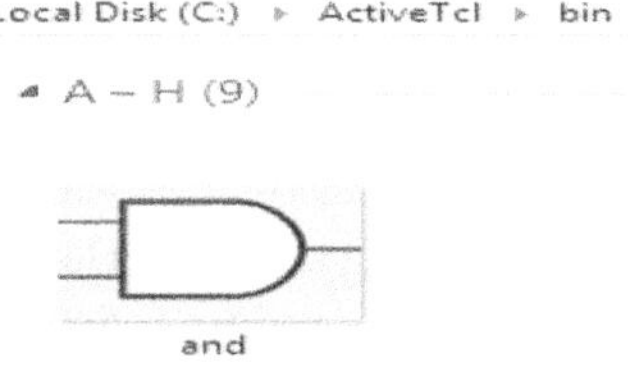

Figure 9.10 Image in the directory.

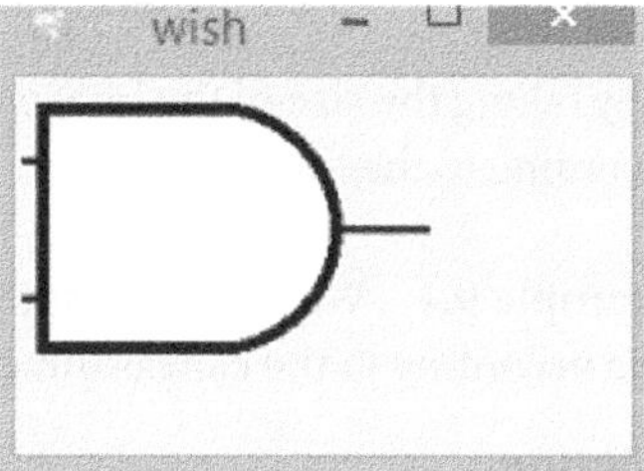

Figure 9.11 Image on the canvas.

Example 9.3 Write a Tcl script to create two different images over the canvas.

Solution

Figure 9.12 shows there are two different images available in the bin directory. The command-line arguments read them one by one and assigns the coordinate location to them. The following script reads the file "and.png" and "or.png" from the directory and places them over the canvas at specified coordinates. The coordinate values must be different to avoid overlapping, as shown in Figure 9.13.

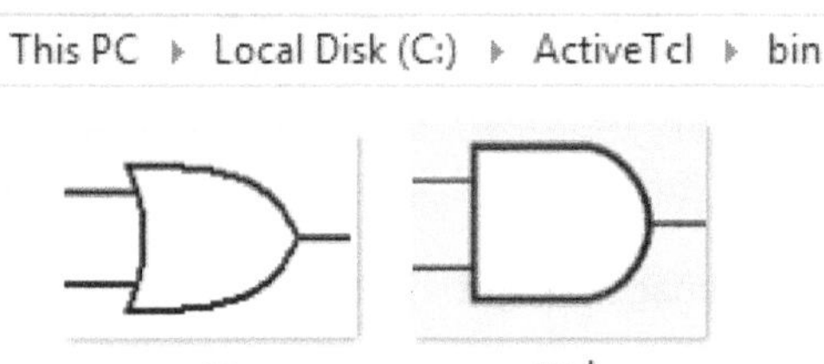

Figure 9.12 Image in the directory.

```
image create photo and -file
"and.png"
image create photo or -file
"or.png"
canvas .c
.c create image 100 100 -image
and
.c create image 200 200 -image
or
pack .c
```

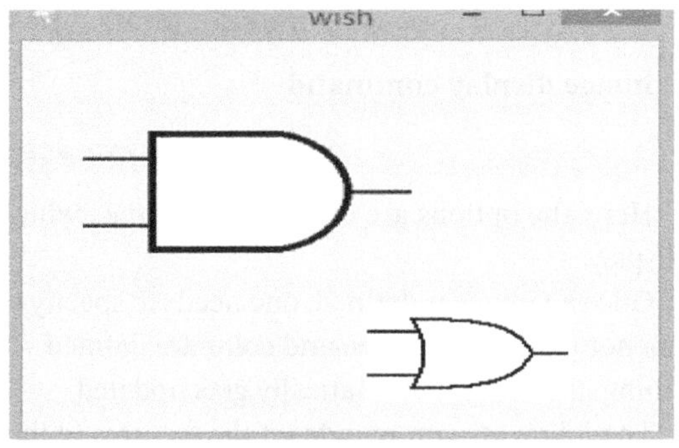

Figure 9.13 Image on the canvas.

The photo image was contributed by Paul Mackerras. It displays a full color image and can undergo dithering and correction. The photo image supports different image formats. The following are attributes to the `image create photo` command.

`-format format`	Specifies the format of the file
`-data string`	Converts the content of the photo to a string
`-file name`	Names the file
`-gamma value`	Gamma correction factor, where a value higher than 1 sets the brightness
`-height value`	Sets the height in screen units
`-width value`	Sets the width in screen units
`-palette spec`	Specifies the number of the gray level

```
canvas .c -height $height -width $width
```

By taking the size of the image into account, this command adjusts the canvas height and width according to the image.

Example 9.4 Write a Tcl script to create an image on the canvas, and auto set the image dimension according to the canvas dimension.

Solution

The following script reads the image file "and.png". Here, the commands `[image height]` and `[image width]` are used to read the height and width, respectively, of a particular image and have been assigned to a variable height and width. During the creation of an image on the canvas, the coordinate value indicates a position from the top left and the command `-image` updates the associated feature, such as the filename height and width via variable substitution, as described in Figure 9.14.

```
image create photo img -file
"and.png"

set height [image height img]
set width [image width img]


canvas .c -height $height -
width $width -bg pink
.c create image 10 10 -image
img  -anchor nw
pack .c
```

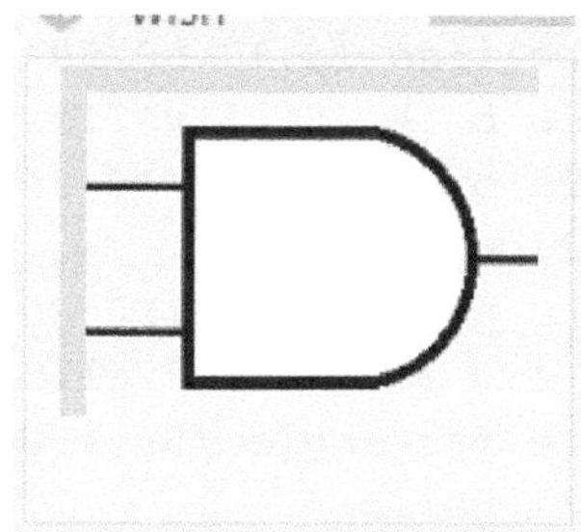

Figure 9.14 Image dimension adjustment.

Example 9.5 Write a script to create two images over the canvas, adjust the image dimension according to the canvas dimension.

Solution

The following example explains the variable height is set as the height of "and.png" and the width is set as the width of "or.png". The canvas dimensions are set to be double the height and width values. During image creation on the canvas, the dimension is set automatically, as presented in Figure 9.15.

```
image create photo and -file
"and.png"
image create photo or -file
"or.png"
set height [image height and]
set width [image width or]
canvas .c -height [expr 2*$height]
-width [expr 2*$width] -bg pink
.c create image 50 50 -image and
.c create image 50 120 -image or
pack .c
```

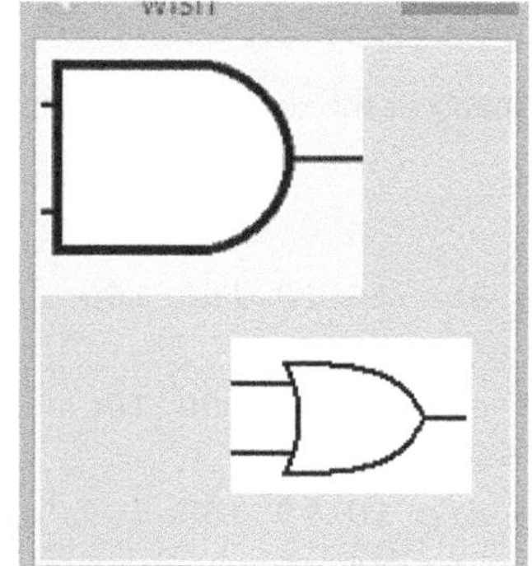

Figure 9.15 Image dimension for each image.

Example 9.6 Write a Tcl script to create all objects on the canvas.

Solution

The following example creates all objects on the canvas (see Figure 9.16).

```
canvas .c -bg red -width 200 -
height 200
pack .c
.c create arc 10 10 50 50 -fill
yellow
.c create line 10 30 50 50 100
10 -arrow both -fill yellow
.c create oval 50 50 100 80 -
fill yellow
.c create polygon 50 150 80 120
120 100 190 180 -fill yellow
.c create rectangle 150 150 170
170 -fill yellow
.c create text 200 50 -text
"Hello" -fill yellow
.c create text 140 50 -text
"Hello" -fill yellow
.c create bitmap 180 50 -bitmap
info
```

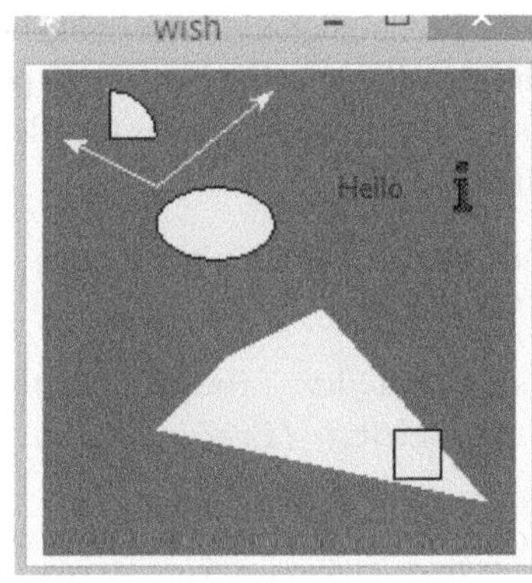

Figure 9.16 Objects on the canvas.

Note – In this example, the polygon and rectangle are overlapping due to coordinate matches.

Example 9.7 Write a script to create a series of arcs on the canvas to obtain a circular shape formed by the arcs.

Solution

Each arc originates at the same coordinate and draws an angle of 45° (see Figure 9.17).

```
canvas .c
pack .c
.c create arc 10 10 100 100 -
start 0 -extent 45
.c create arc 10 10 100 100 -
start 45 -extent 45
.c create arc 10 10 100 100 -
start 90 -extent 45
.c create arc 10 10 100 100 -
start 225 -extent 45
.c create arc 10 10 100 100 -
start 135 -extent 45
.c create arc 10 10 100 100 -
start 180 -extent 45
.c create arc 10 10 100 100 -
start 360 -extent 45
.c create arc 10 10 100 100 -
start 270 -extent 45
.c create arc 10 10 100 100 -
start 315 -extent 45
```

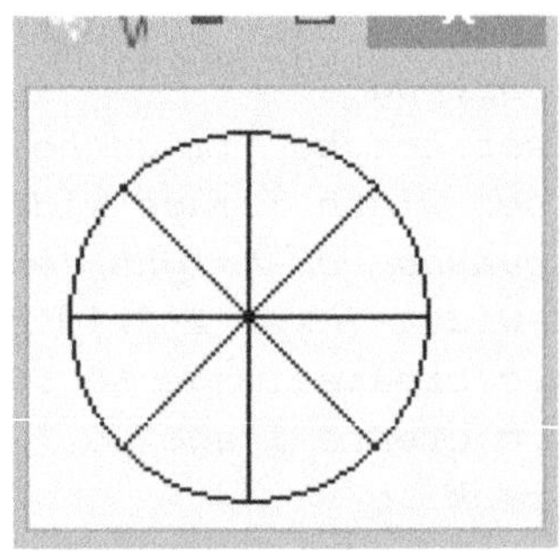

Figure 9.17 Circle using arcs.

9.3 Event Binding of Canvas Object

The `bind` command invokes associated widgets whenever a particular event has occurred. The `bind` command for the widget on canvas is similar to the `bind` command for another widget except that it operates on an object on the canvas rather than the entire widget. Bind permits a manual entry for the event sequence and substitution performed on command before invoking it. Binding events are specified with the keyboard and mouse (such as Enter, Leave, Motion, ButtonPress, and KeyPress) [4]. Mouse-related events Enter, Leave, and Motion direct the current object while the keyboard-related events direct the focused object. If a virtual event is defined, it triggers only when the virtual event sequence occurs via mouse or keyboard.

If binding is created for a canvas window using the `bind` command, triggering will occur in addition to binding created for the canvas object using the `bind widget` command. The binding for an object triggers before any of the bindings for the window as a whole.

Example 9.8 Write a Tcl script to create a canvas and a button which is bonded with text. A mouse action on a button creates the text input over the canvas.

Solution

The following example creates a yellow background canvas and a button widget labeled text. The button is bonded with `<Button-1 >` (left click of the mouse button) and invokes a procedure named plaintext. Figure 9.18 presents that the variables to `proc` are w (window) and name. The provided string "Create a Text" is placeable on the complete window. The `proc` sets the (x, y) coordinate as (50,50) and creates a text widget on the specified coordinate over `$w`.

```
proc paintext {w name} {
    set x 50
    set y 50
    $w create text $x $y -text
$name
    }
canvas .c -bg yellow
pack .c
button  .b1 -text "Text"  -
command {paintext .c "Create a
Text"}
pack .b1
```

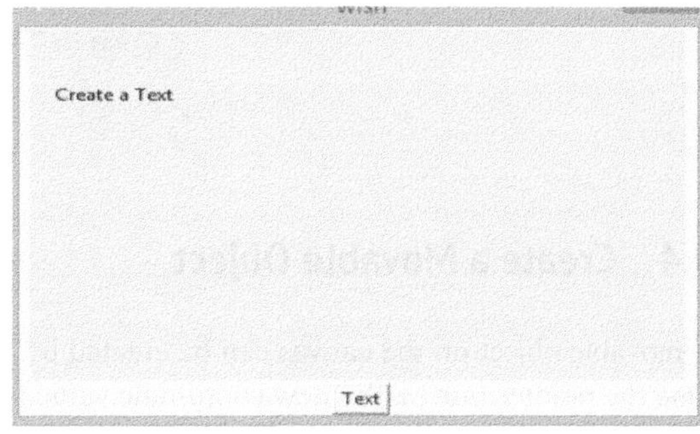

Figure 9.18 Bounded text widget.

Example 9.9 Write a Tcl script to create a canvas and a button which is bonded with text. Text objects are placed in different locations on each action of the mouse.

Solution

In Example 9.8, the coordinate position has been specified by a `set` command to a static value. Its value can dynamically be updated in the following example. A built-in Tcl command `global` declares a global variable inside the procedure in the current namespace, unless a variable by the same name exists in the global namespace, in which case it refers to that variable presented in Figure 9.19. The `incr` command increments the (x, y) coordinate value and creates each object at the updated value.

```
proc paintext {w name} {
     global x 50
     global y 50
    incr x 25
    incr y 25
     $w create text $x $y -text $name
     }
canvas .c -bg yellow
pack .c
button  .b1 -text "Text"  -command {paintext .c "Create a Text"}
pack .b1
```

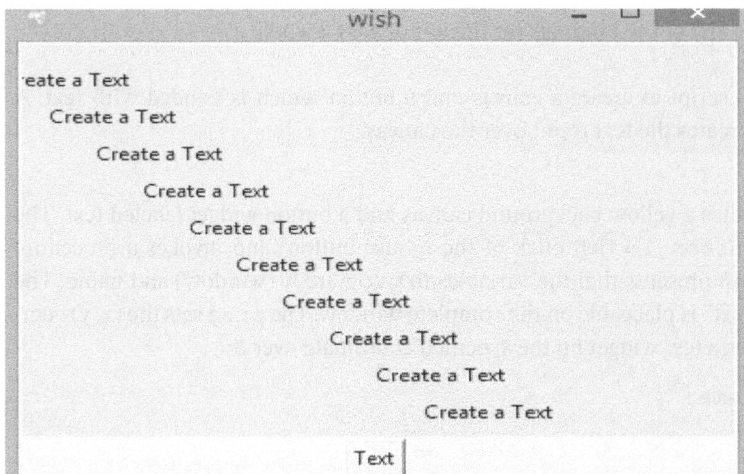

Figure 9.19 Bounded text widget at different locations on the canvas.

9.4 Create a Movable Object

A movable object on the canvas can be created by binding the object with `<B1-Motion>`. Each time the pointer moves, the new coordinate value is updated dynamically with the `cords` operation. The value of x and y is replaced with the pointer's x-coordinate and y-coordinate, respectively. The canvas's object behavior is modeled with a movable tag, where pathname (%w) is passed to the procedures `move` or `drag`. Here, %x and %y is substituted with the (x,y) coordinate of `the event.`

Syntax for binding:

```
.canvasname bind $object <Event> {procname $object  %x %y}
```

Example 9.10 Write a script to create an oval on the canvas and bind it with a mouse action. Create the oval to be movable with the mouse pointer.

Solution

In this example, a white oval has been created over a black canvas screen. The `set` command defines the oval as a variable which is bonded with `< B1-Motion>` and its pointer position is passed to the procedure `moveit`. The `proc` dynamically updates the coordinate value for the oval on a canvas and makes it movable with the mouse pointer (see Figure 9.20).

```
proc moveit {object x y} {
.c coord $object [expr $x - 10]
[expr $y -25] [expr $x +25 ] [expr
$y + 25]
}
canvas .c -width 200 -height 200 -
bg black
pack .c
set oval [.c create oval 10 10 100
100 -fill white]
.c bind $oval <B1-Motion> {moveit
$oval %x %y}
```

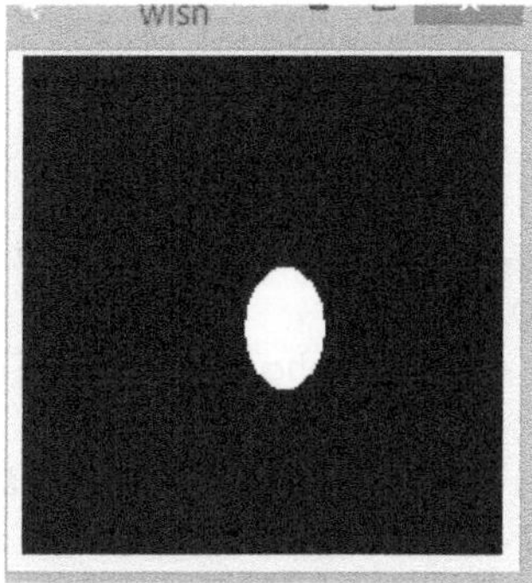

Figure 9.20 Movable oval on the canvas

Example 9.11 Write a Tcl script to create an oval and line on the canvas and bind it with a mouse action and make them movable with the mouse pointer (see Figure 9.21).

Solution

```
proc moveit {object x y} {
   .c coords $object [expr $x-25]
[expr $y-25] [expr $x+25] [expr
$y+25]
}
canvas .c -width 250 -height 100
set myoval [.c create oval 0 0 50
50 -fill orange]
set myline [.c create line 50 50
100 100 -fill blue -width 4]
.c bind $myoval <B1-Motion>
{moveit $myoval %x %y}
.c bind $myline <B1-Motion>
{moveit $myline %x %y}
grid .c -row 0 -column 0
```

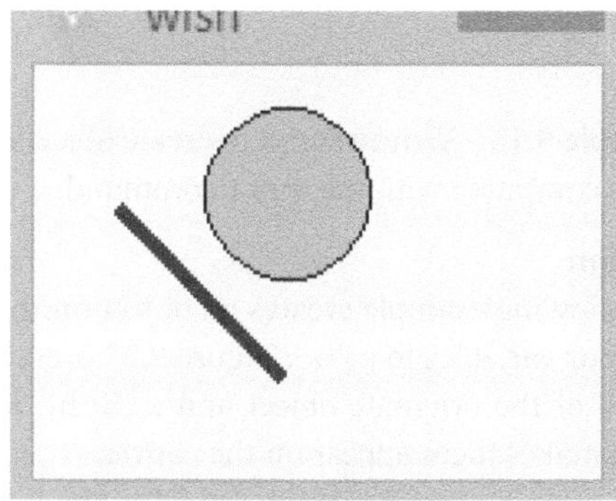

Figure 9.21 Movable oval and line on the canvas.

Example 9.12 Write a Tcl script to create two different images on the canvas and make them moveable with the action of the mouse.

Solution

The following example reads two images “and.png” and “or.png” from the directory with the `photo` command. Creation and dimension of the image on the canvas is associated to variables `and` and `or`. Figure 9.22 shows the images are bounded with `<B1-Motion>` and invoke `proc moveit` when selected by the mouse. The movement of the cursor updates the coordinate value (%x,%y). Command `coords` dynamically updates the coordinate value and makes it movable.

```
proc moveit {object x y} {
.c coord $object [expr $x - 10]
[expr $y -25]
}
image create photo and -file
"and.png"
image create photo or -file
"or.png"
canvas .c -height 500 -width
500 -bg red
set and [.c create image 50 50
-image and]
set or [.c create image 50 120
-image or]
pack .c
.c bind $and <B1-Motion> {moveit
$and %x %y}
.c bind $or <B1-Motion> {moveit
$or %x %y}
```

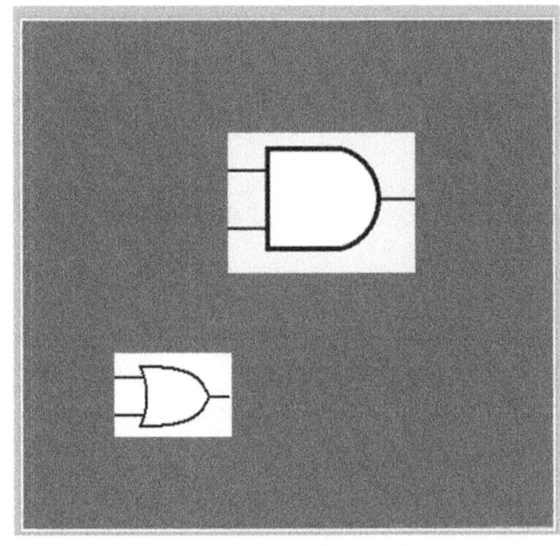

Figure 9.22 Movable image on the canvas.

Example 9.13 Write a script to create objects rectangle and oval on the canvas, while the coordinate is computed with the `eval` command.

Solution

The following example creates an object on the canvas, the `eval` command triggers a procedure with four variables to `proc`. Figure 9.23 presents `centerX centerY`, which provides the coordinates of the originate object and `width, height` calculate the actual coordinate values and return makes them appear on the canvas.

```
canvas .myCanvas
pack .myCanvas
proc CenteredRectangle {centerX
centerY width height} {
return [list [expr $centerX -
$width] \
[expr $centerY - $height] \
[expr $centerX + $width] \
[expr $centerY + $height]]
}
eval .myCanvas create rectangle
[CenteredRectangle 150 100 10 75]
eval .myCanvas create rectangle
[CenteredRectangle 80 80 75 10]
eval .myCanvas create oval
[CenteredRectangle 140 110 75 50]
```

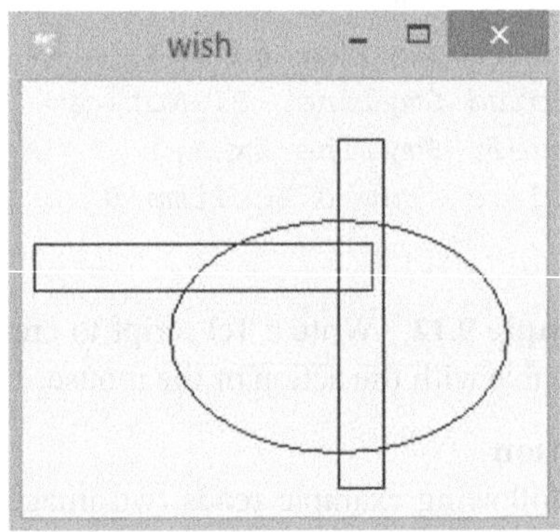

Figure 9.23 Object on the canvas via `eval` command.

9.5 Tk built-in Command

The Tk command provides access to Tk's internal component objects. Most of the information used by this command relates to the entire system, screen, or display, rather than to a specific window. The Tk in-built commands are listed in Appendix 9.A.

9.5.1 Tk_choose Color

`Tk_chooseColor` is an in-built Tk command that invokes a procedure to create a pop-up window to choose the color.

Syntax: `tk_chooseColor option`

The following are options along with command line arguments.

`-initialcolor color`	Specifies the color to display in the pop-up
`-parent window`	Makes a window to the logical parent of the color dialog
`-title titlestring`	Specifies a string to display as the title of the dialog box

Example 9.14 Write a Tcl script to create a GUI of button and label, where an event on button invokes a window to choose the color and change the label's color.

Solution
The following script creates a button "Choose a Color" and label "Change my color" event on the button to execute a command (procedure) `onSelect` on the selected widget (label). Configuration command with `[tk_chooseColor]` provides a pop-up window to select color, and choose the background and foreground colors for the label. The user selects a button pop-up window to choose the color; the first pop-up for background color and the second pop-up for foreground color of the label (Figures 9.24–9.27).

```
button .b -text "Choose a
color" -command "onSelect .l"
place .b -x 20 -y 30
label .l -text "Change my
color"
place .l -x 20 -y 90
proc onSelect {widget} {
    $widget configure -bg
[tk_chooseColor]
    $widget configure -fg
[tk_chooseColor]
}
```

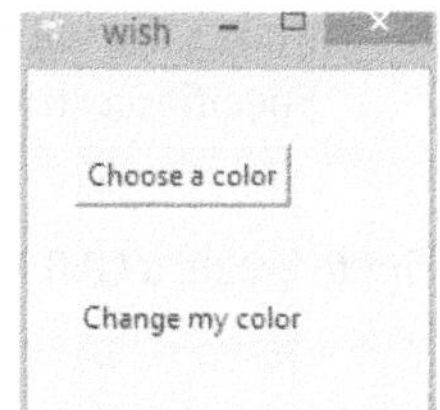

Figure 9.24 GUI before event.

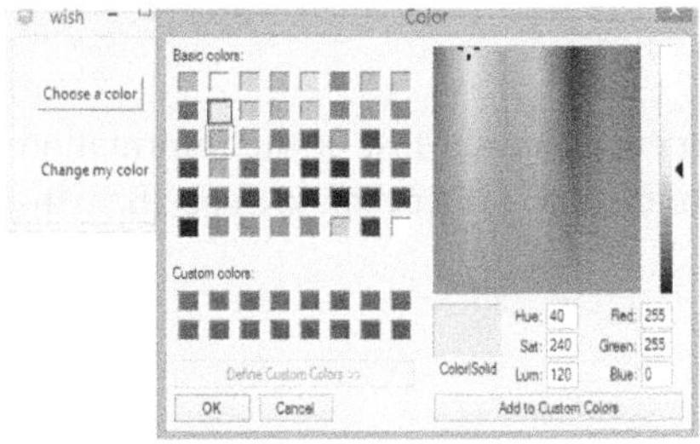

Figure 9.25 GUI during first event.

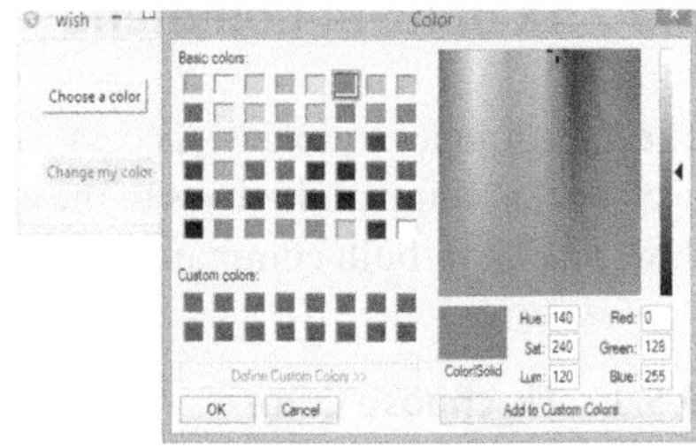

Figure 9.26 GUI during second event.

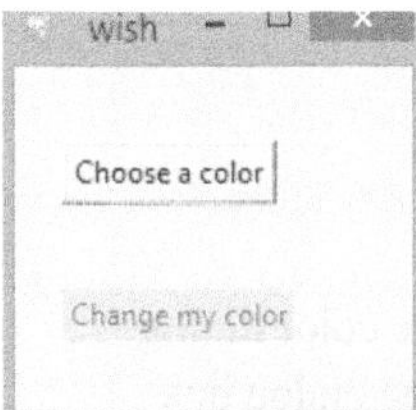

Figure 9.27 GUI after both events.

9.5.2 tk_chooseDirectory

`tk_chooseDirectory` provides a pop-up window to select a file from the directory.

Syntax: `tk_chooseDirectory option`

The following are options along with command line arguments.

`-command string`	Specifies a prefix of the Tcl command when a user closes the dialog
`-initialdir dirname`	Specifies the directory when the dialog pops up
`-message string`	Specifies the message to include for the client
`-mustexist boolean`	One-user may select the existing directory
`-parent window`	Makes the window the logical parent
`-title titelstring`	Specifies a string to display the title of the dialog box

Example 9.15 Write a Tcl script to create a GUI to pop up a dialog box that can select a directory when the event is on a button.

Solution

This example creates an interface consisting of a button and label, An event on the button pops up a dialog box to select a directory. Upon selecting, the text of label changes due to `config` (Figures 9.28–9.30).

```
label .l -text "Select a Directory"
button .b -text "Choose a directory" -command "onSelect .l"
pack .b .l -side left -anchor nw
proc onSelect {widget} {
    set dir [tk_chooseDirectory]
    .l config -text "Directory Selected"
}
```

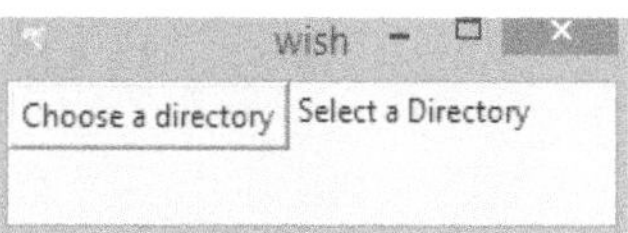

Figure 9.28 Before event.

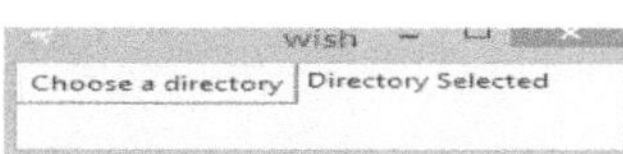

Figure 9.30 After event.

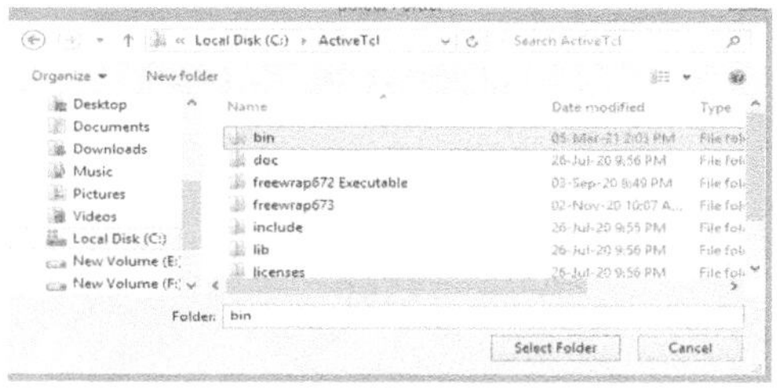

Figure 9.29 Pop-up dialog box.

9.5.3 tk_getOpenFile / tk_getSaveFile

These commands open a dialog box to choose a file to open or save. These commands are associated with the file menu. `tk_getOpenFile` enables users to create an application to select an existing file and `tk_getSaveFile` enables the user to confirm whether the existing file should be overwritten.

Syntax:
```
tk_getOpenFile option
tk_getSaveFile option
```

The following are options along with the command line arguments.

`-command string`	Specifies the prefix of the Tcl command when the user closes the dialog
`-confirmoverwrite boolean`	Reaction of save when the file already exists
`-filetypes filepatternList`	Filetypes listbox exists in the file dialog
`-initialdir directory`	Specifies the file in a directory when dialog pops up
`-initialfile filetype`	Specifies the filename to be displayed when pop up
`-message stringname`	Specifies the message to include in the client area of the dialog
`-multiple boolean`	Allows the user to choose multiple files
`-parent window`	Makes the window the logical parent
`-title titlestring`	Specifies a string to display as the title
`-typevariable variablename`	Global variable to present which filter to use

Example 9.16 Write a Tcl script to create an interface to select a file from a directory upon an event on a button.

Solution

In this example, the interface comprises a button and label. An event on the button pops up a dialog box to prompt the user to select a file from the directory from the list of different types of files. When the user selects the button, it executes command `doit` applied on the label, containing global variable types which list the file to display in the listbox and pops up a window to select the file. The selected file path configures the text on the label (Figures 9.31 and 9.32).

```
set types {
        {"All Source Files"
{.tcl .c .h}}
        {"Image Files"
{.gif}}
        {"All files"
*}
}
proc doIt {label} {
    global types
    set file [tk_getOpenFile -
filetypes $types]
    $label configure -text
$file
}
label .l -text "No File"
button .b -text "Select a
file?" -command {doIt .l}
grid .b -row 0 -column 0
grid .l -row 0 -column 1
```

Figure 9.31 Before event.

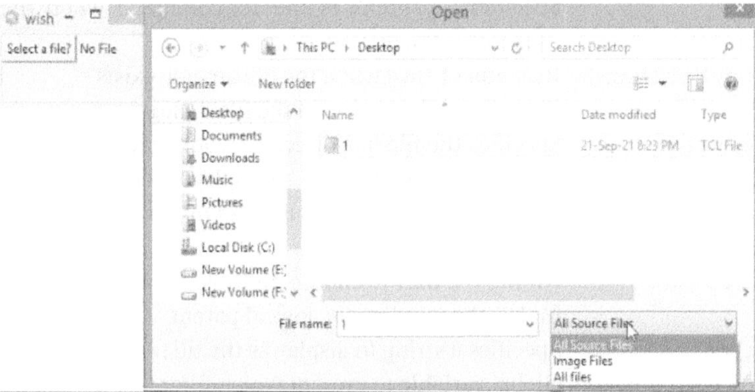

Figure 9.32 Pop-up dialog box to select the file.

9.5.4 tk_messageBox

`tk_messageBox` pops up a message window and waits for the user response. It creates and displays a message window with a specific message and set of buttons (`-type`). Each button has a unique name waiting for the user response and executes the associate command.

Option	Description
`-command string`	Specifies prefix of the Tcl command when user closes dialog box
`-default name`	Symbolic name of the default button
`-icon iconImage`	Specifies an icon to display (bitmap image)
`-message string`	Specifies the message to display in the message box
`-type predefinedType`	Arranges a predefined set of buttons to be displayed

Example 9.17 Write a script to create the interface, which pops up a message box containing two buttons and commands for each button.

Solution

The following example pops up a message box asking "Really quit" and provides two options buttons "Yes" and "No" and waits for a response. There are different commands associated with each button. When the user selects "No," a new window pop-up contains the message "I know you like this application!" and "Yes" exits from the tool (Figures 9.33 and 9.34).

```
set answer [tk_messageBox -message "Really quit?" -type yesno ]
case $answer {
    yes exit
    no {tk_messageBox -message "I know you like this
application!"}
 }
```

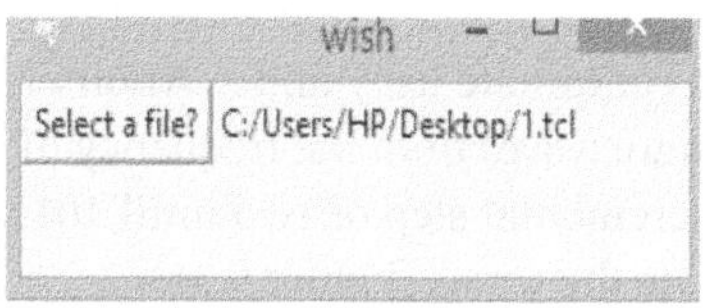

Figure 9.33 After event.

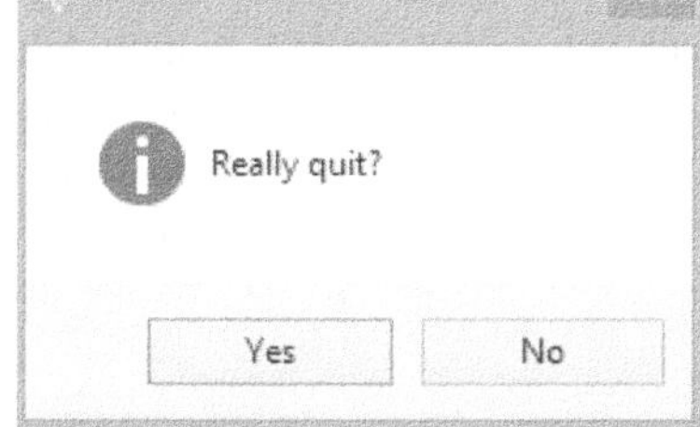

Figure 9.34 Message box before response.

9.6 Solved Problems

[1] Write a Tcl script to create a sine wave on the canvas.

Solution

In Tcl-Tk, a periodic signal is generated using a Fourier series containing sine and cosine functions at harmonic frequencies.

$$F(t) = \sin(t) + \sin(3t)/3 + \sin(5t)/5 + \sin(7t)/7 + \sin(9t)/9 + \ldots$$

$$= \Sigma \sin(nt)/n \text{ (n odd, } 0 < n < \infty).$$

Let the period be 25 ns, then the fundamental frequency $f = 1/(2*\pi*25)$.

```
canvas .sinewave -bg black -width 450 -height 100
pack .sinewave
set coordList {}
for {set x 0} {$x<=450} {incr x} {
lappend coordList $x [expr sin($x/25.0)*50 + 50]
}
eval .sinewave create line $coordList -fill green
```

Create a canvas of height 100 and width 450. For the loop append, the list of coordinates begins from 0 and executes the sin function until 450. Purposefully, the sine function is multiplied by 50 to amplify and then 50 is added to bring the result into the vertical range (Figure 9.35).

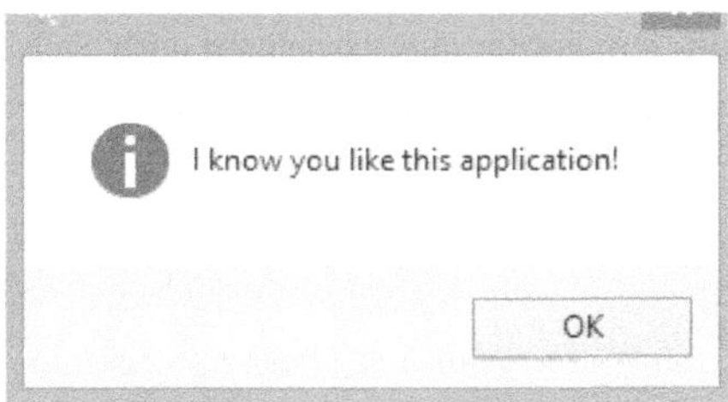

Figure 9.35 Message box after selecting No.

[2] Write a Tcl script to create a square wave on the canvas.

Solution
Create a canvas of height 100 and width 450. The square wave is mapped over a sine wave of frequency 1/(2*π*25). For each value of x, the `for` loop updates the coordinate list y and z. Another `for` loop is used until the *n*th harmonic 101 (creates a perfect square wave) from the frequency of the sine wave. Here, z is updated for the vertical axis with an incremental step of two until 101, then the same process is performed on the horizontal axis to update the y-axis (Figure 9.36).

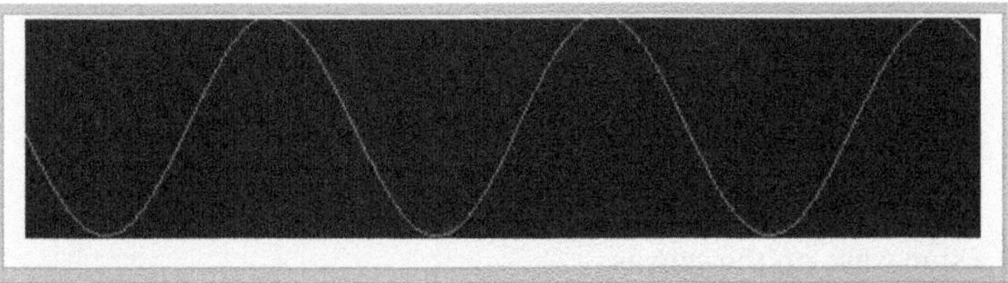

Figure 9.36 Sine wave.

```
canvas .squarewave -bg black -width 450 -height 100
pack .squarewave
set coordList {}
for {set x 0} {$x<=450} {incr x} {
set y 0
set z 0
for {set N 1} {$N<=101} {set N [expr {$N + 2}]} {
set z [expr sin($x*$N/25.0)/$N* 50]
set y [expr $y + $z]
}
lappend coordList $x [expr $y+50]
}
eval .squarewave create line $coordList -fill green
```

[3] Create a symbolic library containing components with the drag and drop feature.

Solution

The following Tcl script creates a symbolic library of canvas widgets, as shown in Figure 9.37. The developed GUI is partitioned into three regions: (i) workspace to draw; (ii) control button on the bottom ribbon; and (iii) left ribbon for the library. Button selection enables the library, a widget is bonded with `<Button-1>` with the drag and drop feature, and a clear button removes all widgets.

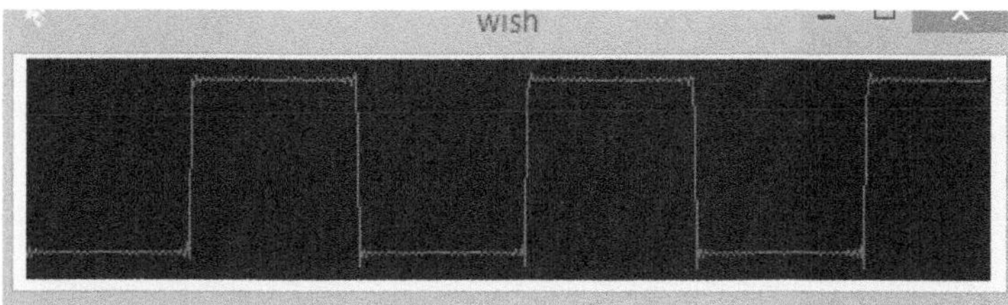

Figure 9.37 Square wave.

```
canvas .c1 -width 460 -height 350 -bg white -relief groove -
borderwidth 4
grid .c1 -row 1 -column 1 -columnspan 2
frame .f1
button .f1.b1 -text "Selection Board" -command {
.c1 create line 55 0 55 350 -width 1
.c1 create rect 10 10 30 30 -fill red -tag movable
.c1 create poly 30 10 30 30 50 30 -fill black -tag movable -outline
black
.c1 create poly 30 10 50 10 50 30 -fill green -tag movable -outline
black
.c1 create rect 10 30 30 50 -fill green -tag movable
.c1 create poly 30 30 30 50 50 30 -fill blue -tag movable -outline
black
.c1 create poly 50 30 30 50 50 50 -fill yellow -tag movable -outline
black
.f1.b1 configure -state disabled
}
button .f1.b2 -text "Clear All" -command {
.c1 delete all
.f1.b1 configure -state normal
}
pack .f1.b1 -side left
pack .f1.b2 -side left
grid .f1 -row 2 -column 1
proc CanvasMarkIt { x y can } {
global canvas
$can raise current
set x [$can canvasx $x]
set y [$can canvasy $y]
```

```
set canvas($can,obj) [ $can find closest $x $y ]
set canvas($can,x) $x
set canvas($can,y) $y
}
proc CanvasDragIt {x y can} {
global canvas
set x [$can canvasx $x]
set y [$can canvasy $y]
set dx [expr $x - $canvas($can,x)]
set dy [expr $y - $canvas($can,y)]
$can move $canvas($can,obj) $dx $dy
set canvas($can,x) $x
set canvas($can,y) $y
}
.c1 bind movable <Button-1> {CanvasMarkIt %x %y %W}
.c1 bind movable <B1-Motion> {CanvasDragIt %x %y %W}
```

[4] Write a Tcl script to create an object on the canvas bonded with a button.

Solution

The following script develops a GUI with five functions bound with buttons on the bottom ribbon. An event on the button makes a particular function appear, as described in Figures 9.38 and 9.39.

```
proc ClrCanvas {w} {
    $w delete "all"
}
proc DrawAxis {w} {
    set midX [expr {
$::maxX / 2 }]
    set midY [expr {
$::maxY / 2 }]
    $w create line 0      $midY
$::maxX   $midY  -tags "axis"
    $w create line $midX 0
$midX $::maxY  -tags "axis"
}
proc PaintText {w Txt} {
    global y
    incr y 10
    $w create text 20 $y -text
$Txt -tags "text"
}
```

```
proc DrawFn2 {w} {
    set offY 0     ;# [expr {
$::maxY / 2 }]
    for { set x 0 } { $x <=
$::maxX } { incr x 5 } {
      set y [expr { rand() *
$::maxY + $offY }]
     #puts "$x $y"
      if {$x>0} { $w create line
$x0 $y0 $x $y -tags "Fn2" }
      set x0 $x
      set y0 $y
    }
}
```

```
proc DrawBox {w} {
    global x1 y1 x2 y2
    $w create rect  50  10  100
60  -tags "box"
    $w create rect $x1 $y1  $x2
$y2  -tags "box"
    incr x1 15
    incr x2 15
    incr y1 10
    incr y2 10
}
proc DrawFn1 {w} {
    $w create line 0 100  50 200
100 50  150 70  200 155  250 50
300 111  350 222
            -tags "Fn1"
-smooth bezier
}
```

```
#: Main :
frame .f1
frame .f2
pack  .f1 .f2

set maxX 320
set maxY 240
set y      0

set x1 120
set x2 150
set y1  50
set y2  80

canvas  .cv -width $maxX -height
$maxY  -bg white
pack    .cv -in .f1

button  .b0 -text "Clear"
-command { ClrCanvas .cv }
button  .b1 -text "Text"
-command { PaintText .cv
"Canvas" }
button  .b2 -text "Axis"
-command { DrawAxis  .cv }
button  .b3 -text "Box"
-command { DrawBox   .cv }
button  .b4 -text "Fn1"
-command { DrawFn1   .cv }
button  .b5 -text "Fn2"
-command { DrawFn2   .cv }
pack .b0 .b1 .b2 .b3 .b4 .b5
-in .f2  -side left -padx 2
```

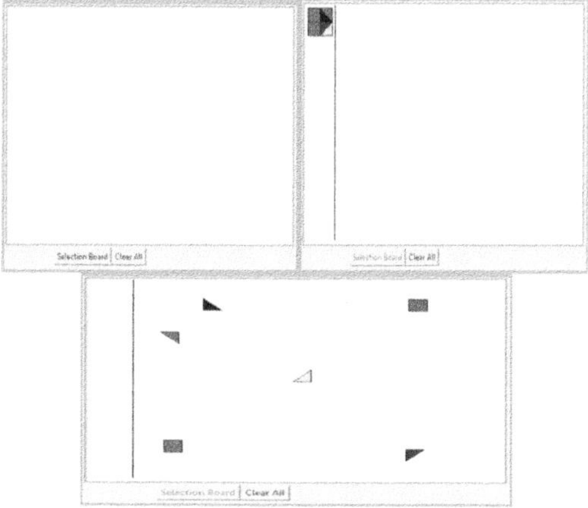

Figure 9.38 Symbolic library interface.

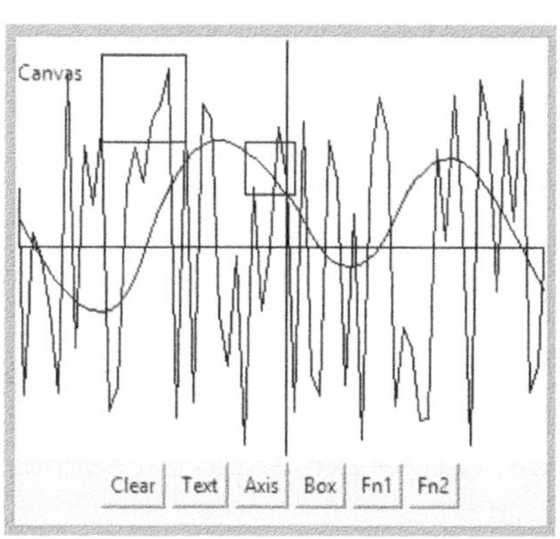

Figure 9.39 Function on the canvas.

[5] Write a Tcl script to create a progress bar.

Solution

The following example creates an interface comprising a progressbar oriented horizontal (with a maximum value of 100), variable `a`, and a button (Figure 9.40). Event on button start counter (Figure 9.41) invokes a `proc Counter`; runs a `for` loop to display 0 to 100 after 25 ns and updates the variable to the progressbar (Figure 9.42).

Figure 9.40 Canvas clear function.

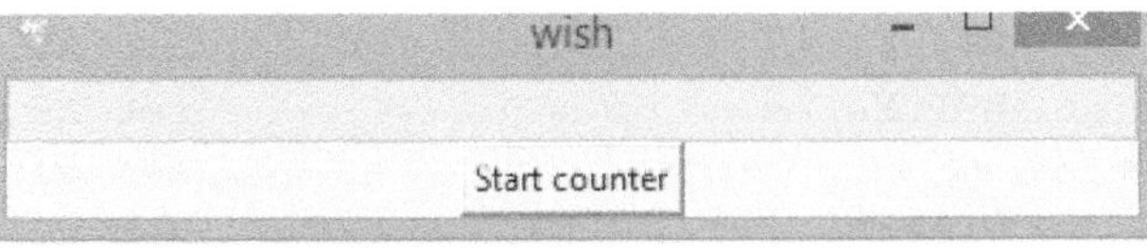

Figure 9.41 Progressbar before event.

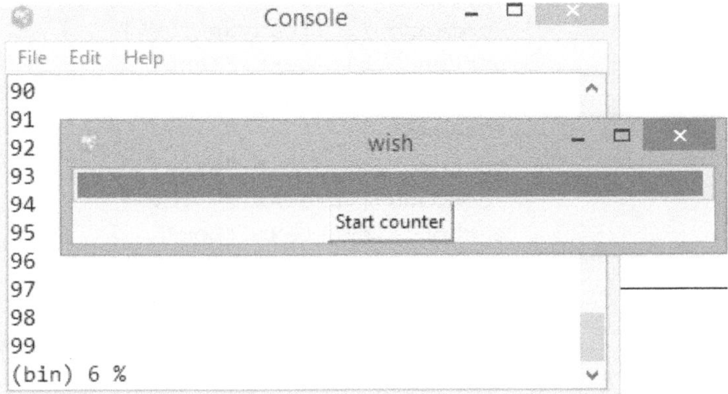

Figure 9.42 Progressbar after event.

```
proc Counter {} {
  for {set i 0} {$i < 100} {incr i} {
    puts "$i"
    after 25
    .pb configure -value $i
    update idletask
  }
}
ttk::progressbar .pb -orient horizontal -maximum 100 -length 400
-value 0 -variable a
button .bt -text "Start counter" -command Counter
pack .pb
pack .bt
```

9.7 Review Problem

Write a script to create a line over the canvas and bind it with a mouse action. Make the line movable with the mouse pointer.

9.8 MCQs of Canvas

[1] `padx n1` and `-pady n2` are used for __________ separation between two widgets

A Internal
B External
C Internal and external
D No

[Solution (c)]

[2] What is the `create` command of the canvas used for?

A Change configuration of canvas
B Manipulate the canvas
C To add a drawing object on the canvas
D None of the above

[Solution (c)]

[3] What does the canvas bitmap create?

A Image graphics
B Icon
C Symbolic name with an icon

[Solution (c)]

[4] What will the following script generate?

```
canvas .c
pack .c
.c create bitmap 10 10 -bitmap info
```

A

B

C

D

[Solution (c)]

[5] What does the canvas `closeenough` attribute measure?

A Distance from mouse to an underlapping object
B Distance from mouse to an overlapping object
C Distance from boundary to an overlapping object
D Distance from boundary to an underlapping object

[Solution (b)]

[6] What is the statement the `bind` command allows commands to be bound to widgets?

A True
B False

[Solution (a)]

[7] The `canvas` command creates a ____________ on which a canvas widget is placed.

A Frame
B Window
C Coordinate
D Box

[Solution (b)]

[8] What are the `xview` and `yview` canvas widget commands used for?

A Scaling
B 3D view
C Scrolling
D Rotation

[Solution (c)]

[9] Select the true statement(s) associated with widget programming.

A Creates an instance of the widget
B Specifies behavior
C Tells the geometry manager to make the widget appear
D All of the above

[Solution (d)]

[10] What will the `button .b` -command exit do?

A Bind a mouse left buttonpress with button
B Bind a mouse left buttonrelease with button
C Bind a mouse right buttonpress with button
D Bind a mouse right buttonrelease with button

[Solution (a)]

9.A Appendix A

Table A.1 Tk in-built command.

Tk command	Description
bell	Rings a display's bell
bind	Arranges for X events to invoke Tcl scripts
bindtag	Determines which bindings apply to a window, and order of evaluation
bitmap	Images display with two colors
button	Creates and manipulates "button" action widgets
busy	Confines pointer-events to a window sub-tree
canvas	Creates and manipulates the drawing surface area
checkbutton	Creates and manipulates "checkbutton" Boolean selection widgets
clipboard	Manipulates Tk clipboard
colors	Symbolizes color names recognized by Tk
console	Controls the console on systems without a real console
cursor	Mouse cursors available in Tk
destroy	Destroys one or more windows
entry	Creates and manipulates "entry" one-line text entry widget
event	Defines and generates an event
focus	Manages the input focus
font	Creates and inspects fonts
fontchooser	Controls font selection dialog
frame	Creates and manipulates frame container widgets
geometry	Variables used or set by Tk
grab	Confines pointer and keyboard events to a window sub-tree
grid	Geometry manager that arranges widgets in a grid
image	Creates and manipulates images
keysyms	Keysyms recognized by Tk
label	Creates and manipulates "label" non-interactive text widget
labelframe	Creates and manipulates labeled container widgets
listbox	Creates and manipulates "listbox" item list widgets
lower	Changes a window's position in the stacking order
menu	Creates and manipulates menu widgets and menubars
menubutton	Creates and manipulates menubutton pop-up menu indicator widgets
message	Creates and manipulates "message" non-interactive text widgets
option	Adds/retrieves window options to/from the option database
options	Standard options supported by widgets
pack	Geometry manager that packs around edges of the cavity

(Continued)

Table A.1 (Continued)

Tk command	Description
panedwindow	Creates and manipulates paned window split container widgets
photo	Full-color images
place	Geometry manager for fixed placement
radiobutton	Creates and manipulates radio button pick-one widgets
raise	Changes a window's position in the stacking order
safe::loaftk	Loads Tk into a safe interpreter
scale	Creates and manipulates scale value-controlled slider widgets
scrollbar	Creates and manipulates scrollbar scrolling control and indicator widgets
selection	Manipulates the X selection
send	Executes a command in a different application
spinbox	Creates and manipulates "spinbox" value spinner widgets
text	Creates and manipulates text editing widgets
tk	Manipulates Tk internal state
tk::mac	Accesses Mac-specific functionality on OS X from Tk
tk_bisque	Modifies the Tk color palette
tk_choosecolor	Pops up a dialog box for the user to select a color
tk_choosedirectory	Pops up a dialog box for the user to select a directory
tk_dialog	Creates modal dialog and waits for the response
tk_focusnext	Utility procedures for managing the input focus
tk_focusprev	Utility procedures for managing the input focus
tk_getopenfile	Pops up a dialog box for the user to select a file to open or save
tk_getsavefile	Pops up a dialog box for the user to select a file to open or save
tk_library	Variables used or set by Tk
tk_menusetfocus	Creates and manipulates "menu" widgets and menubars
tk_messagebox	Pops up a message window and waits for the user response
tk_optionmenu	Creates an option menubutton and its menu
tk_patchlevel	Variables used or set by Tk
tk_popup	Posts a pop-up menu
tk_setpalette	Modifies the Tk color palette
tk_strictmotif	Variables used or set by Tk
tk_textcopy	Creates and manipulates "text" hypertext editing widgets
tk_textcut	Creates and manipulates "text" hypertext editing widgets
tk_textpaste	Creates and manipulates "text" hypertext editing widgets
tk_version	Variables used or set by Tk
tkerror	Command invoked to process background errors
tkwait	Waits for the variable to change or window to be destroyed
toplevel	Creates and manipulates "toplevel" main and pop-up window widgets

(Continued)

Table A.1 (Continued)

Tk command	Description
ttk::buton	Widget that issues a command when pressed
tk::combobox	Text field with dropdown selection list
ttk::entry	Editable text field widget
ttk::frame	Simple container widget
ttk::intro	Introduction to the Tk theme engine
ttk::label	Displays a text string and/or image
ttk::labelframe	Container widget with optional label
ttk::menubutton	A widget that drops down a menu when pressed
ttk::notebook	Multi-paned container widget
ttk::panewindow	Multi-paned container window
ttk::progressbar	Provides progress feedback
ttk::radiobutton	Mutually exclusive option widget
ttk::scale	Creates and manipulates a scale widget
ttk::scrollbar	Controls the viewport of a scrollable widget
ttk::separator	Separator bar
ttk::sizegrip	Bottom-right corner resizes the widget
ttk::spinbox	Selecting text field window
ttk::style	Manipulates style database
ttk::treeview	Hierarchical multicolumn data display widget
ttk::widget	Standard options and commands supported by Tk themed widgets
ttk image	Defines an element based on an image
ttk vsapi	Defines a Microsoft Visual Styles element
winfo	Returns window-related information
wm	Communicates with the window manager

References

1 https://www.tcl.tk/man/tcl/TkCmd/contents.html
2 http://fpgaforum.blogspot.com/2006/02/building-square-wave-from-fourier_21.html
3 Welch, B.B., Jones, K., and Hobbs, J. (2003). *Practical Programming in Tcl/Tk*. Prentice Hall Professional.
4 https://www.tutorialspoint.com/tcl-tk

10

Tcl-Tk for EDA Tool

The Tcl/Tk scripting language has become the de-facto standard for electronic design automation (EDA) tools and computer-aided design (CAD) tool application. Users can interact with the tool via a graphical interface and scripting interface. Tcl is an extension language for EDA created by John Ousterhout in the late 1980s. Along with ASIC industries like Synopsis, Cadence, Mentor, Xilinx's product range encompasses synthesis, verification, report analysis, floorplanning, static timing analysis, place, route, etc. The synopsis suggests the use of Tcl as primary scripting for the EDA interface. Model Technologies uses Tcl/Tk in its most popular tool ModelSim.

Scripting offers a feature to automate the repetitive function and extend the basic function of the application. A tool designer relies on multiple vendors for tool development. It is cumbersome to integrate components developed with different platforms, while blocks developed in the Tcl environment make the design easier. A single common mode language means the designer need only be an expert in Tcl to automate the multiple blocks of the tool.

Xilinx has adopted Tcl as the native programming language for the Vivado design suite [1]. The Tcl interpreter in the Vivado provides the full power and flexibility of Tcl to control the application, and access the design object and properties. Vivado is an EDA tool developed by Xilinx that can be controlled using a Tcl script [2]. There is an in-built command in Tcl to read and write files to a local directory and create a directory dynamically, create a project, add files to the project, then synthesize, implement and generate a report. Tcl command and script are specified to the Vivado design suite. Design constraint files for the Vivado IDE are specified similarly to the Tcl command and are interpreted similarly by the Tcl interpreter [3].

The Vivado tool writes a journal file with extension .jou into the directory from where the tool has been launched. It records the Tcl command run during the session. A log file .log is also created which includes the output of the commands that are executed. Journal and log files verify which commands to run and what results they produced.

10.1 Accessing Vivado Tool via Tcl Script

Figure 10.1 presents the home page of the Vivado design suite; at the bottom, the Tcl Console enables the users to enter the Tcl command. Users can get help directly from the Tcl Console, and every command supports the `-help` command-line argument. The `-help` command provides additional information about the command, syntax, and examples.

```
<command> -help
```

Programming and GUI Fundamentals: Tcl-Tk for Electronic Design Automation (EDA), First Edition.
Suman Lata Tripathi, Abhishek Kumar, and Jyotirmoy Pathak.

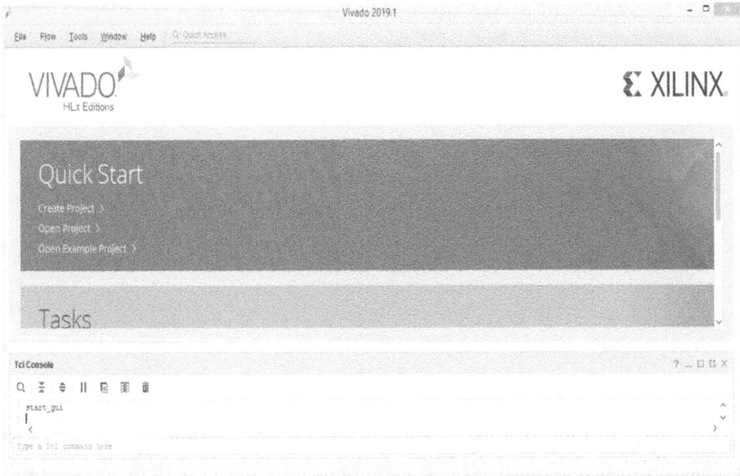

Figure 10.1 Homepage of Vivado Design Suite.

The commands in Table 10.1 are useful while accessing the Vivado tool via Tcl commands (description given in the Appendix).

- **Step 1:** Enter the following command in the Tcl Console to create project FA1 in directory Example, the `-part` adds the FPGA device Artix –7 and the project part xc7a15tcpg236–1, as shown in Figure 10.2.

```
create_project FA -force C:/Xilinx/Example -part xc7a15tcpg236-1
```

Table 10.1 Command to access Vivado Tool.

Command	Property
`create_project`	Creates a new project
`current_project`	Specifies current project
`save_project_as`	Saves the project into the specified directory
`add_files`	Adds Verilog file (.v) into the project
`add_files -fileset constrs`	Adds constraints file (.xdc)
`set_property top`	Defines top module
`launch_simulation`	Simulates design and generates a waveform
`launch_runs`	Synthesizes the active design
`launch_runs`	Implements the active design
`place_design`	Automatically places ports and leaf-level instance
`route_design`	Routes the active design
`phys_opt_desgn`	Optimizes the active design
`close_project`	Closes currently opened project

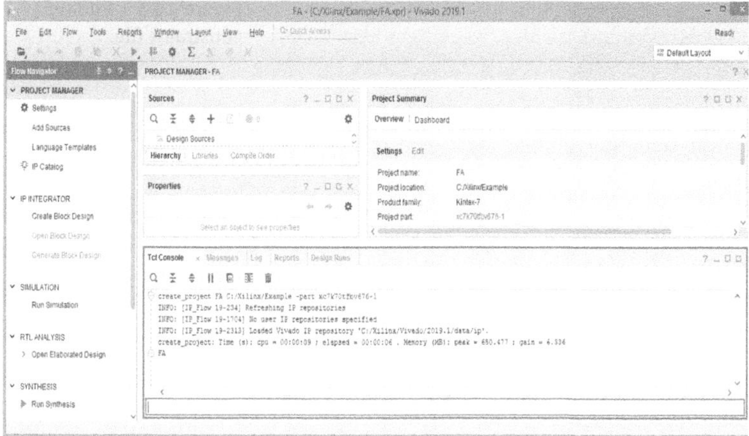

Figure 10.2 Vivado interface after creating project.

- **Step 2:** Create a Verilog file (FA.v) and constraint file (FA_xdc.xdc) physically in the specified directory. Add the following command to add the source file. Double click on the file name to open the source file, as shown in Figures 10.3–10.5.

```
add_files C:/Xilinx/Example/FA.v
add_files C:/Xilinx/Example/FAtb.v
add_files -fileset constrs_1 -norecurse
C:/Xilinx/Example/FA_xdc.xdc
```

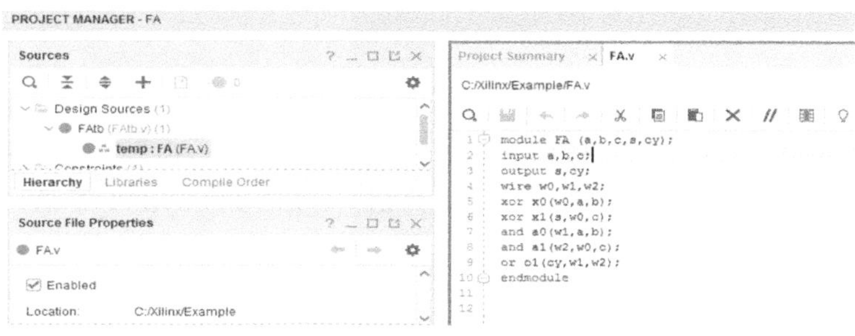

Figure 10.3 Adding FA module.

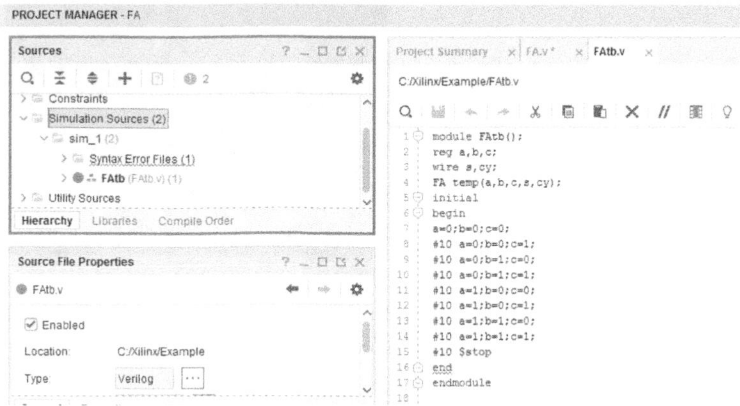

Figure 10.4 Adding stimulus file.

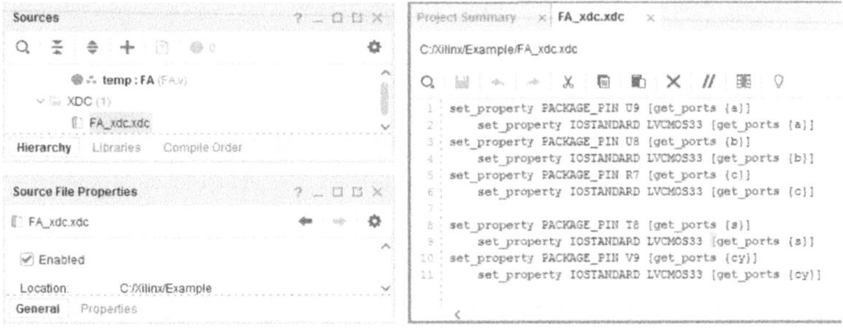

Figure 10.5 Adding constraint file.

- **Step 3:** Save project.

```
save_project_as FA C:/Xilinx/Example
```

- **Step 4:** Update the compile order. The following command sets the top-level module.

```
set_property top FA [current_fileset]
```

- **Step 5:** Synthesize the design via entering the Tcl command, as shown in Figure 10.6.

```
launch_runs synth_1
```

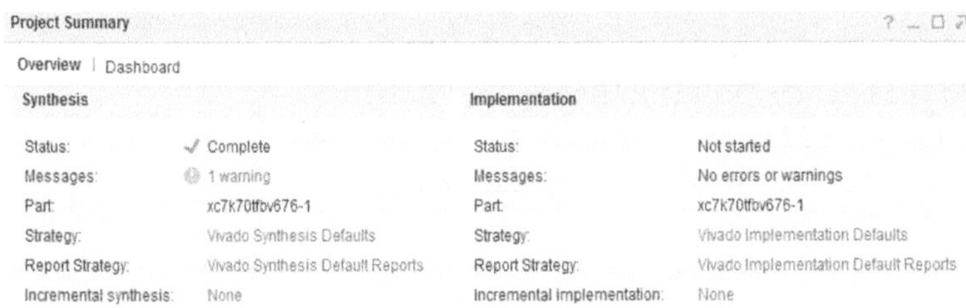

Figure 10.6 Synthesize project summary.

- **Step 6:** `Open_run` displays the devices and packages, as shown in Figure 10.7.

```
open_run -name FA synth_1
```

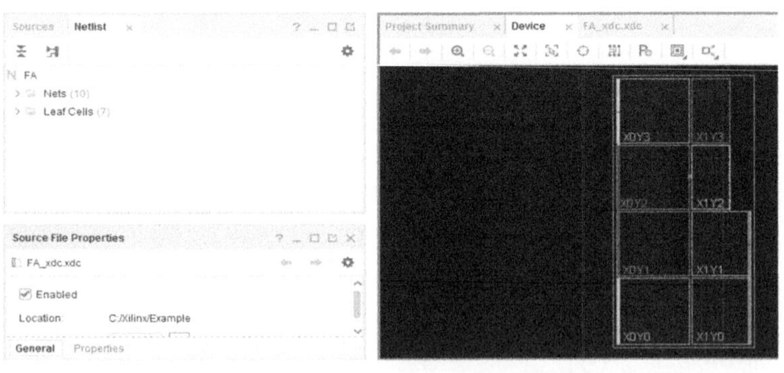

Figure 10.7 FPGA package view.

- **Step 7:** Simulation of the stimulus program executed via the Tcl command. A testbench waveform is shown in Figure 10.8 created with a delay specified in the program.

```
launch_simulation
```

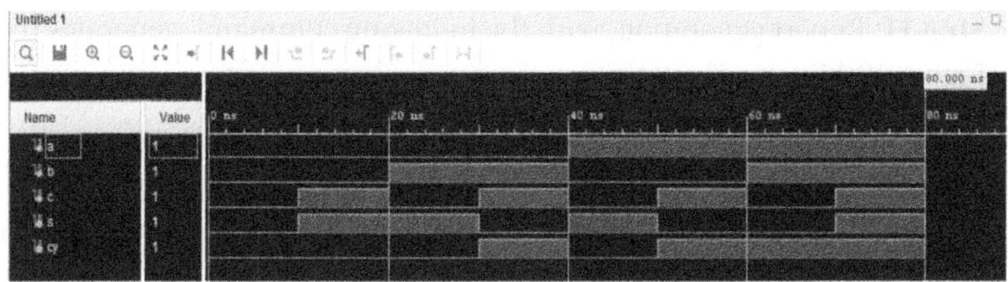

Figure 10.8 Testbench waveform.

- **Step 8:** Implementation step executed via Tcl command.

```
launch_runs impl_1
```

- **Step 9:** Report generation, with the following command, generates the power report shown in Figure 10.9 with the extension .xpe and saves it into the specified directory.

```
report_power -no_propagation -xpe C:/Xilinx/Example/FA.xpe
```

Figure 10.9 Power report.

```
1. Summary
----------

+--------------------------+--------------+
| Total On-Chip Power (W)  | 0.842        |
| Design Power Budget (W)  | Unspecified* |
| Power Budget Margin (W)  | NA           |
| Dynamic (W)              | 0.758        |
| Device Static (W)        | 0.084        |
| Effective TJA (C/W)      | 1.9          |
| Max Ambient (C)          | 83.4         |
| Junction Temperature (C) | 26.6         |
| Confidence Level         | Low          |
| Setting File             | ---          |
| Simulation Activity File | ---          |
| Design Nets Matched      | NA           |
+--------------------------+--------------+
* Specify Design Power Budget using, set_operating_conditions -design_power_budget <value in Watts>
```

- **Step 10:** Report generation, with the following command, generates the timing report, as shown in Figure 10.10.

```
report_timing -nworst 5 -path_type full -input_pins
```

Figure 10.10 Timing report.

```
Timing Report

Slack:                    inf
  Source:                 c
                            (input port)
  Destination:            s
                            (output port)
  Path Group:             (none)
  Path Type:              Max at Slow Process Corner
  Data Path Delay:        6.290ns  (logic 5.123ns (81.444%)  route 1.167ns (18.556%))
  Logic Levels:           3  (IBUF=1 LUT3=1 OBUF=1)

    Location             Delay type                Incr(ns)  Path(ns)    Netlist Resource(s)
  -------------------------------------------------------------------    -------------------
                                                      0.000     0.000 r  c (IN)
                         net (fo=0)                   0.000     0.000    c
                                                                      r  c_IBUF_inst/I
                         IBUF (Prop_ibuf_I_O)         1.688     1.688 r  c_IBUF_inst/O
                         net (fo=2, unplaced)         0.584     2.271    c_IBUF
                                                                      r  s_OBUF_inst_i_1/I0
                         LUT3 (Prop_lut3_I0_O)        0.067     2.338 r  s_OBUF_inst_i_1/O
                         net (fo=1, unplaced)         0.584     2.922    s_OBUF
                                                                      r  s_OBUF_inst/I
                         OBUF (Prop_obuf_I_O)         3.368     6.290 r  s_OBUF_inst/O
                         net (fo=0)                   0.000     6.290    s
                                                                      r  s (OUT)
  -------------------------------------------------------------------    -------------------
```

- **Step 11:** Report generation, with the following command, generates the utilization, as shown in Figure 10.11.

```
report_utilization -file C:/Xilinx/Example/util.txt
```

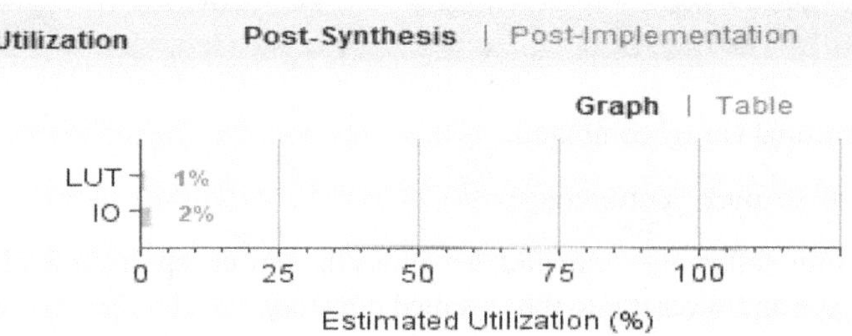

Figure 10.11 Utilization report.

- **Step 12:** Data sheet report generation, with the following command, generates the datasheet report, as shown in Figure 10.12.

```
report_datasheet -sort_by port -show_all_corners
```

From Port	To Port	Max Delay(ns)	Process Corner	Min Delay(ns)	Process Corner
a	cy	2.742	SLOW	2.511	SLOW
a	cy	1.410	FAST	1.172	FAST
a	s	5.140	SLOW	4.669	SLOW
a	s	2.458	FAST	2.066	FAST
b	cy	3.890	SLOW	3.605	SLOW
b	cy	1.799	FAST	1.429	FAST
b	s	6.279	SLOW	5.756	SLOW
b	s	2.846	FAST	2.323	FAST
c	cy	3.890	SLOW	3.605	SLOW
c	cy	1.799	FAST	1.429	FAST
c	s	6.290	SLOW	5.765	SLOW
c	s	2.845	FAST	2.322	FAST

Figure 10.12 Datasheet report.

10.2 Sourcing the Tcl Script with Vivado

In the previous example, all the steps are written separately and their execution result can be visualized. Alternatively, there is a one-step process where all the commands can be written together in a notepad with the extension .tcl and sourced to the Vivado interpreter. First, one needs to create a directory for the module FS (C:/Xilinx/Example/FS). Use WordPad to write the program and save it into the specified directory with the extension (.v). Figure 10.13 shows the three different files required, the main program of the full subtractor (FS.v), the stimulus program (FStb.v), and the constraint file (FS_xdc.xdc). Write the program shown below with help of notepad and save it with

Figure 10.13 Source and constraint file of full subtractor.

the extension .tcl (FS.tcl). The file FS.tcl contains all the steps from the creation of the project to bitstream generation, and is executed in the sequence it is written. Users can visualize the result of each execution one by one. The Project Summary tab on the Vivado homepage contains an overview and dashboard options, where all the reports of the program are summarized. The report of the program is available from the Tcl Console tab of the transcript window too.

FS.tcl script

```
create_project FS -force C:/Xilinx/Example/FS -part xc7a15tcpg236-1
add_files C:/Xilinx/Example/FS/FS.v
add_files C:/Xilinx/Example/FS/FStb.v
add_files -fileset constrs_1 -norecurse C:/Xilinx/Example/FS/
FS_xdc.xdc
set_property top FS [current_fileset]
synth_design -rtl
update_compile_order -fileset sim_1
launch_simulation
```

```
launch_runs synth_1
wait_on_run synth_1
launch_runs impl_1
wait_on_run impl_1

open_run -name FS synth_1
report_power -no_propagation -xpe C:/Xilinx/Example/FS/FS.xpe
report_timing -nworst 5 -path_type full -input_pins
report_utilization -file C:/Xilinx/Example/FS/util.txt
report_datasheet -sort_by port -show_all_corners
launch_runs impl_1 -to_step write_bitstream
```

Source the program FS.tcl in the Vivado interpreter, as shown in Figure 10.14.

```
Tools → Run Tcl Script -→ locate the file (FS.tcl)→    ok
```

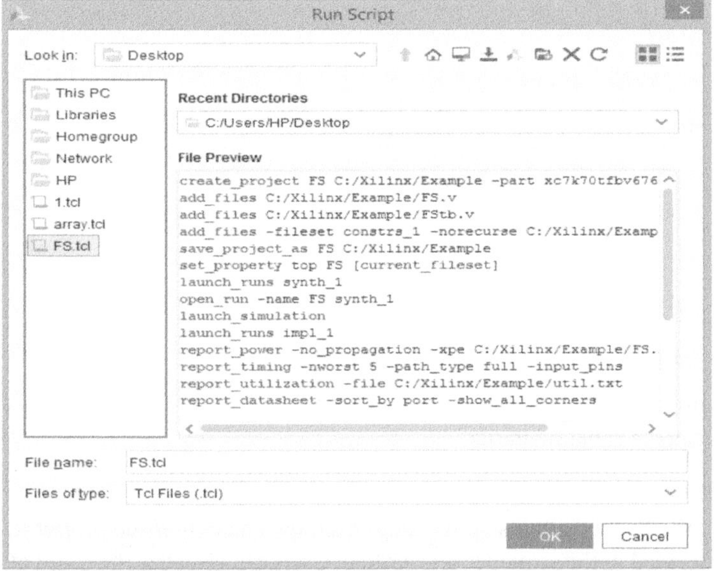

Figure 10.14 Sourcing a .tcl script.

Here, all the steps are executed internally and finally the result appears in the project summary. From the dashboard, different reports can be obtained, as shown in Figures 10.15–10.19.

(A) Simulation waveform

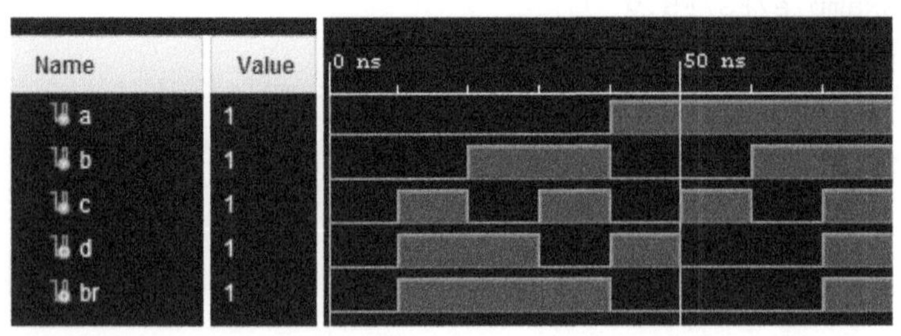

Figure 10.15 Simulation waveform of FS.

(B) Utilization Report

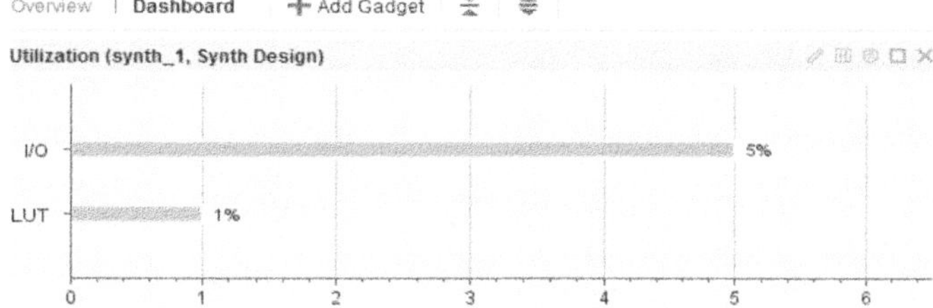

Figure 10.16 Utilization reports of FS.

(C) Timing Report

Figure 10.17 Timing report of FS.

```
Timing Report

Slack:                   inf
  Source:                b
                           (input port)
  Destination:           d
                           (output port)
  Path Group:            (none)
  Path Type:             Max at Slow Process Corner
  Data Path Delay:       6.722ns  (logic 5.123ns (76.207%)  route 1.599ns (23.793%))
  Logic Levels:          3  (IBUF=1 LUT3=1 OBUF=1)

    Location             Delay type                Incr(ns)  Path(ns)    Netlist Resource(s)
  -------------------------------------------------------------------    -------------------
    U8                                                0.000     0.000 r  b (IN)
                         net (fo=0)                   0.000     0.000    b
    U8                                                                 r  b_IBUF_inst/I
    U8                   IBUF (Prop_ibuf_I_O)         1.480     1.480 r  b_IBUF_inst/O
                         net (fo=2, unplaced)         0.800     2.280    b_IBUF
                                                                     r  d_OBUF_inst_i_1/I0
                         LUT3 (Prop_lut3_I0_O)        0.150     2.430 r  d_OBUF_inst_i_1/O
                         net (fo=1, unplaced)         0.800     3.230    d_OBUF
                                                                     r  d_OBUF_inst/I
                         OBUF (Prop_obuf_I_O)         3.492     6.722 r  d_OBUF_inst/O
                         net (fo=0)                   0.000     6.722    d
                                                                     r  d (OUT)
  -------------------------------------------------------------------    -------------------
```

(D) Power Report

Figure 10.18 Power report of FS.

Power | Summary | On-Chip

Total On-Chip Power:	**2.771 W**
Junction Temperature:	**38.9 °C**
Thermal Margin:	46.1 °C (9.2 W)
Effective ϑJA:	5.0 °C/W
Power supplied to off-chip devices:	0 W
Confidence level:	Low

(E) **DataSheet Report**

```
Data Sheet Report

Combinational Delays

-----+------+-----------+---------+-----------+---------+
From | To   |    Max    | Process |    Min    | Process |
Port | Port | Delay(ns) | Corner  | Delay(ns) | Corner  |
-----+------+-----------+---------+-----------+---------+
a    | br   |     6.653 | SLOW    |     6.277 | SLOW    |
a    | br   |     2.552 | FAST    |     2.119 | FAST    |
a    | d    |     6.679 | SLOW    |     6.298 | SLOW    |
a    | d    |     2.553 | FAST    |     2.120 | FAST    |
b    | br   |     6.696 | SLOW    |     6.320 | SLOW    |
b    | br   |     2.595 | FAST    |     2.161 | FAST    |
b    | d    |     6.722 | SLOW    |     6.341 | SLOW    |
b    | d    |     2.591 | FAST    |     2.158 | FAST    |
c    | br   |     6.653 | SLOW    |     6.277 | SLOW    |
c    | br   |     2.552 | FAST    |     2.119 | FAST    |
c    | d    |     6.647 | SLOW    |     6.272 | SLOW    |
c    | d    |     2.556 | FAST    |     2.122 | FAST    |
-----+------+-----------+---------+-----------+---------+
```

Figure 10.19 Datasheet report of FS.

10.3 Implementing Counter Program with Vivado Tcl Console

Following the step mentioned in section 10.2, store the three files counter.v, countertb.v, and counter_const.xdc into the directory C/Xilinx/Example/counter (Figure 10.20).

Source the program FS.tcl in the vivado interpreter, as shown in Figure 10.21.

```
Tools → Run Tcl Script -→ locate the file (counter.tcl)→   ok
```

Counter.tcl Script

```
create_project counter -force C:/Xilinx/Example/counter -part
xc7a15tcpg236-1
add_files C:/Xilinx/Example/counter/counter.v
add_files C:/Xilinx/Example/counter/countertb.v
add_files -fileset constrs_1 -norecurse C:/Xilinx/Example/counter/
counter_const.xdc
set_property top counter [current_fileset]
synth_design -rtl
update_compile_order -fileset sim_1
launch_simulation
launch_runs synth_1
wait_on_run synth_1
launch_runs impl_1
wait_on_run impl_1
```

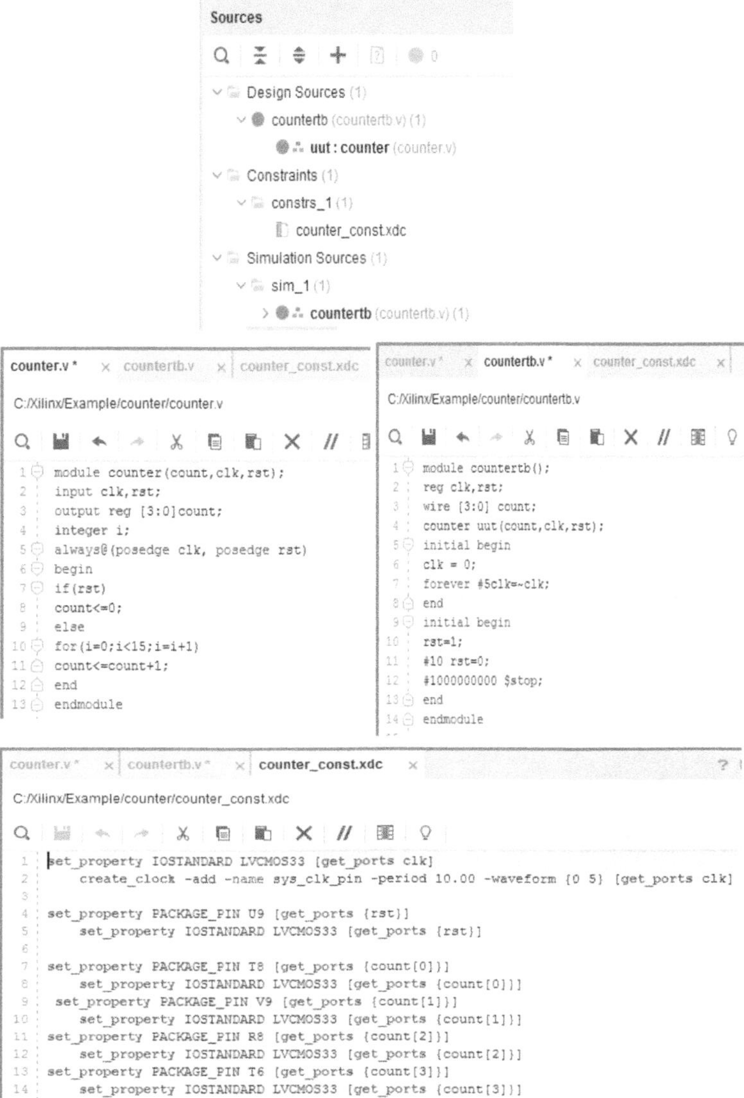

Figure 10.20 Source and constraint file of counter.

```
open_run -name counter synth_1
report_power -no_propagation -xpe C:/Xilinx/Example/counter/
counter.xpe
report_timing -nworst 5 -path_type full -input_pins
report_utilization -file C:/Xilinx/Example/FS/util.txt
report_datasheet -sort_by port -show_all_corners

launch_runs impl_1 -to_step write_bitstream
```

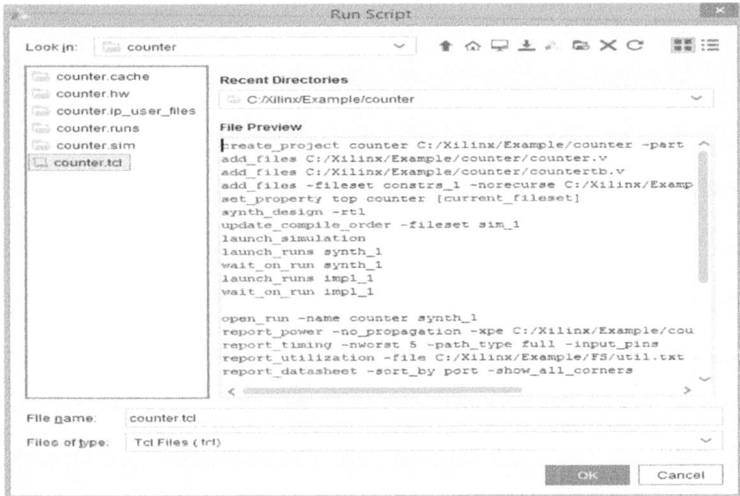

Figure 10.21 Sourcing of counter.tcl.

Here, all the steps are executed internally and finally the result appears in the project summary. From the dashboard, different reports can be obtained as shown in Figures 10.22–10.26.

(A) **Simulation waveform**

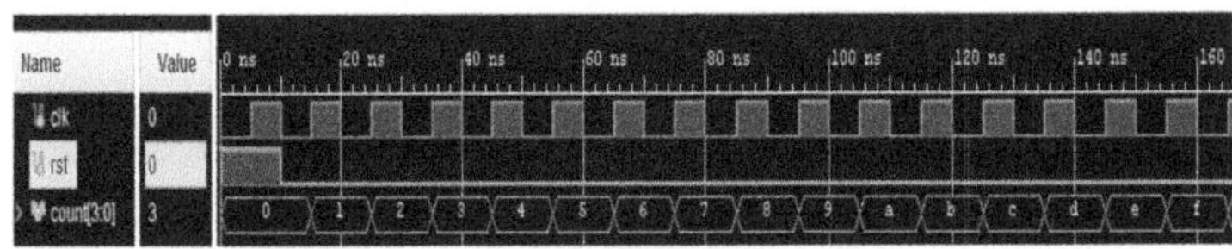

Figure 10.22 Simulation waveform of the counter.

(B) **Utilization Report**

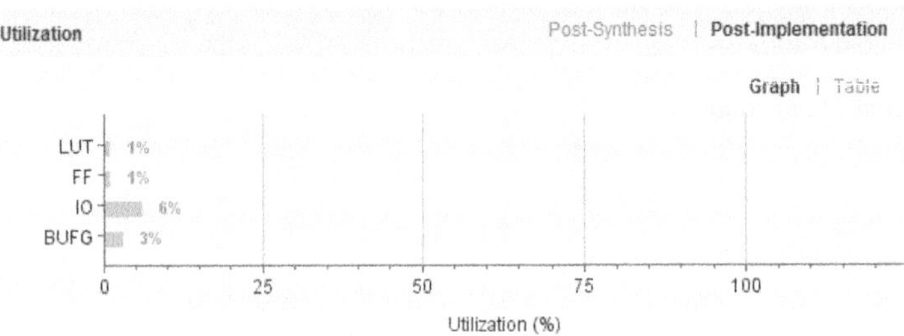

Figure 10.23 Utilization report of counter.

(C) Power Report

Power	
Total On-Chip Power:	0.083 W
Junction Temperature:	25.4 °C
Thermal Margin:	59.6 °C (11.9 W)
Effective ϑJA:	5.0 °C/W
Power supplied to off-chip devices:	0 W
Confidence level:	Medium

```
+--------------------------+--------------+
| Total On-Chip Power (W)  | 0.075        |
| Design Power Budget (W)  | Unspecified* |
| Power Budget Margin (W)  | NA           |
| Dynamic (W)              | 0.004        |
| Device Static (W)        | 0.072        |
| Effective TJA (C/W)      | 5.0          |
| Max Ambient (C)          | 84.6         |
| Junction Temperature (C) | 25.4         |
| Confidence Level         | Medium       |
| Setting File             | ---          |
| Simulation Activity File | ---          |
| Design Nets Matched      | NA           |
+--------------------------+--------------+
```

Figure 10.24 Power report of counter.

(D) Timing Report

Setup

Timing	
Worst Negative Slack (WNS):	8.213 ns
Total Negative Slack (TNS):	0 ns
Number of Failing Endpoints:	0
Total Number of Endpoints:	4

Hold

Timing	
Worst Hold Slack (WHS):	0.251 ns
Total Hold Slack (THS):	0 ns
Number of Failing Endpoints:	0
Total Number of Endpoints:	4

Pulse Width

Timing	
Worst Pulse Width Slack (WPWS):	4.5 ns
Total Pulse Width Negative Slack (TPWS):	0 ns
Number of Failing Endpoints:	0
Total Number of Endpoints:	5

Figure 10.25 Timing report of counter.

(E) Datasheet Report

```
Input Ports Setup/Hold

------------+-------+---------+-------+---------------+---------+---------------+---------+----------+
Reference   | Input | IO Reg  | Delay |      Setup(ns) | Process |       Hold(ns) | Process | Internal |
Clock       | Port  | Type    | Type  | to Clk (Edge) | Corner  | to Clk (Edge) | Corner  | Clock    |
------------+-------+---------+-------+---------------+---------+---------------+---------+----------+
sys_clk_pin | rst   | FDCE    | -     |   -0.015 (r) | SLOW    |     0.582 (r) | SLOW    |          |
sys_clk_pin | rst   | FDCE    | -     |    0.218 (r) | FAST    |     0.401 (r) | FAST    |          |
------------+-------+---------+-------+---------------+---------+---------------+---------+----------+

Output Ports Clock-to-out

------------+----------+---------+-------+-----------------+---------+-----------------+---------+----------+
Reference   | Output   | IO Reg  | Delay | Max Clk (Edge)  | Process | Min Clk (Edge)  | Process | Internal |
Clock       | Port     | Type    | Type  |     to port(ns) | Corner  |     to port(ns) | Corner  | Clock    |
------------+----------+---------+-------+-----------------+---------+-----------------+---------+----------+
sys_clk_pin | count[0] | FDCE    | -     |       7.865 (r) | SLOW    |       7.190 (r) | SLOW    |          |
sys_clk_pin | count[0] | FDCE    | -     |       3.052 (r) | FAST    |       2.384 (r) | FAST    |          |
sys_clk_pin | count[1] | FDCE    | -     |       7.865 (r) | SLOW    |       7.190 (r) | SLOW    |          |
sys_clk_pin | count[1] | FDCE    | -     |       3.052 (r) | FAST    |       2.384 (r) | FAST    |          |
sys_clk_pin | count[2] | FDCE    | -     |       7.865 (r) | SLOW    |       7.190 (r) | SLOW    |          |
sys_clk_pin | count[2] | FDCE    | -     |       3.052 (r) | FAST    |       2.384 (r) | FAST    |          |
sys_clk_pin | count[3] | FDCE    | -     |       7.865 (r) | SLOW    |       7.190 (r) | SLOW    |          |
sys_clk_pin | count[3] | FDCE    | -     |       3.052 (r) | FAST    |       2.384 (r) | FAST    |          |
--                                                                    -----------------+---------+----------+
```

```
Setup between Clocks

------------+-------------+--------------+---------+
Source      | Destination |  Src:Rise    | Process |
Clock       | Clock       | Dest:Rise(ns) | Corner  |
------------+-------------+--------------+---------+
sys_clk_pin | sys_clk_pin |        1.697 | SLOW    |
sys_clk_pin | sys_clk_pin |        0.806 | FAST    |
------------+-------------+--------------+---------+
```

```
Max / Min delays for output bus
Clocked by: sys_clk_pin
Bus Skew: 0.000 ns (slow corner)
Bus Skew: 0.000 ns (fast corner)
-------------------+-------------+---------+-------------+---------+----------+
                   |     Max     | Process |     Min     | Process | Edge     |
Pad                |   Delay(ns) | Corner  |   Delay(ns) | Corner  | Skew(ns) |
-------------------+-------------+---------+-------------+---------+----------+
count[0]           |   7.865 (r) | SLOW    |   7.190 (r) | SLOW    |    0.000 |
count[0]           |   3.052 (r) | FAST    |   2.384 (r) | FAST    |    0.000 |
count[1]           |   7.865 (r) | SLOW    |   7.190 (r) | SLOW    |    0.000 |
count[1]           |   3.052 (r) | FAST    |   2.384 (r) | FAST    |    0.000 |
count[2]           |   7.865 (r) | SLOW    |   7.190 (r) | SLOW    |    0.000 |
count[2]           |   3.052 (r) | FAST    |   2.384 (r) | FAST    |    0.000 |
count[3]           |   7.865 (r) | SLOW    |   7.190 (r) | SLOW    |    0.000 |
count[3]           |   3.052 (r) | FAST    |   2.384 (r) | FAST    |    0.000 |
-------------------+-------------+---------+-------------+---------+----------+
Worst Case Summary |   7.865 (r) | SLOW    |   7.190 (r) | SLOW    |    0.000 |
Worst Case Summary |   3.052 (r) | FAST    |   2.384 (r) | FAST    |    0.000 |
-------------------+-------------+---------+-------------+---------+----------+
```

Figure 10.26 Datasheet report of counter.

10.4 Advantage of Vivado in Tcl Mode

In an earlier section, the Tcl script for every step was explained to implement a digital circuit with the Vivado EDA tool. There is also a graphical feature available to access them. In Tcl mode, all the steps can be assembled once and all the steps will be executed in the background. The Tcl mode offers the following advantages:

i) fast execution;
ii) does not require to look at internal execution;

iii) result and report are accessible at summary;
iv) easy to update the device.

Reference

1 https://www.xilinx.com/support/documentation/sw_manuals/xilinx2018_3/ug894-vivado-tcl-scripting.pdf
2 https://www.xilinx.com/support/documentation/sw_manuals/xilinx2019_2/ug835-vivado-tcl-commands.pdf
3 https://www.doulos.com/knowhow/tcltk

10.A Appendix

A few important and repetitively used Tcl commands [1, 2] are explained here.

1. **`create_project`** Creates a new project.

This creates a Vivado Design Suite project file (.xpr) or a project file for the Vivado Lab Edition (.lpr), in the specified directory. There is different command syntax for the Vivado Lab Edition; `[-part]` and `[-ip]` are not supported in Vivado Lab Edition.

Syntax: `create_project [-part <arg>] [-force] [-in_memory] [-ip] [-rtl_kernel] [-quiet] [-verbose] [<name>] [<dir>]`

Name	Description
[-part]	Targets part
[-force]	Overwrites existing project directory
[-in_memory]	Creates an in-memory project
[-ip]	Default GUI behavior is for a managed IP project
[-rtl_kernel]	Default GUI behavior is for an RTL Kernel project
[-quiet]	Ignores command errors
[-verbose]	Suspends message limits during command execution
[<name>]	Project name
[<dir>]	Directory where the project file is saved

The default Vivado Design Suite creates an RTL project which manages the RTL source file. After creating a project, the project type can be changed by using the `set_property` command to set the `DESIGN_MODE` property on the `current_fileset`.

```
*  RTL Project - set_property DESIGN_MODE RTL [current_fileset]
*  Netlist Project - set_property DESIGN_MODE GateLvl [current_
   fileset]
*  I/O Planning Project - set_property DESIGN_MODE PinPlanning
   [current_fileset]
```

Example:

```
create_project project1 myDesigns // creates a project project1.xpr
in directory  // myDesigns in the current working directory
```

2. **`close_project`** Closes the currently opened project.

   Syntax: `close_project [-delete] [-quiet] [-verbose]`

Name	Description
`[-delete]`	Deletes the project from disk
`[-quiet]`	Ignores command errors
`[-verbose]`	Suspends message limits during command execution

3. **`current_project`** Specifies the current project or sets the current project when no project is specified.

   Syntax: `current_project [-quiet] [-verbose] [<project>]`

Name	Description
`[-quiet]`	Ignores command errors
`[-verbose]`	Suspends message limits during command execution
`[<project>]`	Project to set as current

```
current_project project_1          //set project_1 as current project
current_project                   // returns the name of current
project in the tool
```

Name	Description
`[-quiet]`	Ignores command errors
`[-verbose]`	Suspends message limits during command execution
`[<design>]`	Name of the current design to be set

4. **`current_design`** Defines the current design or returns the name of the current design in an active project.

Example:

current_design rtl_1 // set rtl_1 as current design

5. **`create_port`** Creates a port and specifies its parameter such as direction, width, single-ended, or differential ended. Newly created ports are added at the top level of the design.

   Syntax: `create_port -direction <arg> [-from <arg>] [-to <arg>] [-diff_pair] [-interface <arg>] [-quiet] [-verbose] <name> [<negative_name>]`

Name	Description
`-direction`	Direction of port IN, OUT, or INOUT
`[-from]`	Starting bus index
`[-to]`	Ending bus index
`[-diff_pair]`	Creates a differential pair of ports
`[-interface]`	Assigns a new port to interface
`[-quiet]`	Ignores command errors
`[-verbose]`	Suspends message limits during command execution
`<name>`	Name of the port
`[<negative_name>]`	Optional negative name of a diff-pair

```
create_port -direction IN PORT0                       //creates a new
input port named PORT0

create_interface Group1                               //Creates a new
interface named Group1

create_port -direction OUT -diff_pair data            //creates
differential pair ended output port   data

create_port -direction OUT -from 0 -to 3 -diff_pair -interface
Group1 D_BUS

      //creates a 4 bit wide differential pair ended output bus
using interface Group1 D_BUS

create_port -direction OUT -diff_pair data_P data_N

                         //creates differential pair ended output port
named data_P ,       data_N
```

6. **`create_net`** creates a new net in the current netlist of synthesized/implemented design.

   Syntax: `create_net [-from <arg>] [-to <arg>] [-quiet] [-verbose] <nets>`

Name	Description
`[-from]`	Starting bus index
`[-to]`	Ending bus index
`[-quiet]`	Ignores command errors
`[-verbose]`	Suspends message limits during command execution
`<nets>`	Names of nets

Example:

```
create_net tempBus -from 23 -to 0          //creates 24-bit bus
```

7. **`create_pin`** Adds a single pin or bus pins to the current netlist of an open synthesized/implemented design.

   Syntax: `create_pin [-from <arg>] [-to <arg>] -direction <arg> [-quiet] [-verbose] <pins>`

Name	Description
[-from]	Starting bus index
[-to]	Ending bus index
-direction	Pin direction values: IN, OUT, INOUT
[-quiet]	Ignores command errors
[-verbose]	Suspends message limits during command execution
<pins>	Names of pins to create

Examples:

```
create_pin -direction IN cpuEngine/inPin     //creates input pin
IN on the module

     cpuEngine named inPin

create_pin -direction INOUT -from 0 -to 23 usbEngine0|myDMA|dataBus
                                  //creates 24-bit bidirectional bus
to the instance
```

8. **`create_clock`** Creates a clock object with a specified period of nanoseconds.

   `create_clock` generates a virtual clock, which can be used as a time reference for setting input and output delays.

   `create_generated_clock` derives a clock from a physical clock and derives properties from the master clock.

   Syntax: `create_clock -period <arg> [-name <arg>] [-waveform <args>] [-add] [-quiet] [-verbose] [<objects>]`

Name	Description
-period <argument>	Specifies a clock period in nanoseconds(ns)
[-name]	Name of the clock
[-waveform]	Specifies rising/falling edge times of the defined clock
[-add]	Add the existing clock to source objects
[-quiet]	Ignores command errors
[-verbose]	Suspends message limits during command execution
[<objects>]	List of clock source ports, pins, or nets

```
create_clock -name bftClk -period 5.000 [get_ports bftClk]
                              // creates a clock named bftClk with
period 5ns
create_clock -name clk -period 10.000 -waveform {2.4 7.4} [get_
ports bftClk]
      //creates a clock named clk with period 10 ns, rising edge 2.4
ns and falling edge 7.4 ns.
create_clock -name virtual_clock -period 5.000
                        //creates a virtual clock with period 5 ns
since no clock source specified
create_clock -name clk -period 10.000 -waveform {7 2} [get_
ports bftClk]
       //creates a clock named clk with period 10 ns and rising
edge at 7 ns and falling edge at 2 ns
```

9. **`read_verilog`** Reads one or more Verilog or SystemVerilog source file.

   Syntax: `read_verilog [-library <arg>] [-sv] [-quiet] [-verbose] <files>`

Name	Description
[-library]	Library name, Default: default lib
[-sv]	Enables system Verilog compilation
[-quiet]	Ignores command errors
[-verbose]	Suspends message limits during command execution
<files>	Name of one or more Verilog files to be read
[-quiet]	Ignores command errors

```
read_verilog C:/Data/FPGA_Design/new_module.v
                    // reads the Verilog file new_module  and adds
it to the source fileset
read_verilog { file1.v file2.v file3.v}                  //reads
one and more verilog files
```

10. **`add_files`** Adds one or more source file to the specified fileset in the current project.

    Syntax: `add_files [-fileset <arg>] [-of_objects <args>] [-norecurse] [-copy_to <arg>] [-force] [-scan_for_includes] [-quiet] [-verbose] [<files>...]`

Name	Description
[-fileset]	Fileset name
[-of_objects]	Filesets or sub-designs or RMs to add the files to
[-norecurse]	Does not recursively search in specified directories
[-copy_to]	Copies the file to the specified directory before adding it to project
[-force]	Overwrites the existing file when -copy_to is used
[-scan_for_includes]	Scans and adds any included files found in the fileset's RTL sources
[-quiet]	Ignores command errors
[-verbose]	Suspends message limits during command execution
[<files>]	Name of the files and/or directories to add

```
    add_files rtl.v          // adds a file called rtl.v to the
current project
```

11. **`write_verilog`** Exports the current netlist in Verilog format.

```
write_verilog [-cell <arg>] [-mode <arg>] [-lib] [-port_diff_
buffers] [-write_all_overrides]                       [-keep_
vcc_gnd] [-rename_top <arg>] [-sdf_anno <arg>] [-sdf_file <arg>]
[-force] [-include_xilinx_libs] [-logic_function_stripped] [-quiet]
[-verbose] <file>
```

Name	Description
[-cell]	Root of the design to write
[-mode]	Values: design, pin_planning, synth_stub, sta, funcsim, timesim
[-lib]	Writes each library into a separate file
[-port_diff_buffers]	Outputs differential buffers when writing in -port mod
[-write_all_overrides]	Writes parameter overrides on Xilinx primitives
[-keep_vcc_gnd]	Do not replace VCC/GND instances with literal constants on load terminals.
[-rename_top]	Replaces top module name with custom name
[-sdf_anno]	Specifies if sdf_annotate system task statement is generated
[-sdf_file]	Full path to sdf file location
[-force]	Overwrites existing file
[-include_xilinx_libs]	Includes simulation models directly in netlist instead of linking to the library
[-logic_function_stripped]	Converts INIT strings on LUTs & RAMBs to fixed values
[-quiet]	Ignores command errors
[-verbose]	Suspends message limits during command execution
<file>	Defines which file to write

```
write_verilog C:/Data/my_verilog.v
          // writes a Verilog simulation netlist file for the whole
design to the specified file and path
```

12. **`save_project_as`** saves the current project under a new name.

    Syntax: `save_project_as [-scan_for_includes] [-exclude_run_results] [-include_local_ip_cache] [-force] [-quiet] [-verbose] <name> [<dir>]`

Name	Description
[-scan_for_includes]	Scans for include files and add them to the new project
[-exclude_run_results]	Excludes run results in the new project
[-include_local_ip_cache]	Includes IP cache results in the new project
[-force]	Overwrites existing project directory
[-quiet]	Ignores command errors
[-verbose]	Suspends message limits during command execution
<name>	New name for the project to save
[<dir>]	Directory where the project file is saved

Examples:

```
save_project_as myProject myProjectDir
    //saves the active project as a new project named myProject in a
directory called myProjectDir
```

13. **`close_design`** Closes the currently active design.

    Syntax: `close_design [-quiet] [-verbose]`

Name	Description
[-quiet]	Ignores command errors
[-verbose]	Suspends message limits during command execution

In the case where multiple designs open, `current_design` specifies the active design.

Example:

```
current_design rtl_1
      close_design
```

14. **`save_constraints`** Saves any changes to the constraints files of the active constraints set.

    Syntax: `save_constraints [-force] [-quiet] [-verbose]`

Name	Description
[-force]	Forces constraints save
[-quiet]	Ignores command errors
[-verbose]	Suspends message limits during command execution

15. **synth_design** Synthesizes a design using Vivado Synthesis and opens that design. Launches the Vivado synthesis engine to compile and synthesize a design in either Project Mode or Non-Project Mode in the Vivado Design Suite.

    Syntax: synth_design [-name <arg>] [-part <arg>] [-constrset <arg>] [-top <arg>] [-include_dirs <args>] [-generic <args>] [-verilog_define <args>] [-flatten_hierarchy <arg>] [-gated_clock_conversion <arg>] [-directive <arg>] [-rtl] [-bufg <arg>] [-no_lc] [-fanout_limit <arg>] [-shreg_min_size <arg>] [-mode <arg>] [-fsm_extraction <arg>] [-rtl_skip_ip] [-rtl_skip_constraints] [-keep_equivalent_registers] [-resource_sharing <arg>] [-cascade_dsp <arg>] [-control_set_opt_threshold <arg>] [-incremental <arg>] [-max_bram <arg>] [-max_uram <arg>] [-max_dsp <arg>] [-max_bram_cascade_height <arg>] [-max_uram_cascade_height <arg>] [-retiming] [-no_srlextract] [-assert] [-no_timing_driven] [-sfcu] [-quiet] [-verbose]

Name	Description
[-name]	Design name
[-part]	Target part
[-constrset]	Constraint fileset to use
[-top]	Specifies the top module name
[-include_dirs]	Specifies Verilog search directories
[-generic]	Specifies generic parameters
[-verilog_define]	Specifies Verilog defines
[-flatten_hierarchy]	Flattens hierarchy during LUT mapping
[-gated_clock_conversion]	Converts clock gating logic to flop enable (on/off/auto)
[-directive]	Synthesis directive
[-rtl]	Elaborates and opens an RTL design
[-bufg]	Max number of global clock buffers used by synthesis (Default 12)
[-no_lc]	Disables LUT combining
[-fanout_limit]	Fanout limit
[-shreg_min_size]	Minimum length for a chain of registers to be mapped onto SRL (Default 3)
[-mode]	Design mode (default, out_of_context)
[-fsm_extraction]	FSM extraction encoding (off, one_hot, sequential, johnson, gray, user_encoding, auto)
[-rtl_skip_ip]	Excludes sub design checkpoints in the RTL elaboration of the design
[-rtl_skip_constraints]	Do not load and validate constraints against elaborated design
[-keep_equivalent_registers]	Prevents registers sourced by the same logic from being merged
[-resource_sharing]	Shares arithmetic operators (auto, on, off)
[-cascade_dsp]	Controls how adders summing DSP block outputs will be implemented (auto, tree, force)

Name	Description
[-control_set_opt_threshold]	Threshold for synchronous control set optimization to lower the number of control sets
[-incremental]	DCP file for incremental flow value of this is the file name
[-max_bram]	Maximum number of block RAM allowed in design (default -1n −1 means that the tool will choose the max number allowed)
[-max_uram]	Maximum number of Ultra RAM blocks allowed in design (default -1n −1 means that the tool will choose the max number allowed)
[-max_dsp]	Maximum number of block DSP allowed in design (default −1 means that the tool will choose the max number allowed)
[-max_bram_cascade_height]	Controls the maximum number of BRAM that can be cascaded by the tool (default −1 means that the tool will choose the max number allowed)
[-max_uram_cascade_height]	Controls the maximum number of URAM that can be cascaded by the tool default −1 means that the tool will choose the max number allowed)
[-retiming]	Seeks to improve circuit performance for intra-clock sequential paths by automatically moving registers (register balancing) across combinatorial gates or LUTs
[-no_srlextract]	Prevents the extraction of shift registers so that they get implemented as simple registers
[-assert]	Enables VHDL to assert statements to be evaluated
[-no_timing_driven]	Do not run in timing-driven mode
[-sfcu]	Run in single-file compilation unit mode
[-quiet]	Ignores command errors
[-verbose]	Suspends message limits during command execution

```
synth_design -rtl -name rtl_1                    //elaborates the
source files and opens an RTL design
synth_design -top [lindex [find_top] 0]      //defines the top of the
current design for synthesis
```

16. **`open_run`** Opens a run into a netlist or implementation design.

    Syntax: `open_run [-name <arg>] [-pr_config <arg>] [-quiet] [-verbose] <run>`

Name	Description
[-name]	Design name
[-pr_config]	PR configuration to apply while opening the design
[-quiet]	Ignores command errors
[-verbose]	Suspends message limits during command execution
<run>	Run to open into the design

```
open_run -name synthPass1 synth_1          //opens the specified
synthesis run into a Netlist
Design named synthPass1

open_run impl_1                            //opens an Implemented
Design for impl_1
```

17. **`create_run`** Defines a synthesis or implementation run.
    Syntax: `create_run [-constrset <arg>] [-parent_run <arg>] [-part <arg>] -flow <arg> [-strategy <arg>] [-report_strategy <arg>] [-pr_config <arg>] [-quiet] [-verbose] <name>`

Name	Description
`[-constrset]`	Constraint fileset to use
`[-parent_run]`	Synthesis runs to link to new implementation run
`[-part]`	Target part
`-flow`	Flow name
`[-strategy]`	Strategy to apply to the run
`[-report_strategy]`	Reports strategy to apply to the run
`[-pr_config]`	Partition configuration to apply to the run
`[-quiet]`	Ignores command errors
`[-verbose]`	Suspends message limits during command execution
`<name>`	Name for a new run

```
create_run -flow  synth_1                   //creates a run
named synth_1
create_run impl_2 -parent_run synth_1 -flow
    //creates an implementation run and attaches it to the synth_1
synthesis run previously created
```

18. **`launch_runs`** Launches synthesis and implementation runs.

    Syntax: `launch_runs [-jobs <arg>] [-scripts_only] [-lsf <arg>] [-sge <arg>] [-dir <arg>] [-to_step <arg>] [-next_step] [-host <args>] [-remote_cmd <arg>] [-email_to <args>] [-email_all] [-pre_launch_script <arg>] [-post_launch_script <arg>] [-custom_script <arg>] [-force] [-quiet] [-verbose] <runs>`

Name	Description
`[-jobs]`	Number of jobs (default 1)
`[-scripts_only]`	Only generates scripts
`[-lsf]`	Uses LSF to launch jobs
`[-sge]`	Uses SGE to launch jobs
`[-dir]`	Launches directory

Name	Description
[-to_step]	Last step to run
[-next_step]	Runs next step
[-host]	Launches on the specified remote host with a specified number of jobs
[-remote_cmd]	Command to log in to remote hosts
[-email_to]	List of email addresses to notify when jobs complete
[-email_all]	Sends an email after each job completes
[-pre_launch_script]	Script to run before launching each job
[-post_launch_script	Script to run after each job completes
[-custom_script]	User run script map file which contains run name to user-run script mapping
[-force]	Runs the command
[-quiet]	Ignores command errors
[-verbose]	Suspends message limits during command execution
<runs>	Runs to launch

```
 launch_runs synth_1 synth_2 synth_4 -jobs 2
                                        //launches 3 different synthesis
runs with 2 parallel jobs
```

19. **`set_property`** Sets property on object(s)

    Syntax: `set_property [-dict <args>] [-quiet] [-verbose] <name> <value> <objects>`

Name	Description
[-dict]	List of name/value pairs of properties to set
[-quiet]	Ignores command errors
[-verbose]	Suspends message limits during command execution
<name>	Name of property to set
<value>	Value of property to set
<objects>	Objects to set properties on

```
create_property -type bool truth cell          //creates a user-
defined boolean property, TRUTH
 set_property truth false [lindex [get_cells] 1]   //sets  the
property on a cell
```

20. **`get_property`** Gets the current value of the specified properties of object

    Syntax: `get_property [-min] [-max] [-quiet] [-verbose] <name> <object>`

Name	Description
[-min]	Returns only the minimum value
[-max]	Returns only the maximum value
[-quiet]	Ignores command errors
[-verbose]	Suspends message limits during command execution
<name>	Name of property whose value is to be retrieved
<object>	Object to query for properties

```
get_property NAME [lindex [get_cells] 3]          //gets the NAME
property from the specified cell
get_property -min PERIOD [get_clocks]      //smallest PERIOD prop-
erty from specified clock
```

Index

Programming and GUI Fundamentals: Tcl-Tk for Electronic Design Automation (EDA), First Edition.
Suman Lata Tripathi, Abhishek Kumar, and Jyotirmoy Pathak.

Printed and bound by CPI Group (UK) Ltd, Croydon, CR0 4YY

27/10/2024

14580677-0002